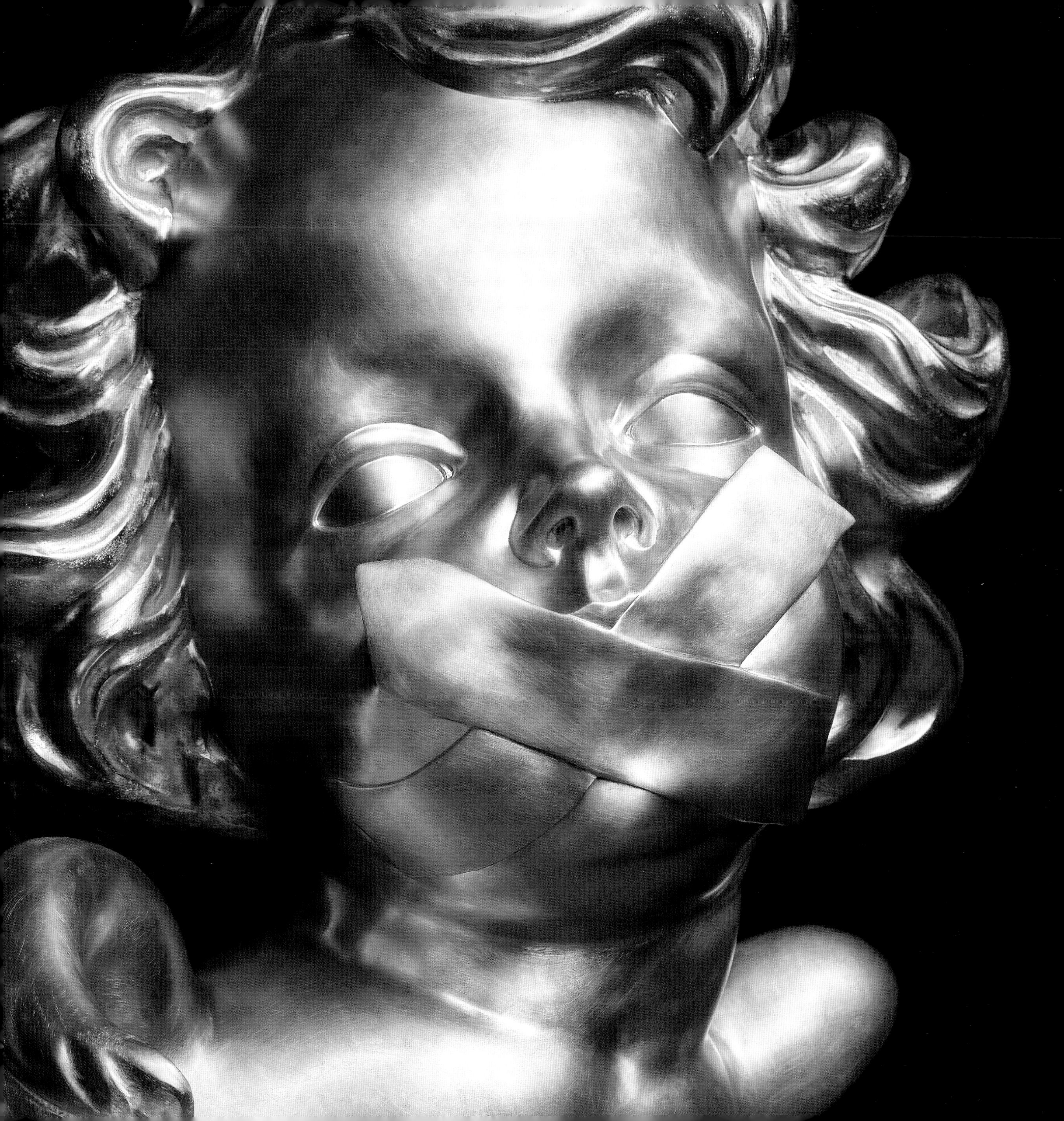

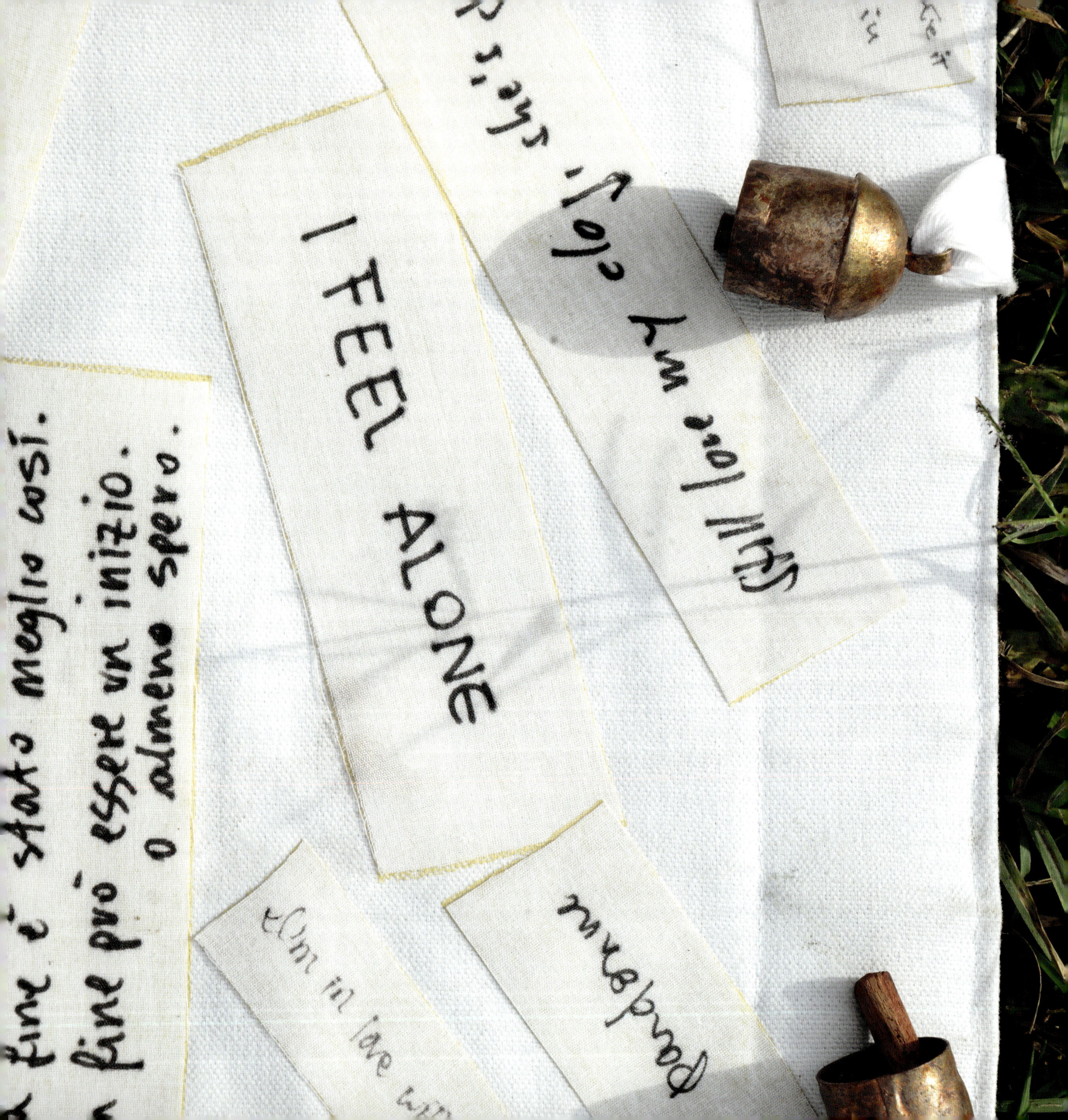
fine è stato meglio così.
fine può essere un inizio.
o almeno spero.
I FEEL ALONE
Still love my
I'm in love wi

Rachel Lee Hovnanian

YOU ARE NOT ALONE

ANGELS LISTENING

Mandragora

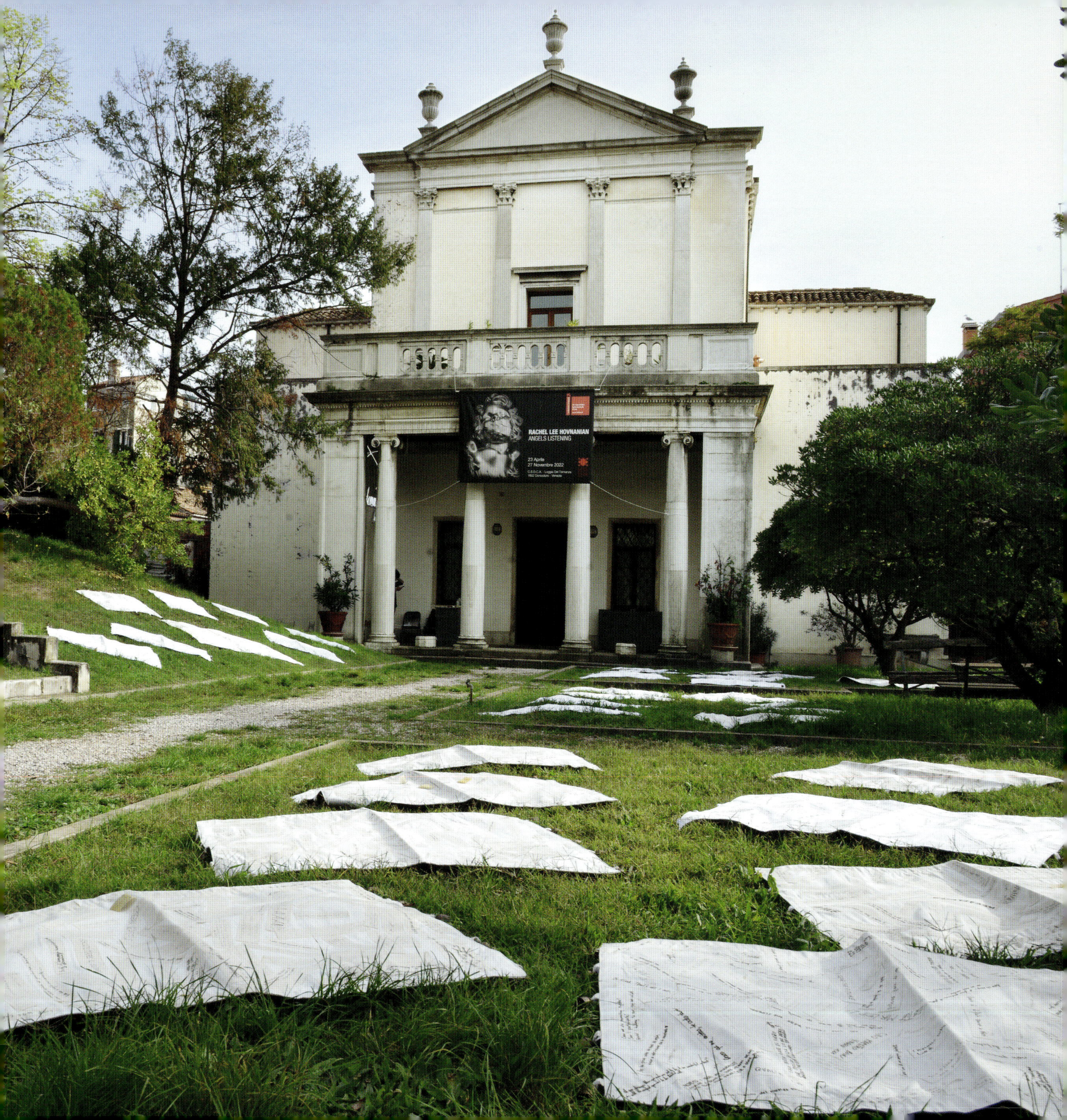
RACHEL LEE HOVNANIAN
ANGELS LISTENING
23 Aprile
27 Novembre 2022

Rachel Lee Hovnanian: *Angels Listening*

Collateral Event of the 59th International Art Exhibition – La Biennale di Venezia

April 23, 2022 to November 27, 2022

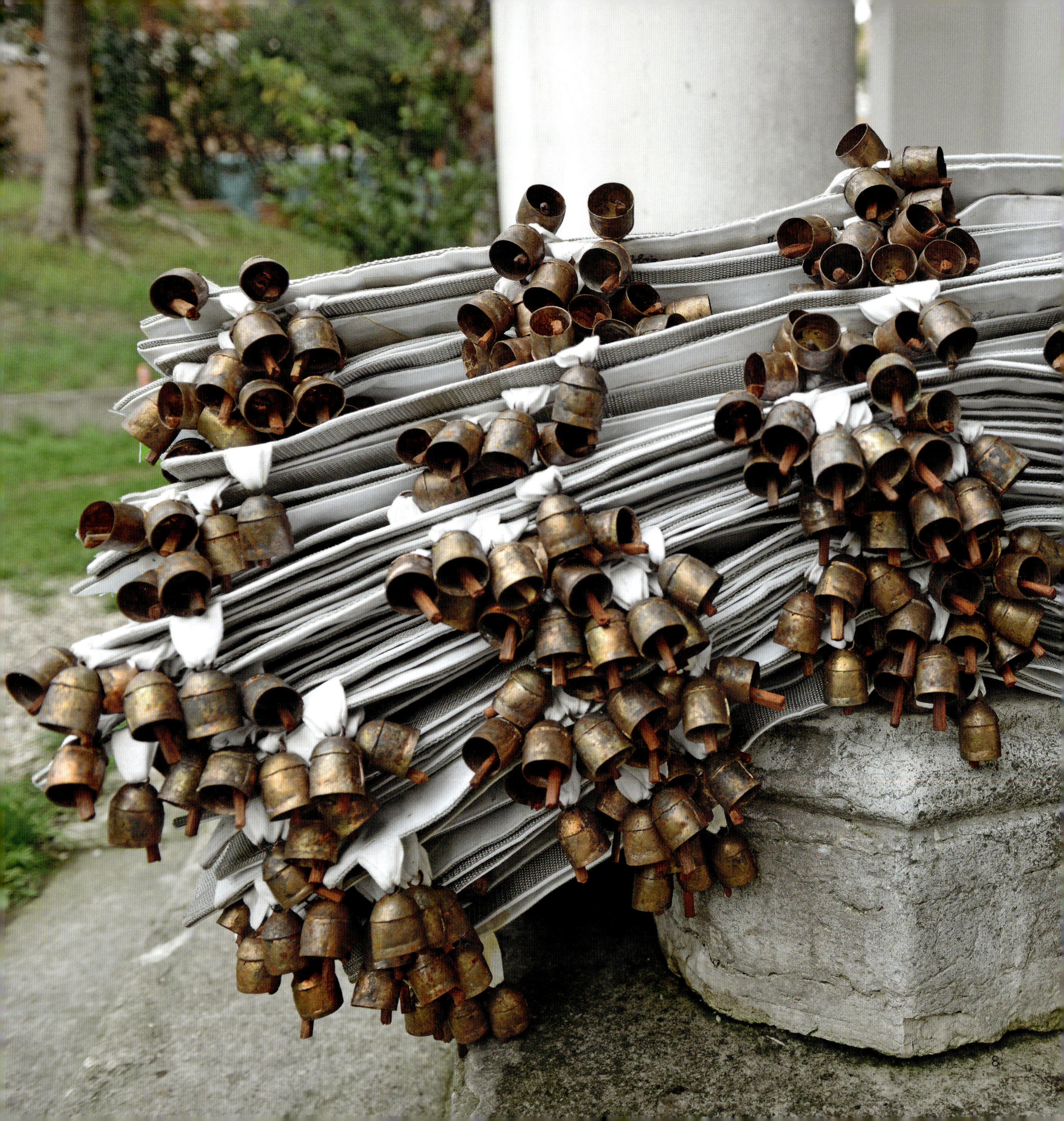

First presented at the 59th Venice Biennale in 2022, Venice

For her presentation at the 59th Venice Biennale, Hovnanian presented "Angels Listening" (2022), an interactive exhibition featuring seven large-scale bronze angels staged around a silver confessional box, each figure rendered in silence with its mouth "taped" shut.

Viewers were invited to participate by relinquishing their innermost thoughts, whether repressed due to fear of judgement or sheer inability, by writing them onto pieces of ribbon, placing these ribbons into "La Scatola Catartica" (The Cathartic Box), and ringing the awakening bell, a symbol of the role of the angels as mute listeners.

At the end of each day all of the new messages were compiled onto prayer-like mats and dispersed throughout the exterior gardens for future visitors to encounter and share as a collective stream-of-consciousness.

Curated by Annalisa Bugliani

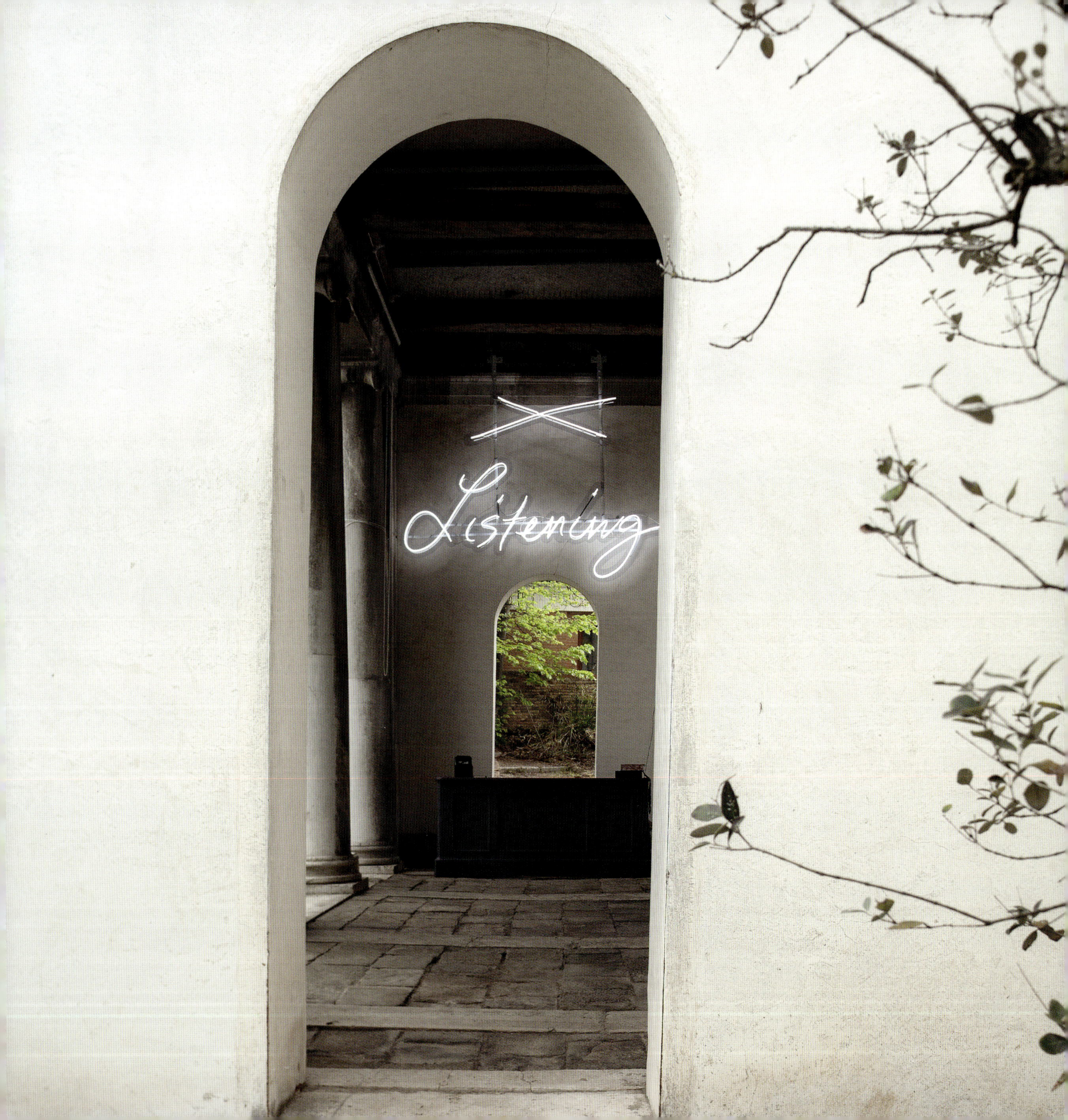
Listening

ARTIST STATEMENT | YOU ARE NOT ALONE

Rachel Lee Hovnanian

When I was a little girl, my father had a disease that affected his personality. I did not want to tell anyone about this, so I hid it.

His disease, which caused him to be violent, affected all of us. Yet, it was not discussed in the family. As a child, it seemed all my friends and neighbors had "perfect lives". I wanted to be like them, so I hid this secret; carrying it deep inside of me.

In January 2021, I was asked to do an installation in a 13th century gothic church. I began to wonder what could be created. It was still the time of the pandemic, and it almost seemed that the world had "shut down". Italy was one of the hardest hit countries. People were still wearing masks; everyone was instructed to remain at least 6 feet apart.

Here we were, due to the pandemic, in large part, only able to speak with one another through technology. A mode of communication, which lacked a human touch. The situation reminded me of a small marble sculpture that I created in Italy about being silenced as a woman. An angel with its mouth taped shut.

An angel is a messenger that appears in every religion. And, here in the time of the shut-down, everyone had an experience of not being able to speak. This sculpture now had a new meaning. We were all being silenced!

I was moved to recreate the sculpture of the Angel. Yet, this time on a much larger scale accompanied by a "cathartic box", where people could leave a message of something that they didn't say or couldn't say; something that they felt could never be heard.

When I took the messages out and read them, I realized that they were the show's essence. These anonymous messages needed to be heard. When I was asked to propose a show for the 2022 Venice Biennale, "Angels Listening" was born.

I dedicate this book to those who courageously shared their secrets surrounded by the angels that I created. For me, each writing represents a life whose story deserves to be told. In listening to these stories, perhaps it is we who become the angels listening.

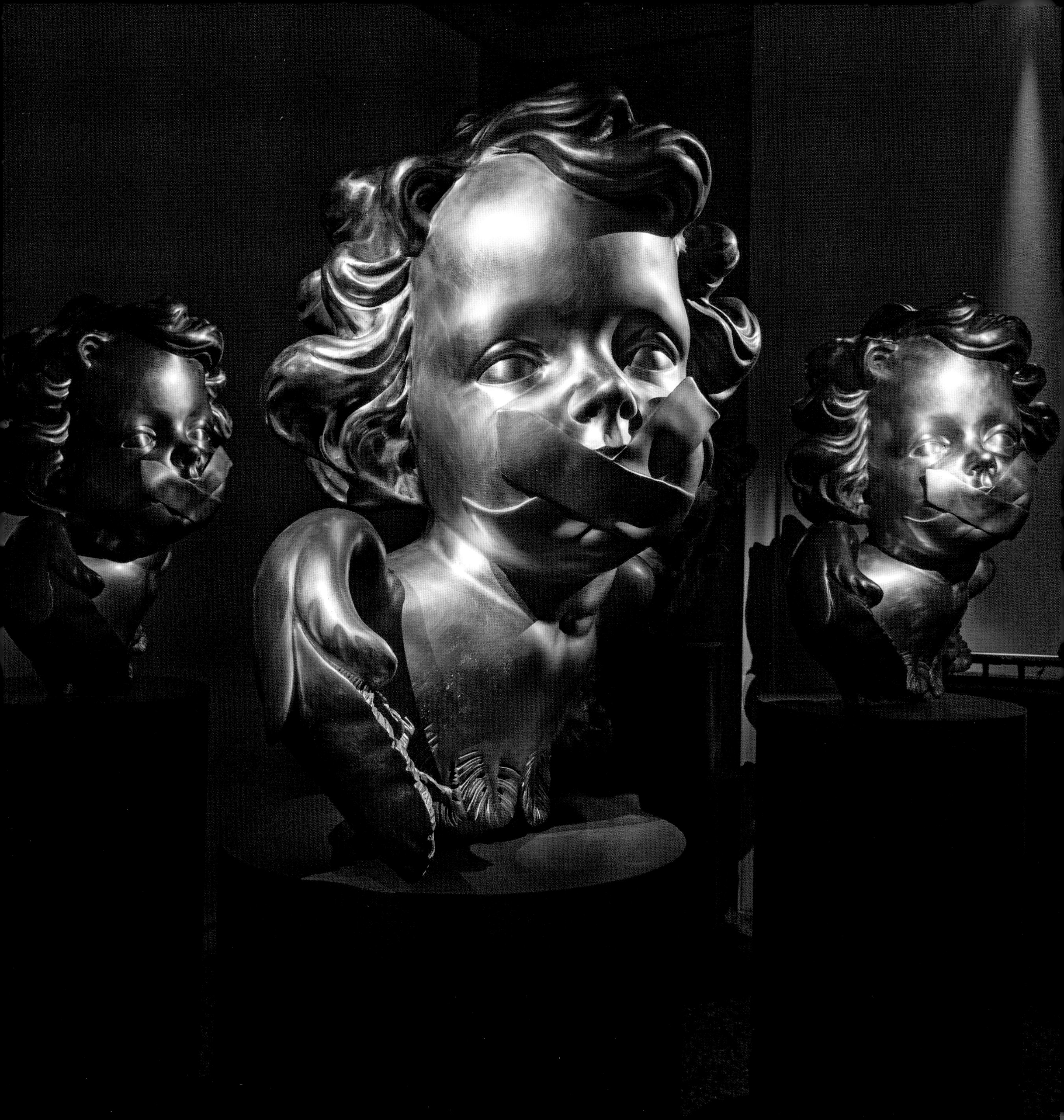

RACHEL LEE HOVNANIAN : YOU ARE NOT ALONE, OR THE CATHARTIC POWER OF ART AND HOW TO RECREATE CONTEMPORARY RITES

For many years, with uncommon persistence and acuity, the artist Rachel Lee Hovnanian has been analyzing the drifts of our hyper-technological and hyper-connected, but completely "liquid"—as Baumann tells us—society that has folded in on itself in a compulsive solipsism that generates a solitary crowd much in the way David Riesmann anticipated[1] many decades ago. The analysis and reworking of these topical issues are even more effective in her work because they are conducted not through the written word, but through the synthetic and metaphorical power of images. Whether in photos, sculptures, paintings, multimedia installations, or performative interventions, she produces devices that "force" the viewer to build a sensorial map of autonomous meanings; a powerful stimulus for reflection that encourages the observer to free himself from the state of sensorial and relational passivity typical of mass-media and social networking. Her works of art provide a specific path for the viewer, who becomes an active element and co-author called upon to complete the meaning of the work itself. Thus, the combination of the performative, "time-based" dimension with the eminently physical and visual one becomes a determining element of the artist's poetics and, above all, a highly effective expressive strategy in the context of practical and effective intervention in social and relational dynamics.

The artist's works furthermore recreate a ritual system which in turn activates a symbolic system. As is known, rites are symbolic actions—they produce, pass on, and represent those shared values that give life and support to a community. Rites provide access to community without need for communication while, as the philosophy of Korean writer Byung-Chul Han explains, today we are dominated by communication without access to community. Rachel Lee Hovnanian's recent works, such as the cathartic performance of "Angels Listening," produced on the occasion of the 2022 Venice Biennale, offer an effective and successful attempt to reactivate the elements of sublimation inherent to social rituals and that create networks of a symbolic dimension.

Symbolic perception builds symbols, and the artist has developed a refined ability to build what Thomas Stearns Elliot called the objective correlative, a concept that has similarly been effectively employed in the poetry of Eugenio Montale and the artistic expression of Marcel Duchamp. Rachel Lee Hovnanian has developed the capacity to individualize both the objective and formal dimensions, as a means to effectively build a symbolic universe that creates a dialectic with the observer, thereby activating a process of sublimation and relational creation.

The symbol (from the Greek *symbolon*) originally indicated the signal of recognition between guests (*tessera hospitalis*), referencing a clay tablet that was broken in half and offered as a sign of hospitality. Similarly, the artist activates a system of understanding that accesses the knowing of something that is already known, and it is in this context that the authentic process that Hegel called human "settlement" (*Einhausung*) occurs.

Rites, such as the one structured by the artist in the Venice performance, are symbolic techniques of "settling in," becoming in space what the house is in space, that is, they make time habitable. In these creative processes the artist renders time a designed and defined construction, repeatable within the context of this stable duration. Today, time lacks a stable structure—it is not "inhabitable" but rather a constant flow, reduced to a mere repetition of episodes that proceed forward, toppling without offering a handhold. Objects and language stabilize life, and rites have the same function by virtue of their recurrence. The artist's installations and performances offer the visitor the chance to experience a sense of duration and lingering—sensations that have been erased by contemporary trends of consumption; ritual practices with their cathartic effects allow us to relate harmoniously not only with one another but also with the objects that surround us, attributing to them a weighted significance.

The "ritual" actions imposed by the artist force us to reflect but also to execute structured actions, the repetition of which leads us to become aware of ourselves as we take note of the procedures; in fact, the term religion also derives from the Latin *relegere*, that is, to take note. As Kierkegaard reminded us, repetition, like recognition, is a "compacting" form, such that in these dynamics the past and the future are brought together in a living and participatory present. These installations and performances aim to reunite oneself with the essence of one's own self, a self that has otherwise been set aside or even canceled by the circadian rhythms of production, consumption, and communication with others. Rites create embodied knowledge and memory, allowing them to become physically integrated into the self.

Rachel Lee Hovnanian addresses through ethical and aesthetic formations within her creative process the problematic of a society that rejects rituals for their affiliation with conformity and thereby inadvertently paves the way for an atomization of society.

From the famous separation of man, carried out by Zeus and remembered in Plato's *Symposium*, man has become a *symbolon* who pines in the search for his other half, to achieve salvific completeness. In Greek, to bring together, "to put together," is called *symballein* and in this sense the rites, the performances implemented by the artist, become a symbolic practice, a practice of *symballein* as they bring people together and create a bond, a totality, and ultimately atomization of community. Rites and ceremonies are actions that humans have carried out since ancient times to make life appear complete and interpretable through a magical key and their appearance in our contemporary society, also induced by the pervasive "virtual" communication deprived of real relational consistency, desecrates life itself and relegates it to simple survival.

Art, as Rachel Lee Hovnanian demonstrates, has the task and the power to re-awe the world through that healing energy that was already attributed to it by the primitive peoples who adorned caves, and can heal the widespread collective narcissism that produces incommunicability.

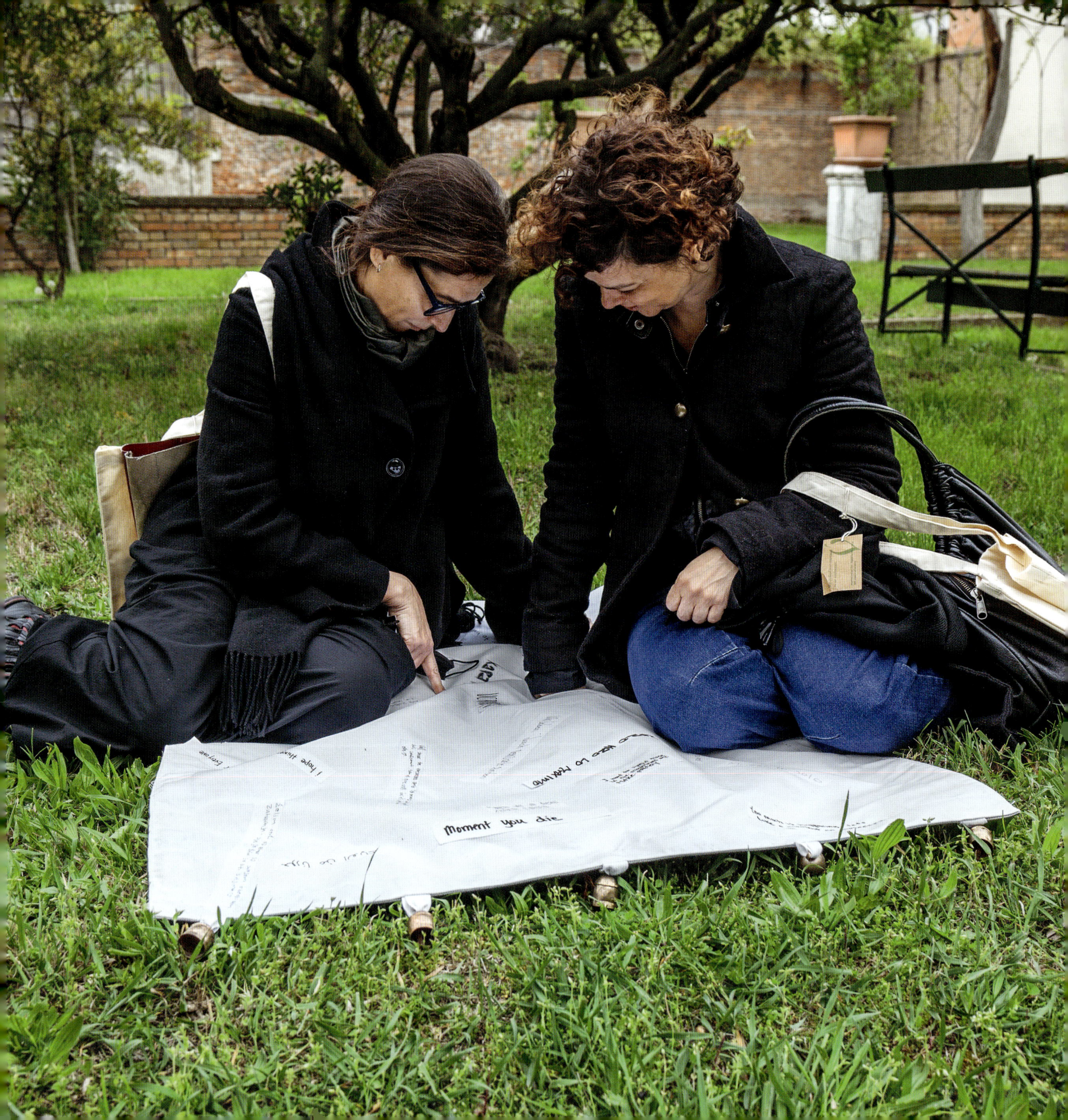
Moment you die

RACHEL LEE HOVNANIAN: ANGELS LISTENING

Samantha Boardman, MD

As human beings, we crave communication. But most of communication isn't speaking, it's listening. Feeling heard is a cornerstone of connection. So much in our lives is left unsaid and what is said is not always heard. Even when someone summons the courage to speak up, their confession, revelation or reflection may not elicit the hoped for response.

It's human to crave understanding. We all long to be seen, to be known, to be listened to. Because when we feel heard, we are not alone. Nearly 1 in 4 adults across the world have reported feeling very or fairly lonely[1]—that's more than a billion people who don't feel there is anyone in their life to confide in.

In "Angels Listening",[2] Rachel Lee Hovnanian invites viewers to "write down what you could not say, what you did not say". The act of anonymously expressing one's innermost thoughts can be cathartic—an unearthing and letting go of what has never been articulated. Sometimes feeling heard is all we need to feel unburdened. Hovnanian's angels bear witness without judging. They hear without probing. A listening ear can be a life raft when a person feels adrift.

Hovnanian's angels may be mute but are, in many ways, active listeners. They are quite literally "all ears". There is no threat of betrayal or criticism. They occupy a liminal space between innocence and all-knowing. According to research,[3] attention, empathy, and respect are the key ingredients of feeling heard. Hovnanian's angels embody all three.

Psychologist Harriet Lerner observed, "If we only listened with the same passion that we feel about being heard". We all long to be heard. Hovnanian's angels have a great deal to teach us about how to listen deeply.

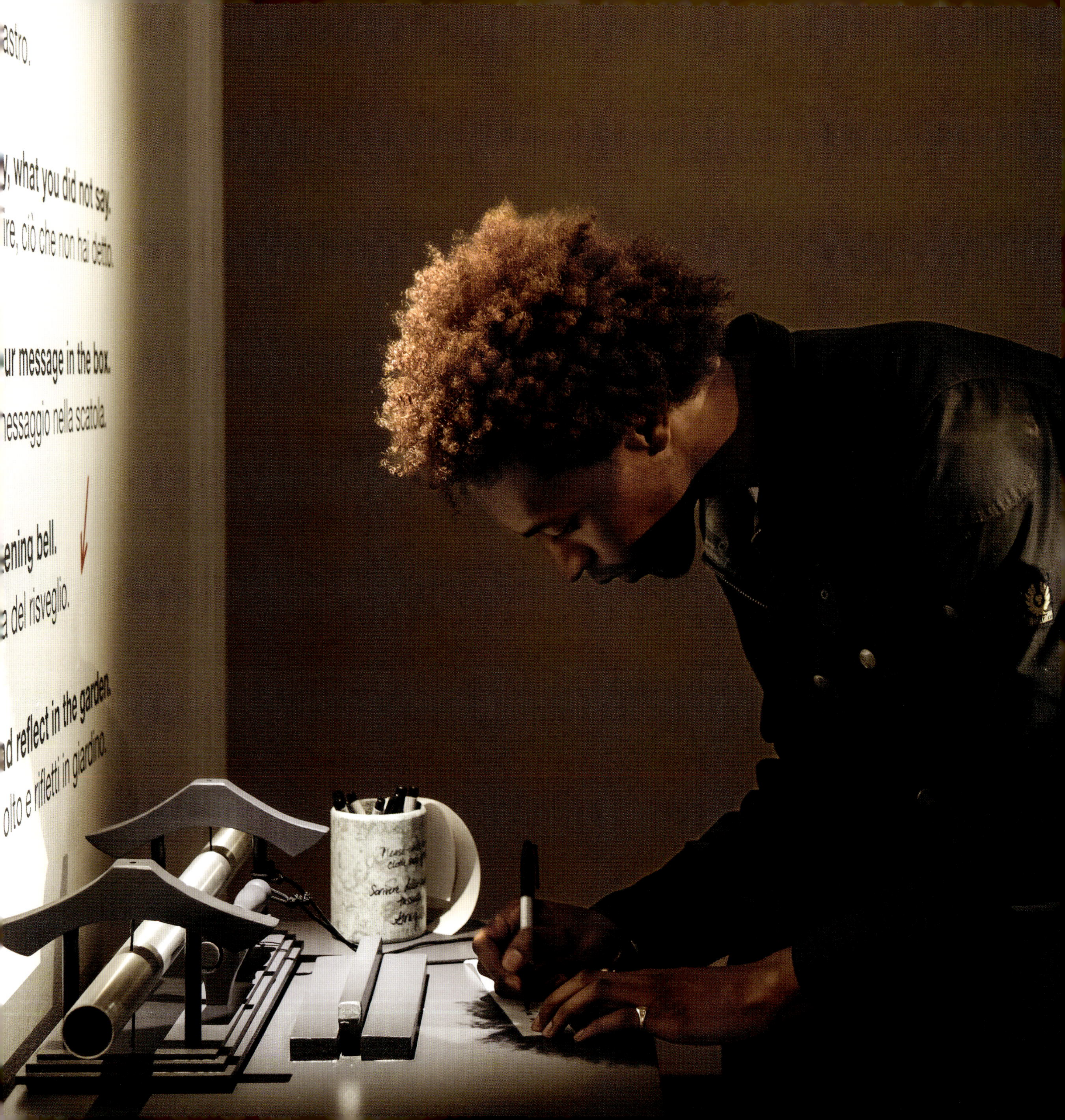
astro.
y, what you did not say.
ire, ciò che non hai detto.
ur message in the box.
nessaggio nella scatola.
ening bell.
a del risveglio.
d reflect in the garden.
olto e rifletti in giardino.

CATHARTIC PERFORMANCE

La performance catartica

Approach either side of the confessional.
Avvicinati a entrambi i lati del confessionale.

Take a ribbon.
Prendi un nastro.

Write what you could not say, what you did not say.
Scrivi ciò che non hai potuto dire, ciò che non hai detto.

Open the door and leave your message in a box.
Apri la porta e lascia il tuo messaggio nella scatola.

Ring the awakening bell.
Suona la campana del risveglio.

Take a listening blanket and reflect in the garden.
Prendi una coperta da ascolto e rifletti in giardino.

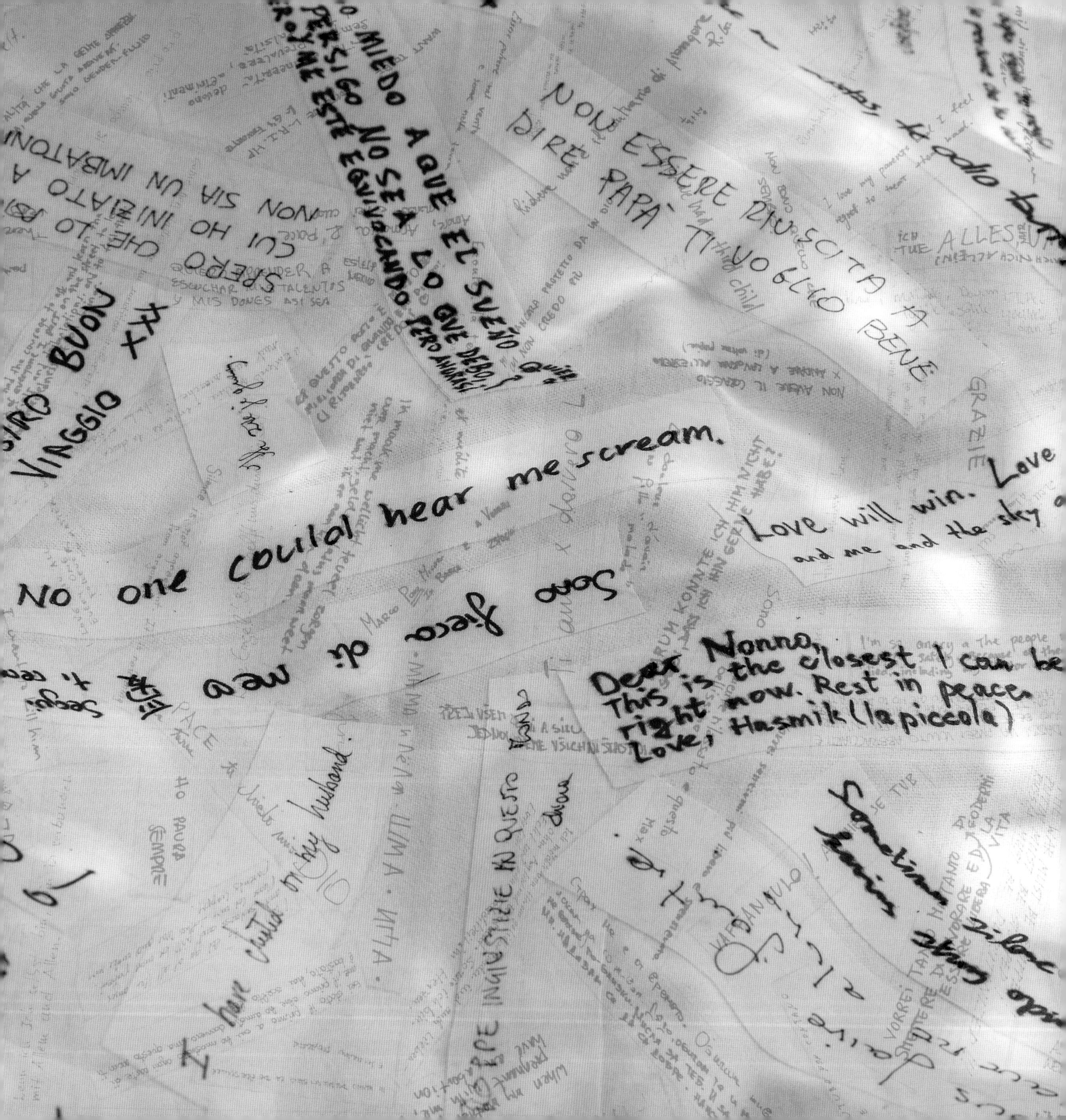

NON ESSERE RIUSCITA A DIRE PAPÀ TI VOGLIO BENE
No one could hear me scream.
Love will win. Love
and me and the sky
Dear Nonno,
This is the closest I can be
right now. Rest in peace.
Love, Hasmik (la piccola)

MESSAGES

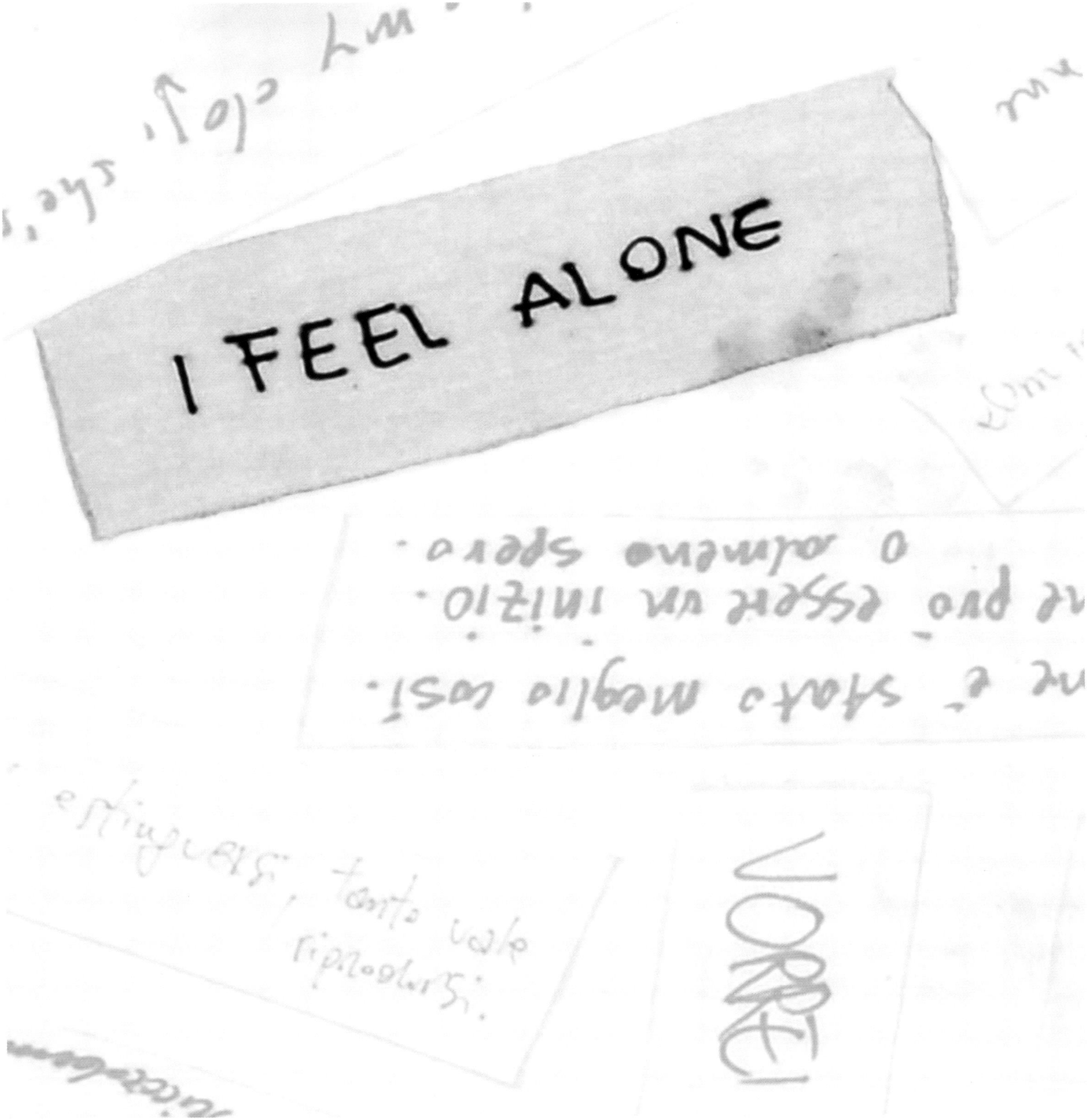
I FEEL ALONE
è stato meglio così.
può essere un inizio.
o almeno spero.
VORREI

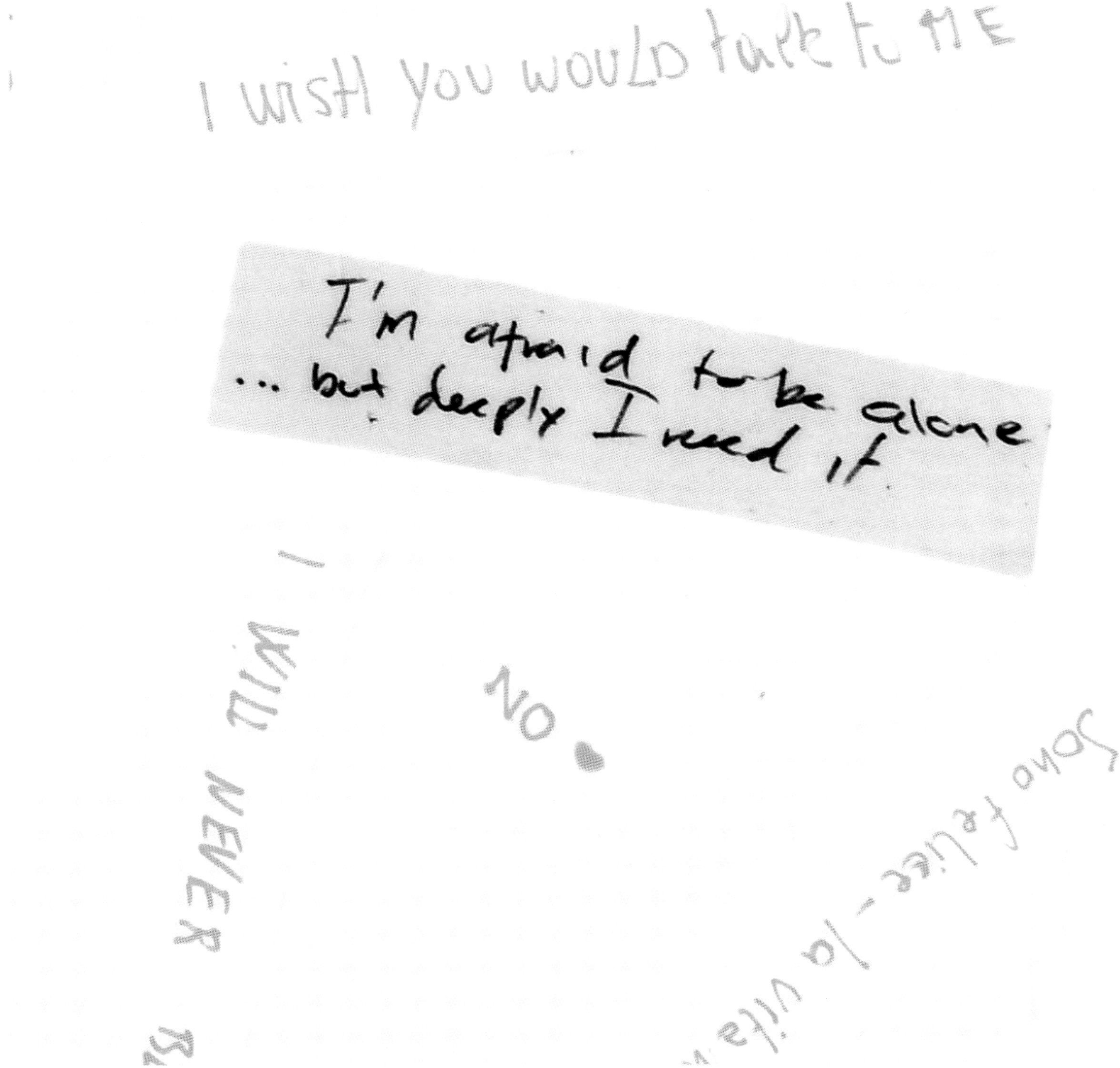
I WISH YOU WOULD talk to ME
I'm afraid to be alone
... but deeply I need it
I WILL NEVER
NO
Sono felice - la vita

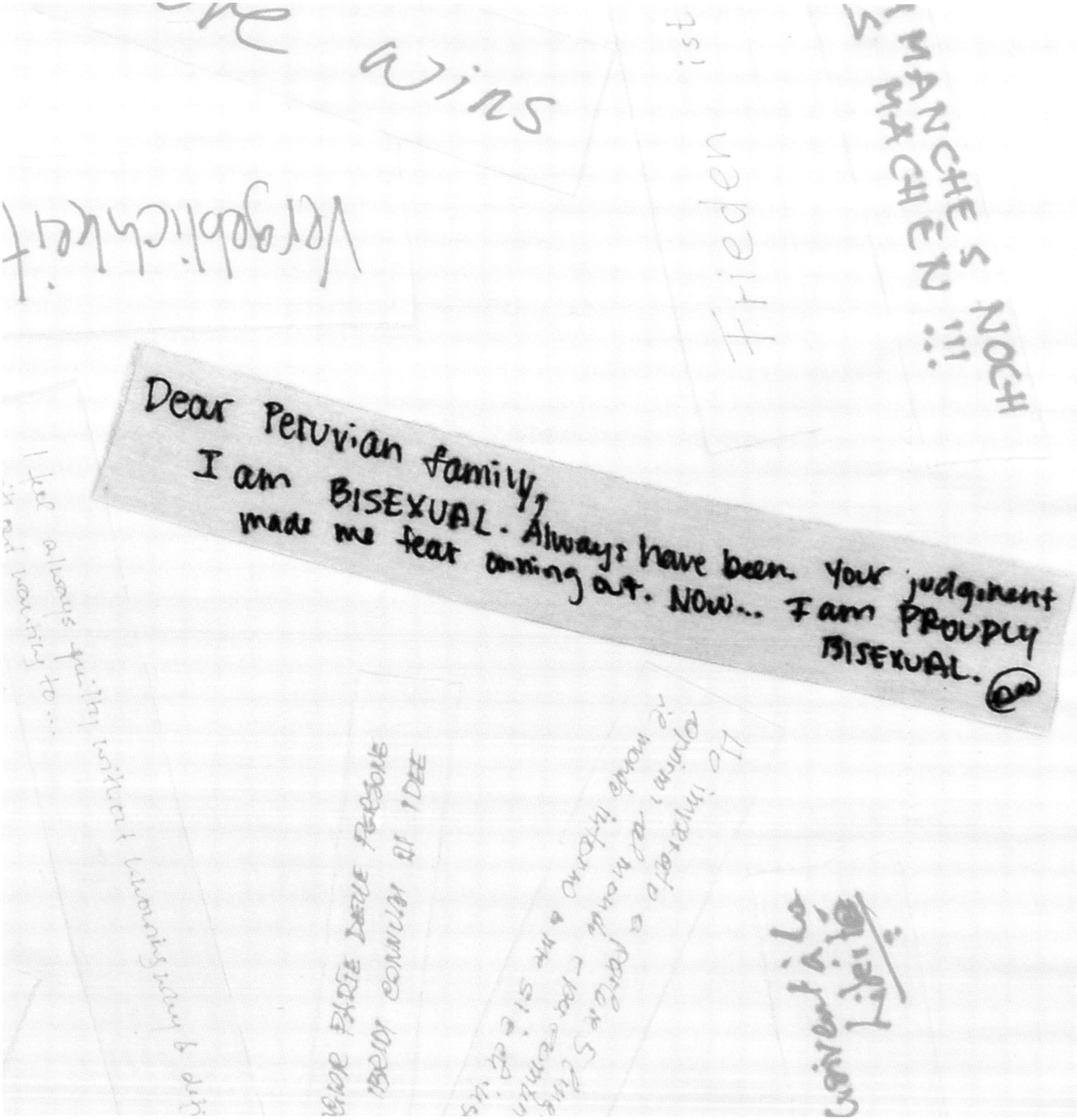
Dear Peruvian family,
I am BISEXUAL. Always have been. Your judgment made me fear coming out. NOW... I am PROUDLY BISEXUAL.
wins
Frieden ist
MANCHES NOCH MACHEN !!!

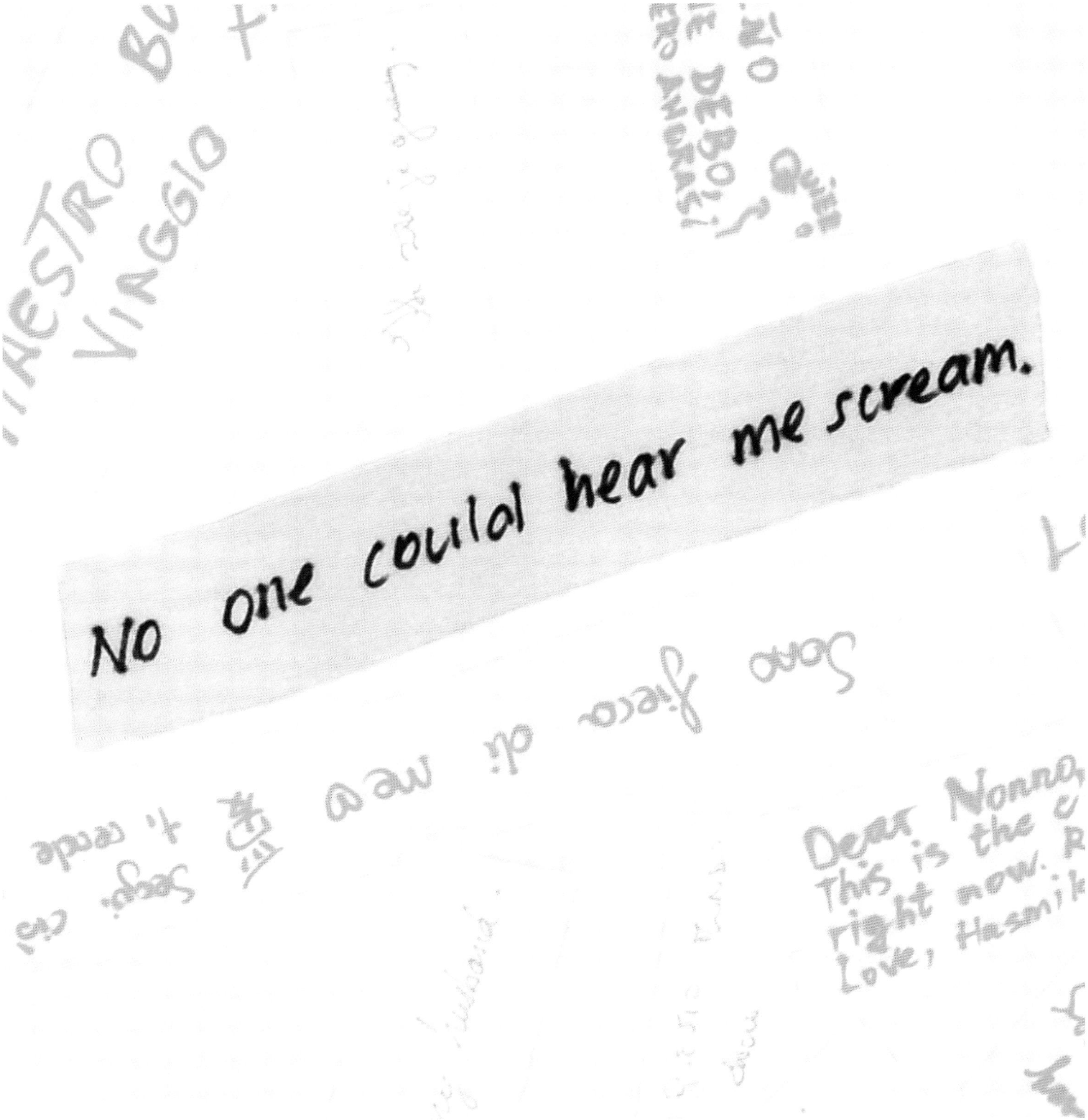
No one could hear me scream.

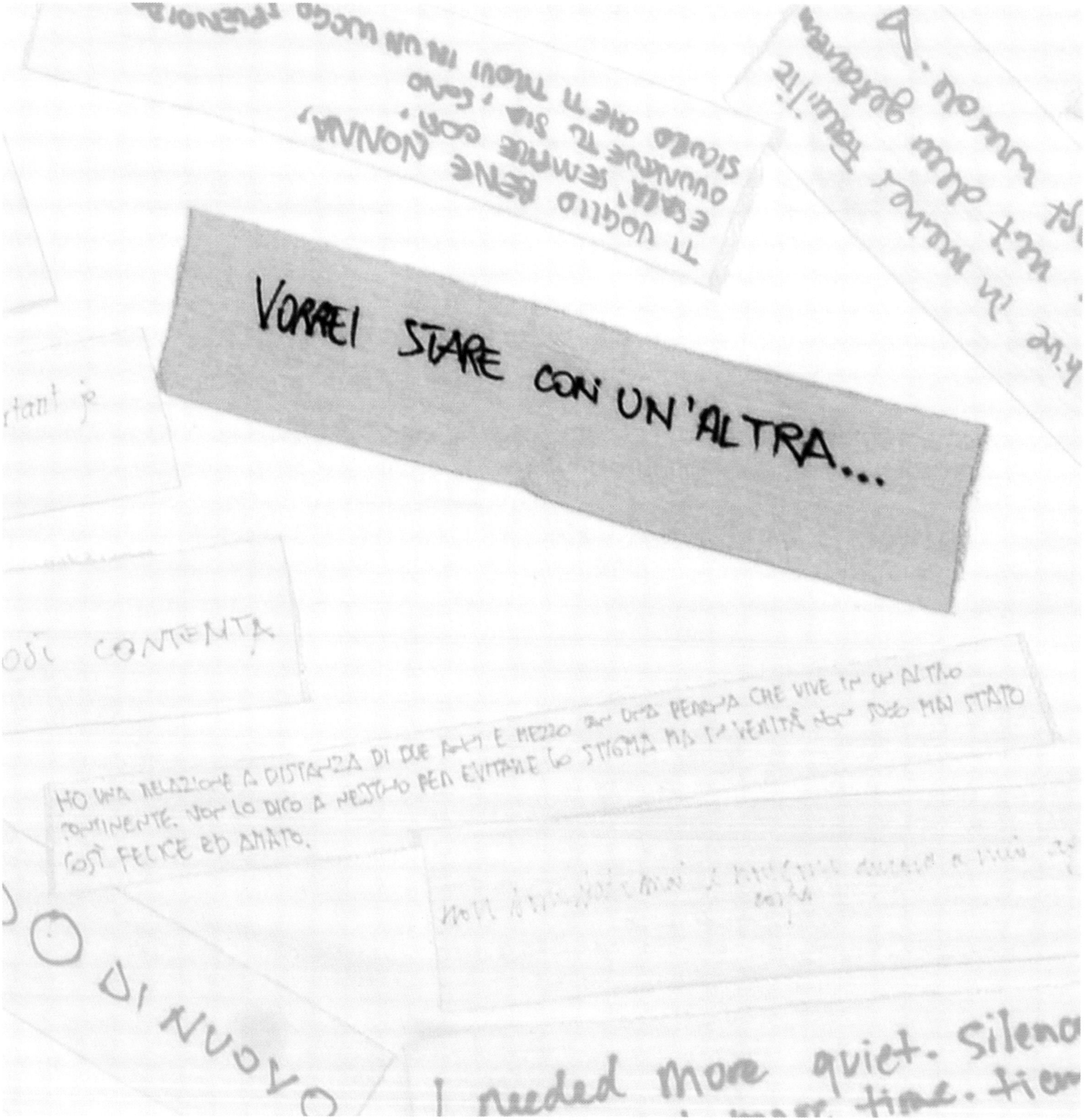
VORREI STARE CON UN'ALTRA...
OSÌ CONTENTA
DI NUOVO
I needed more quiet.

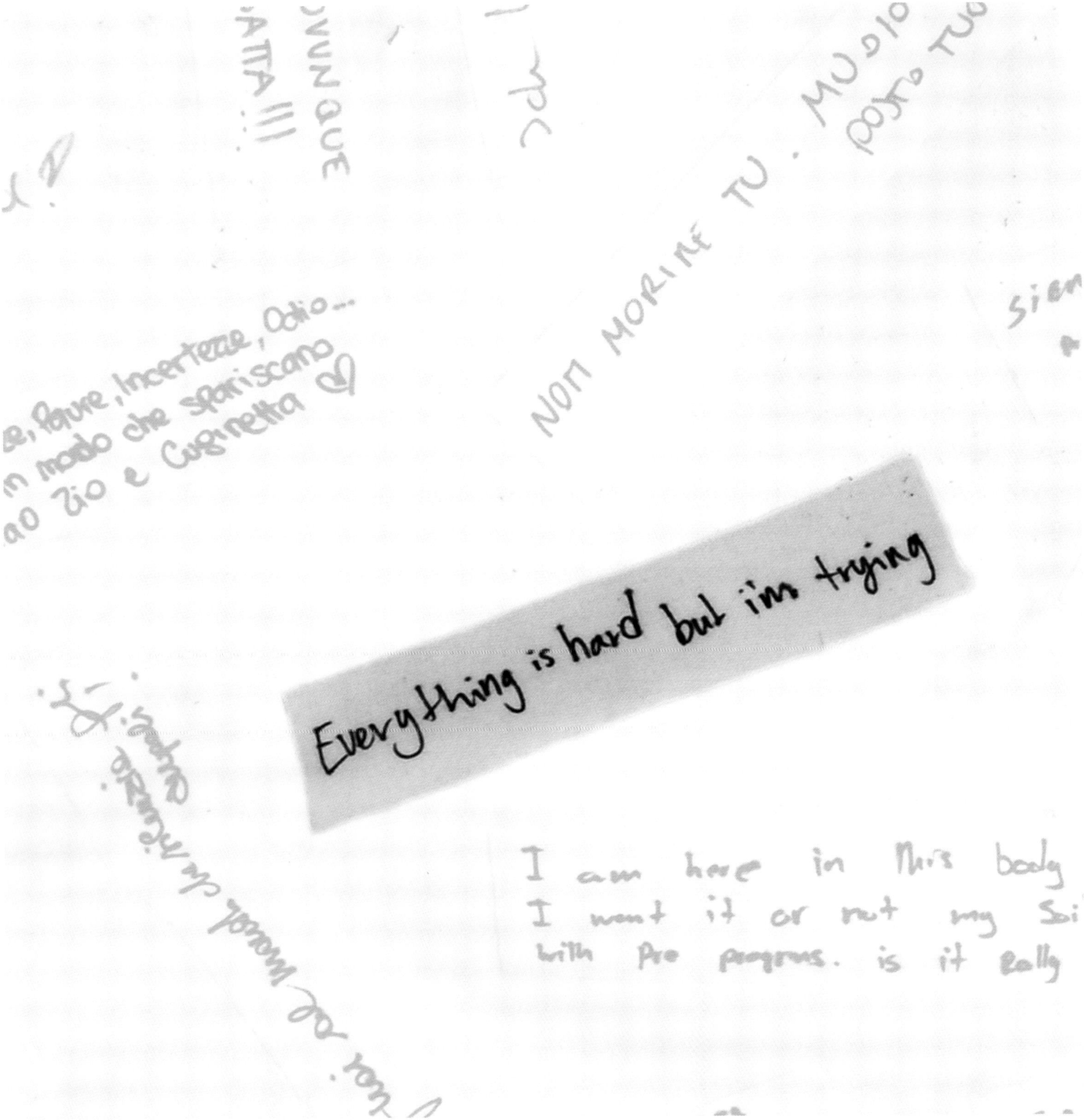
Everything is hard but im trying
NON MORIRE TU.
POSTO TUO
e, Paure, Incertezze, Odio...
n modo che spariscano
ao Zio e Cuginetta
I am here in this body
I want it or not
with the progress. is it Really

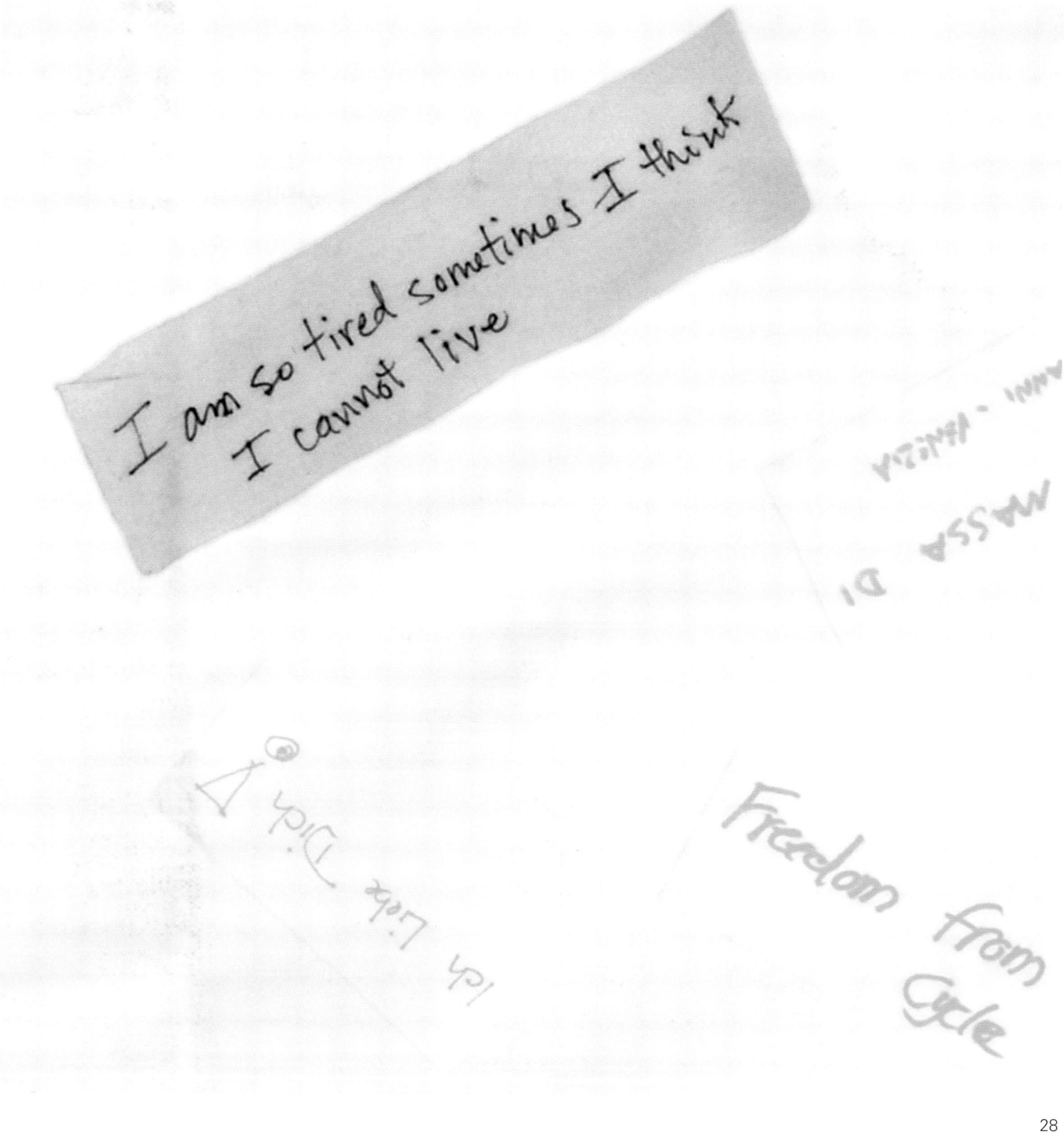
I am so tired sometimes I think
I cannot live
Freedom from Cycle

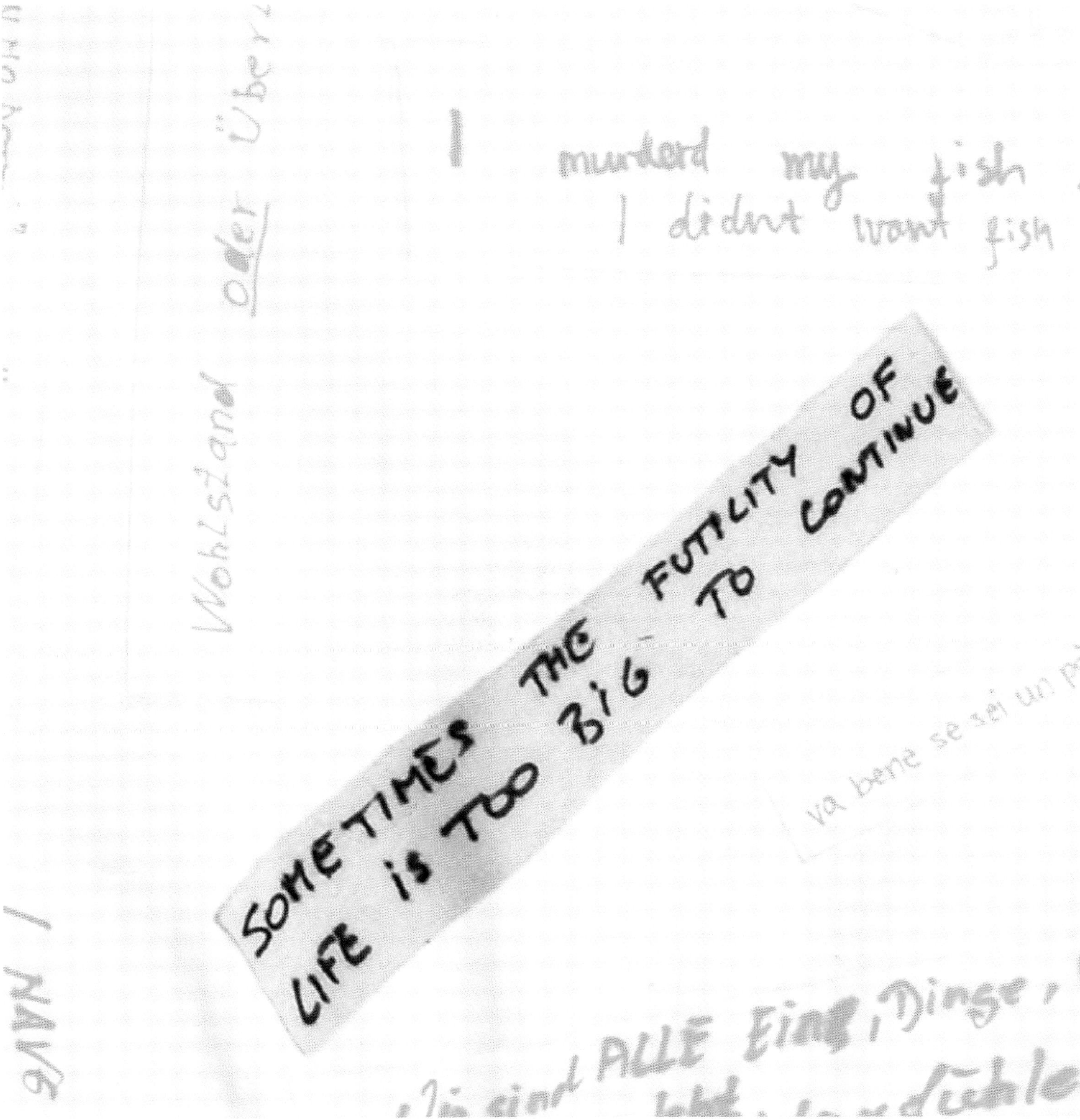
I murderd my fish
I didnt want fish
SOMETIMES THE FUTILITY OF
LIFE IS TOO BIG TO CONTINUE
Wohlstand oder
va bene se sei un

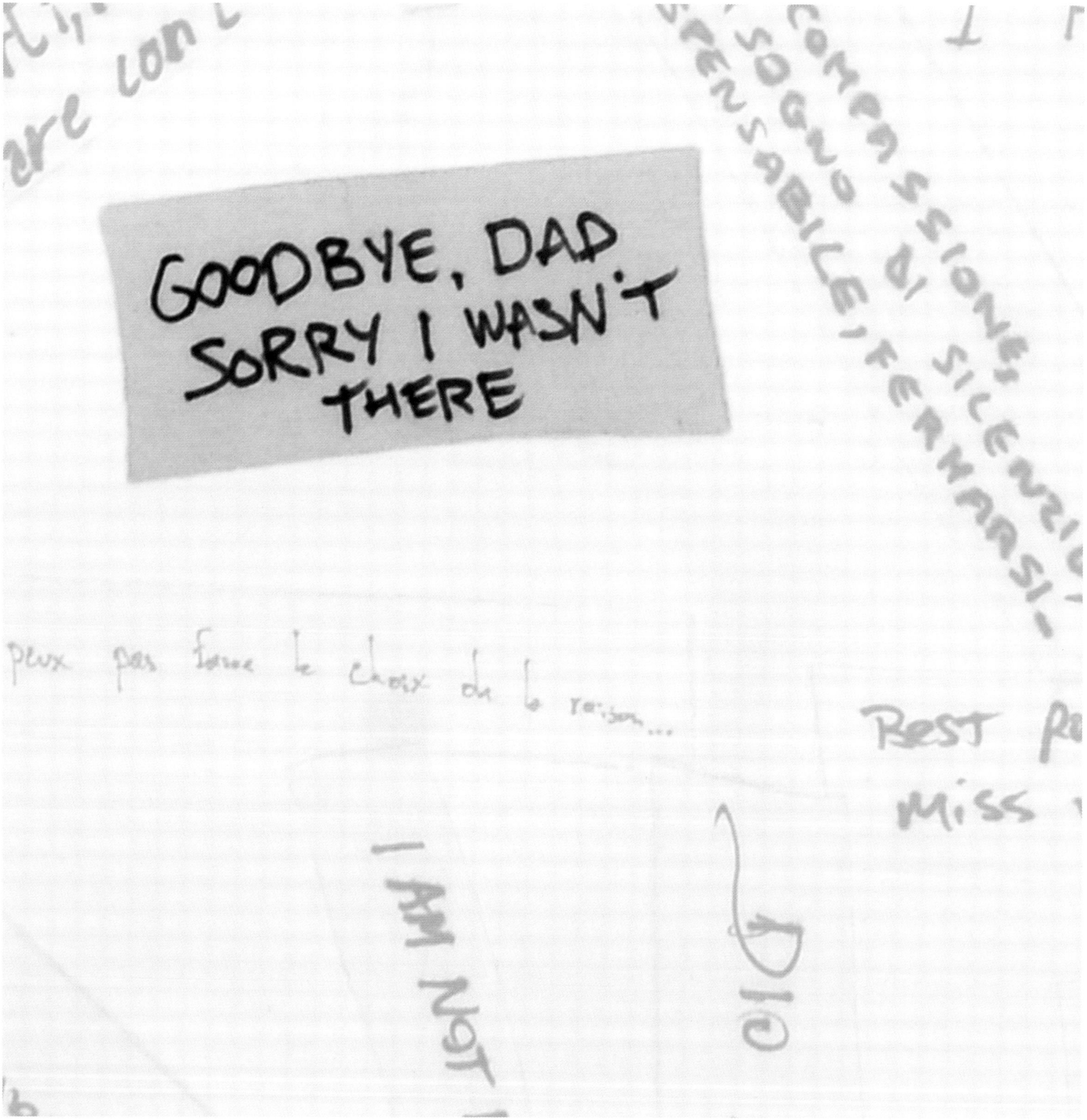
GOODBYE, DAD
SORRY I WASN'T
THERE
COMPASSIONE
SOGNO DI SILENZIO
FERMARSI-
BEST
MISS
I AM NOT
DIO

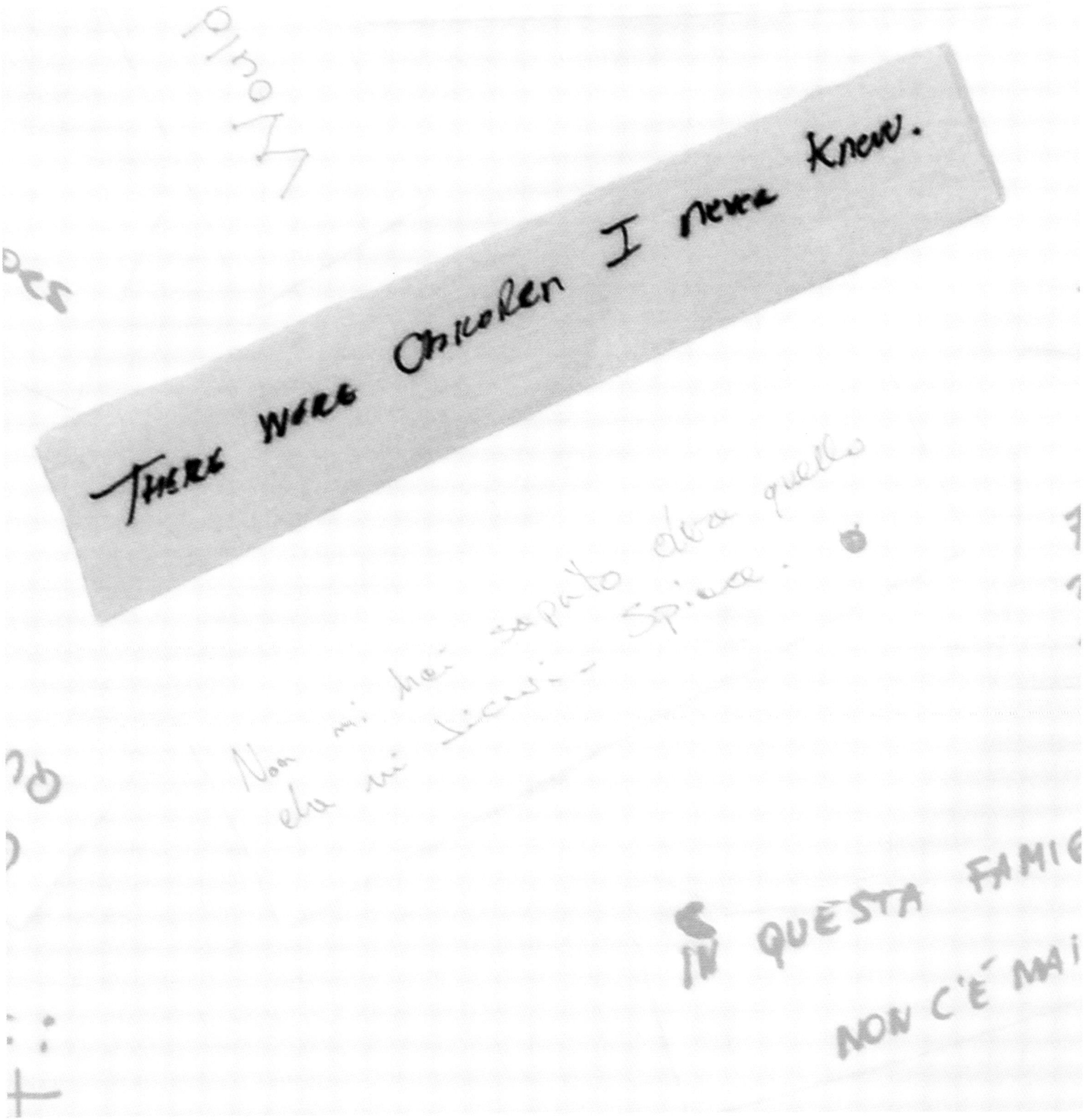
THERE WERE CHILDREN I NEVER KNEW.
IN QUESTA FAMIG
NON C'É MAI

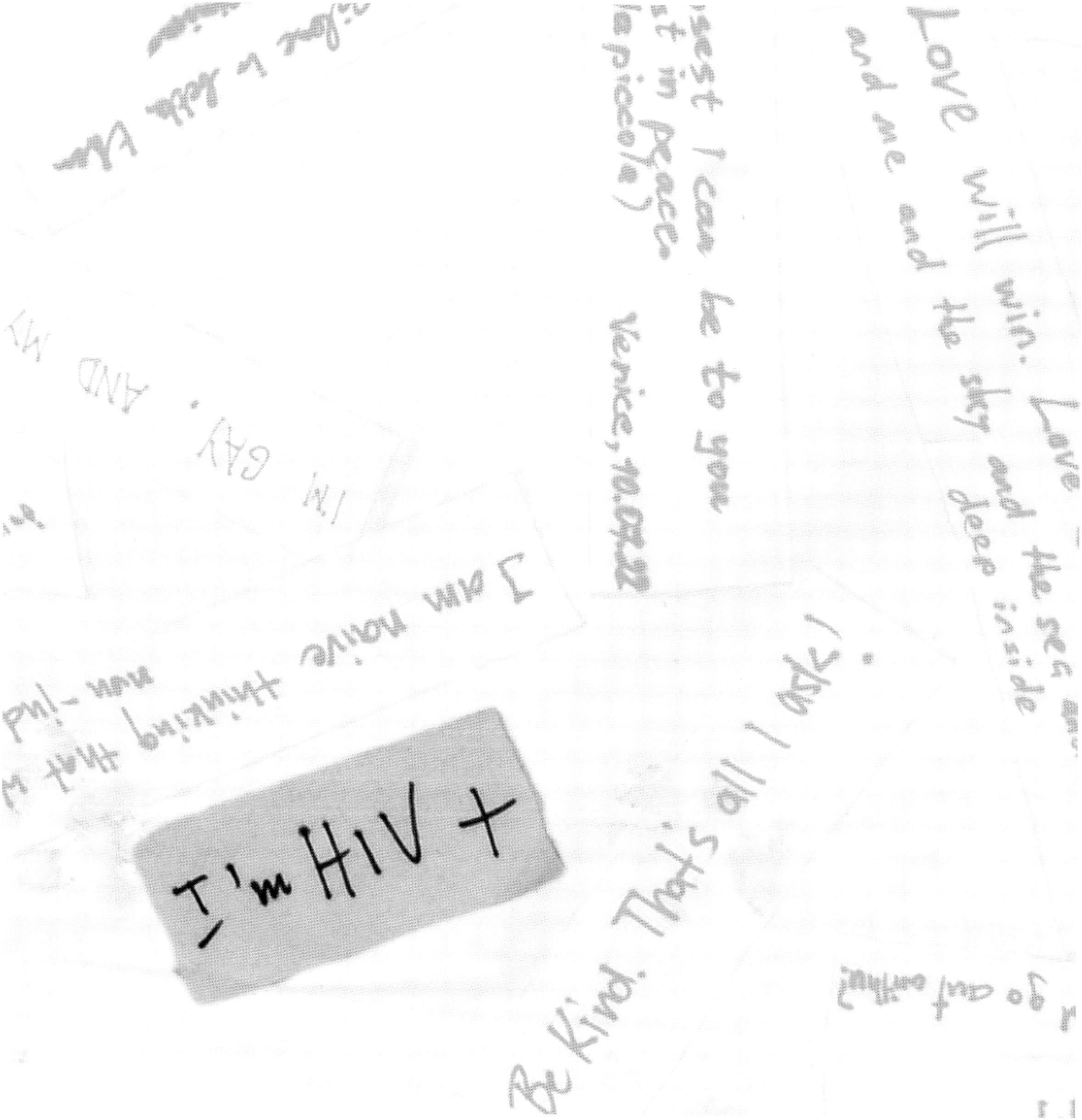
I'm HIV +
Love will win. Love
and me and the sky and deep inside
I am naive
Be Kind. That's all I ask!
Venice, 10.07.22
I'M GAY. AND MY

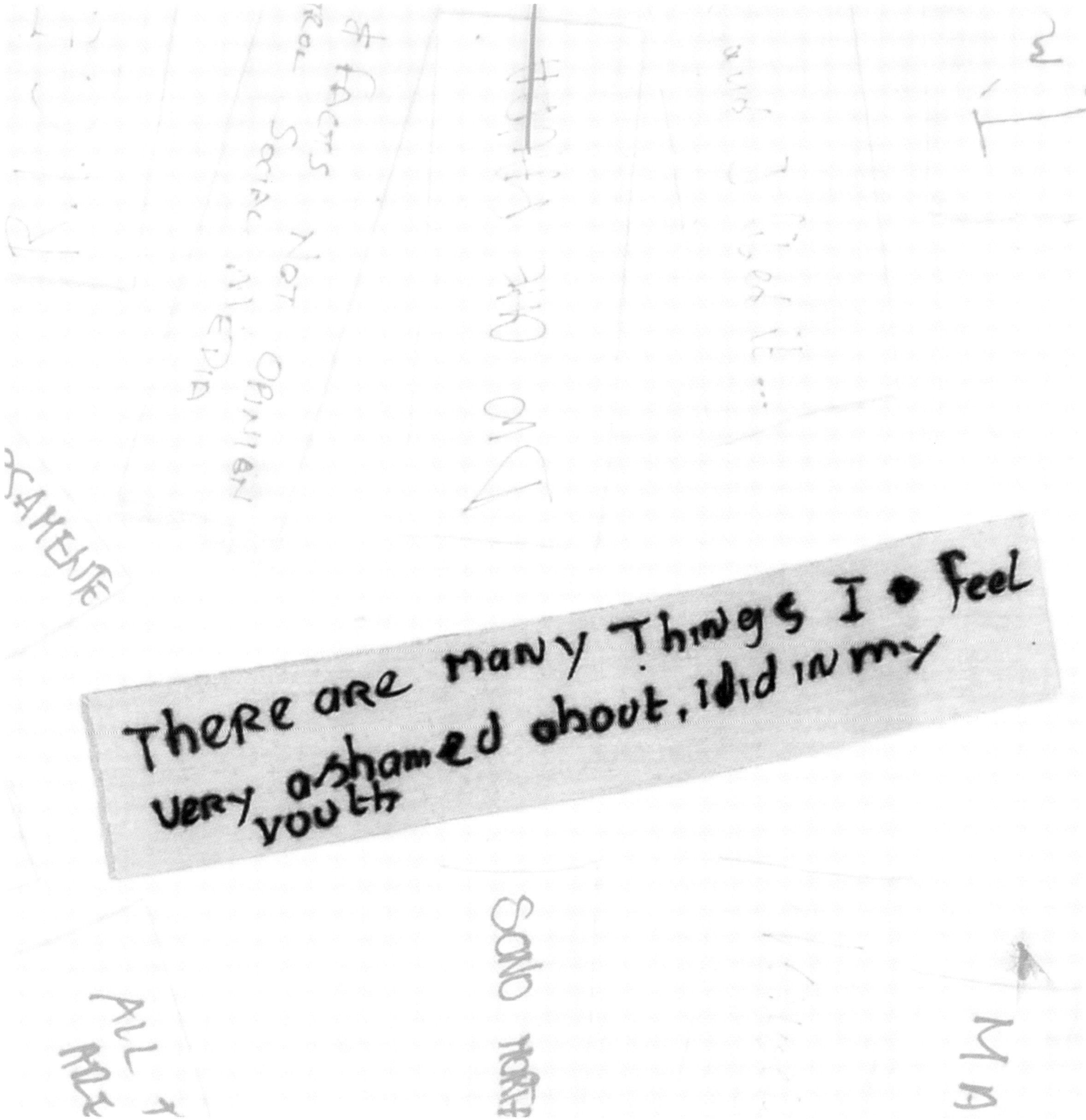
There are many Things I feel
very ashamed about, I did in my youth

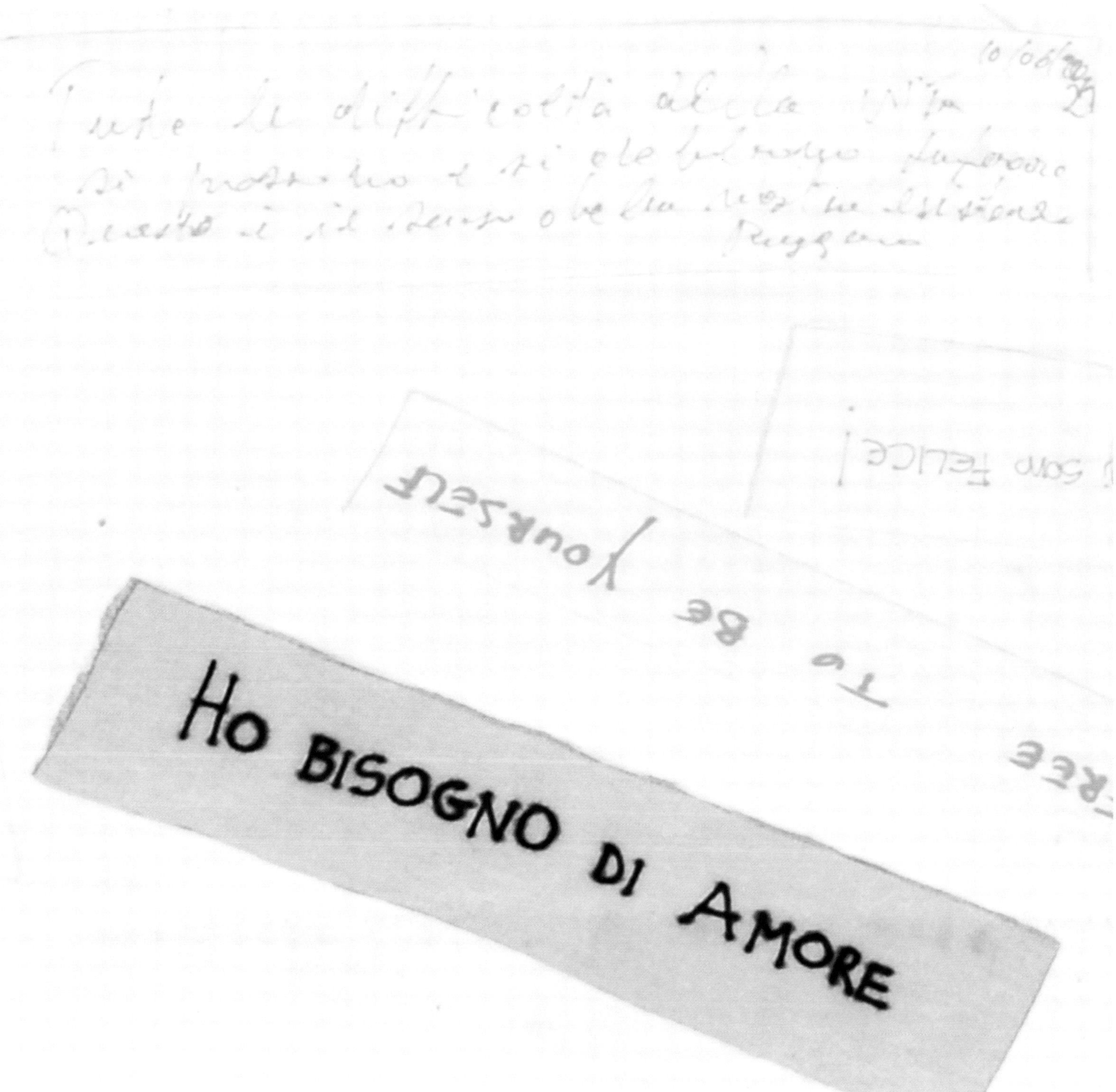
HO BISOGNO DI AMORE

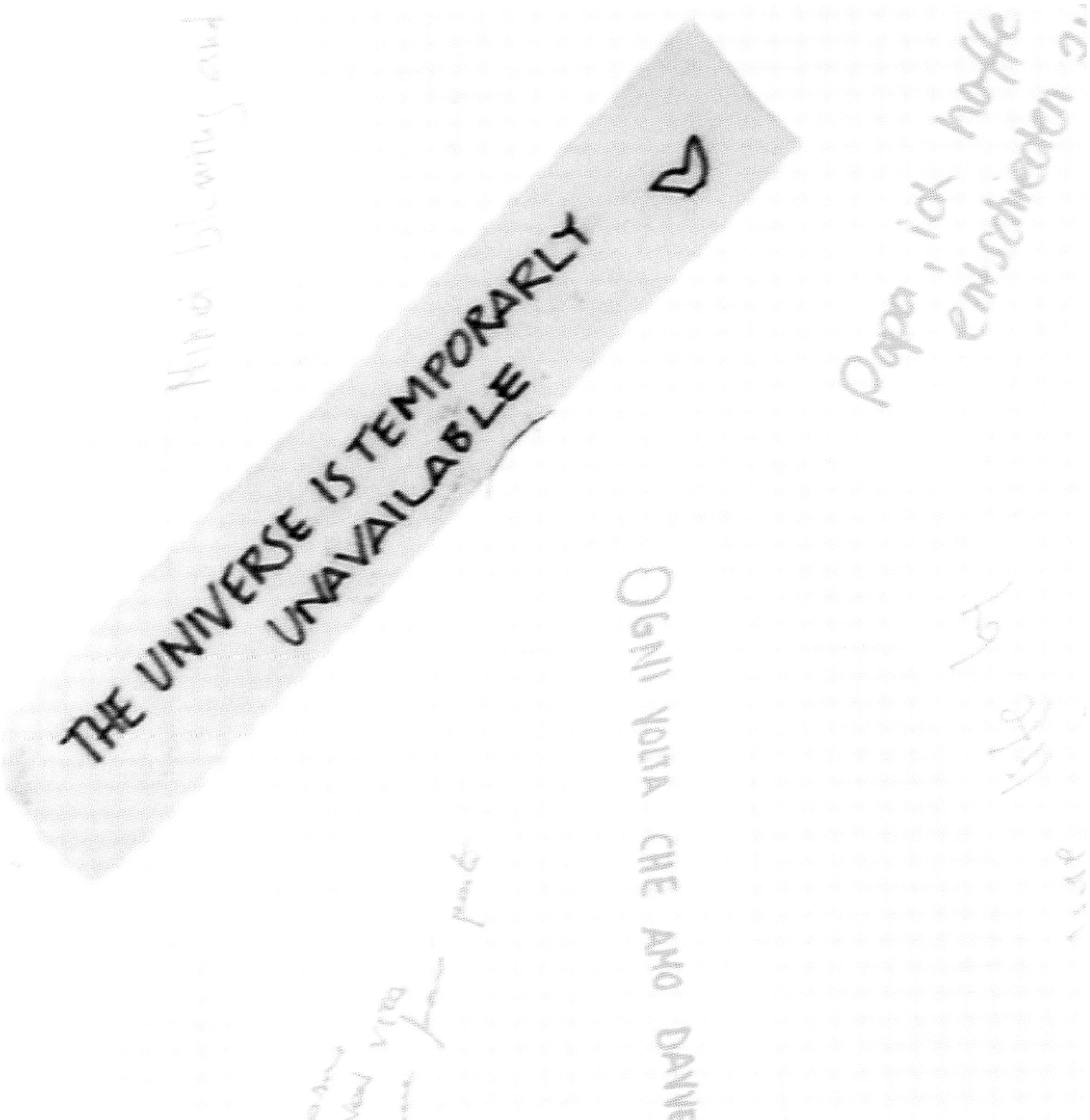
THE UNIVERSE IS TEMPORARLY
UNAVAILABLE
OGNI VOLTA CHE AMO DAVVE
Papa, ich hoffe
entschieden

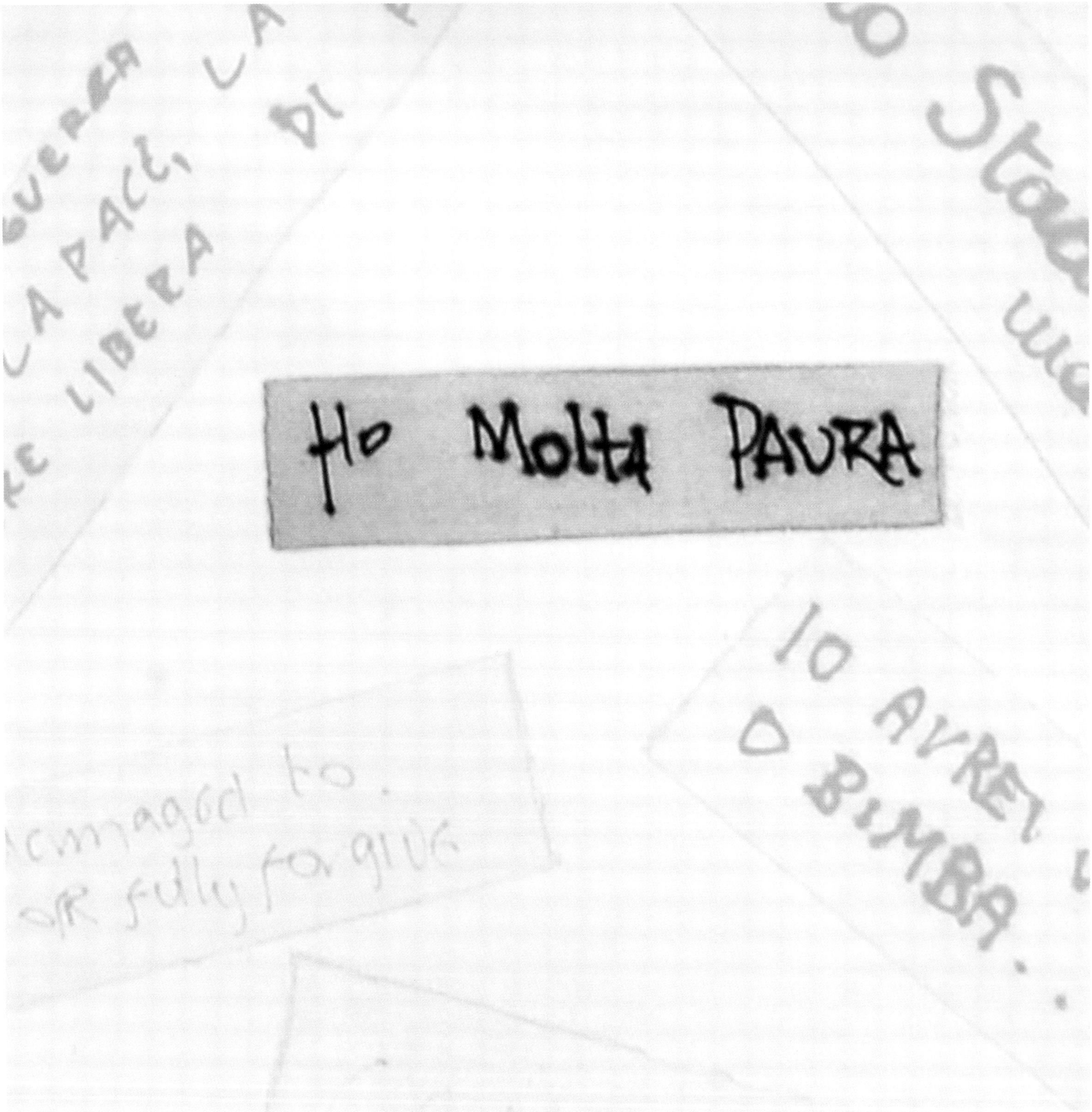
Ho Molta PAURA

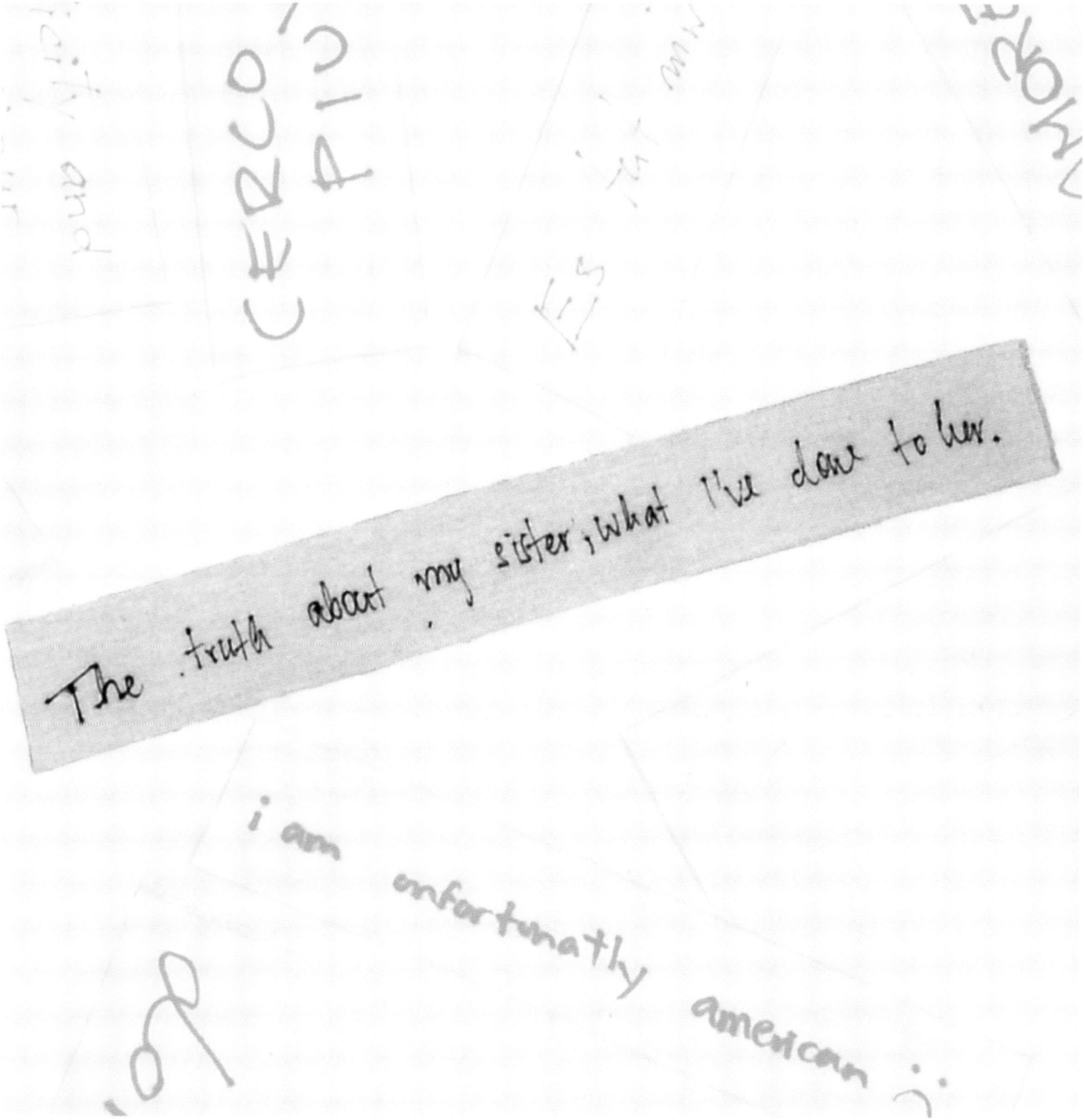
The truth about my sister, what I've done to her.
i am unfortunatly american

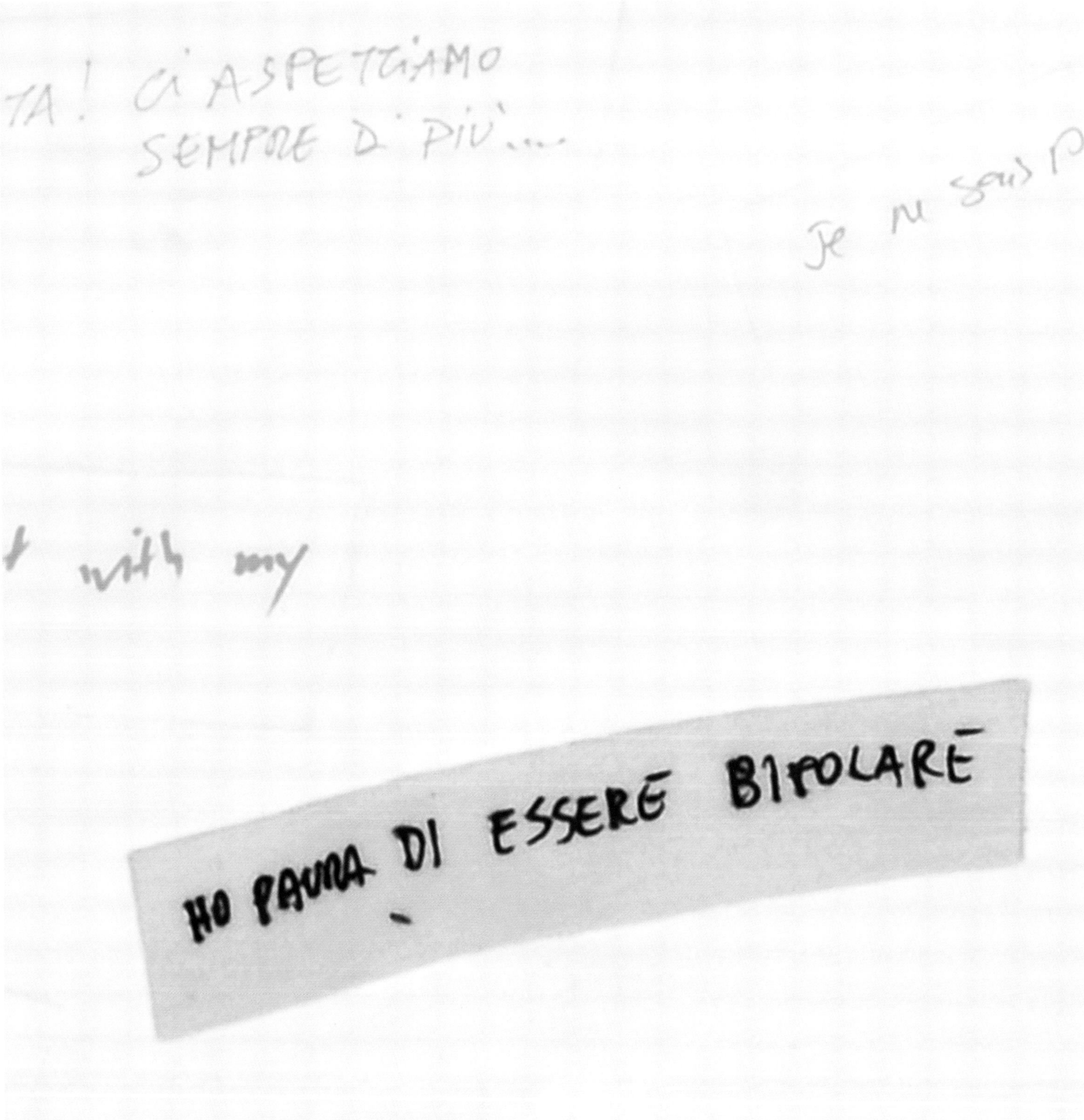
TA! CI ASPETTIAMO
SEMPRE DI PIÙ...
Je ne sais p
with my
HO PAURA DI ESSERE BIPOLARE

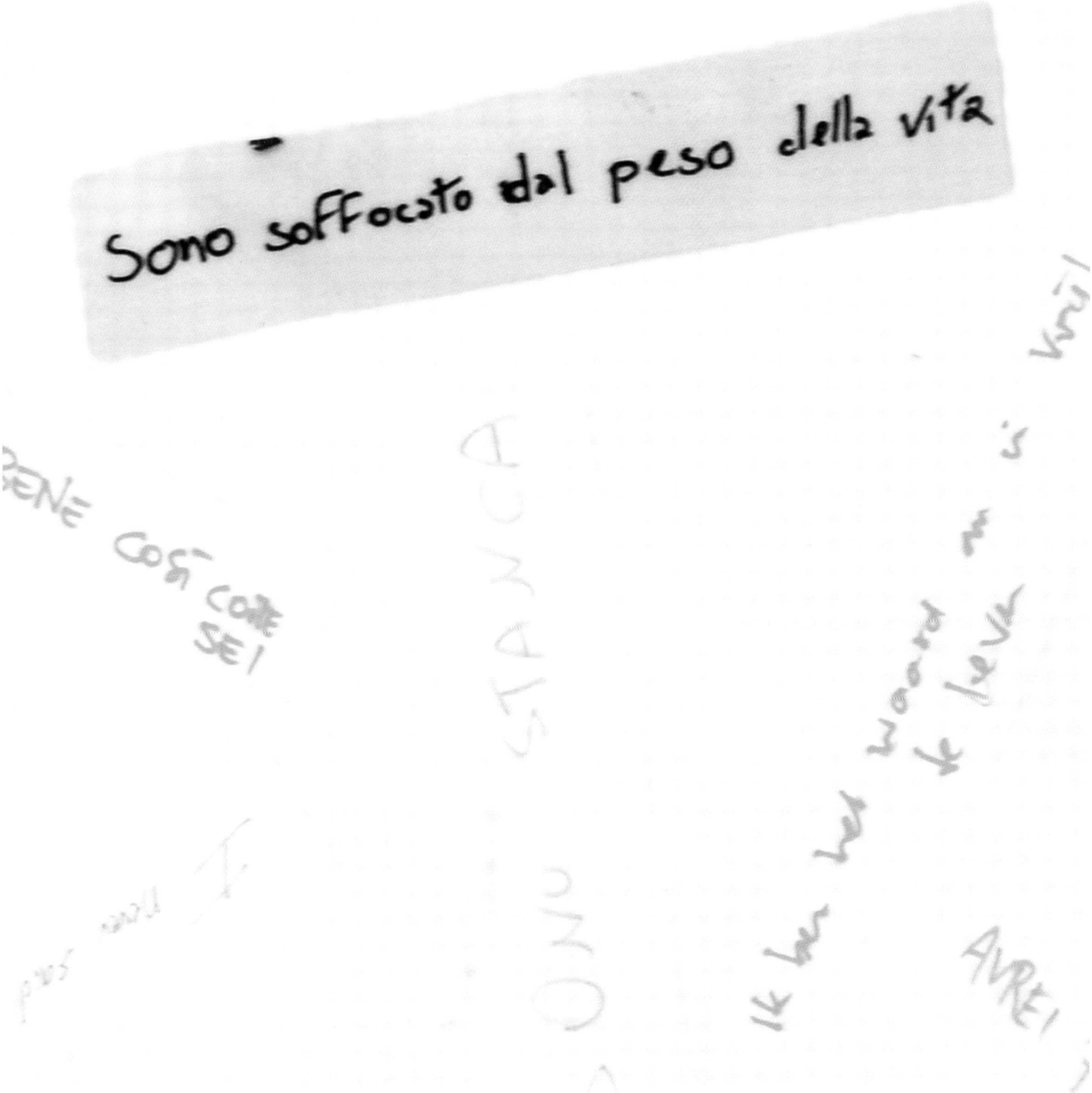
Sono soffocato dal peso della vita

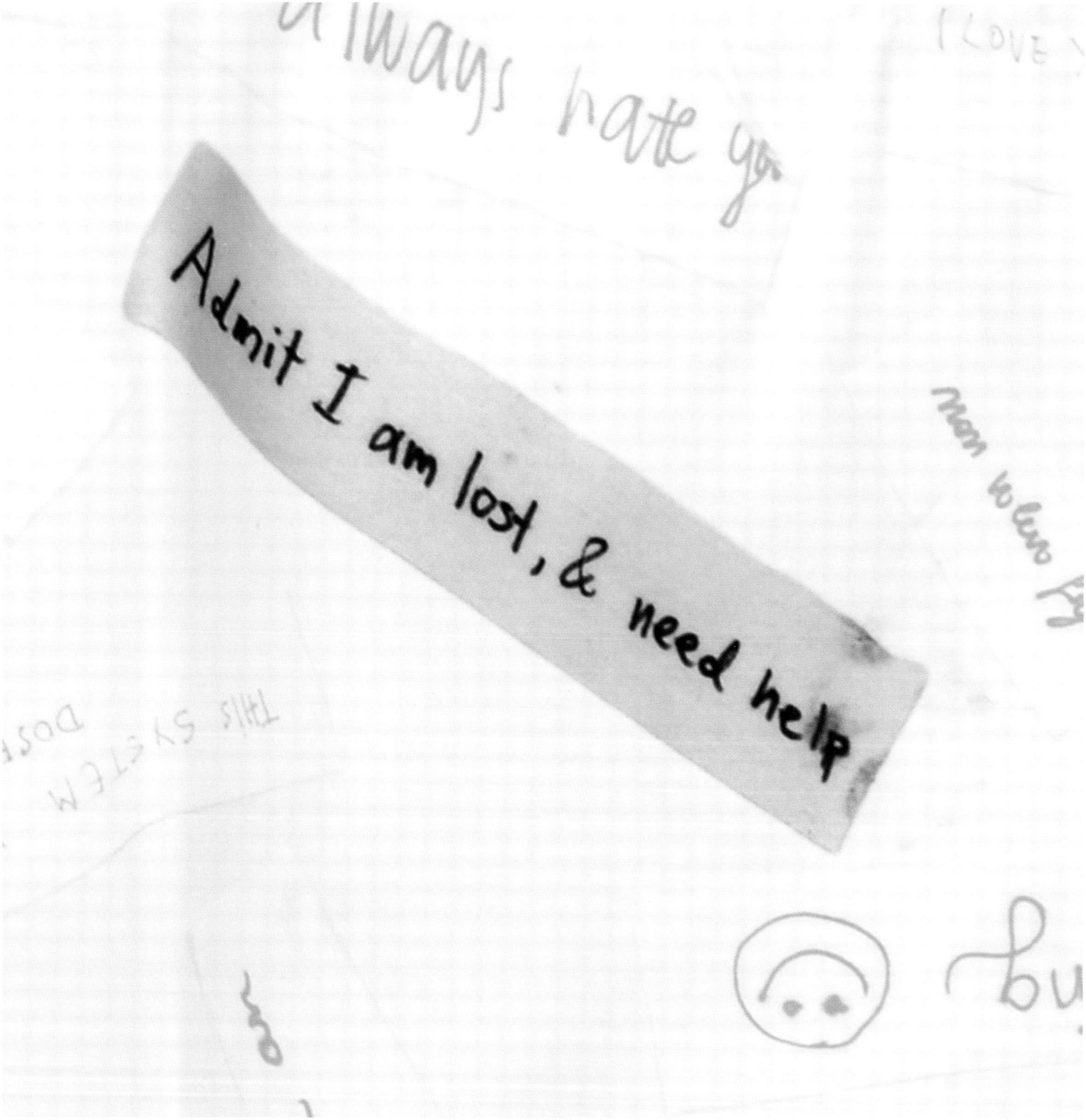
Admit I am lost, & need help

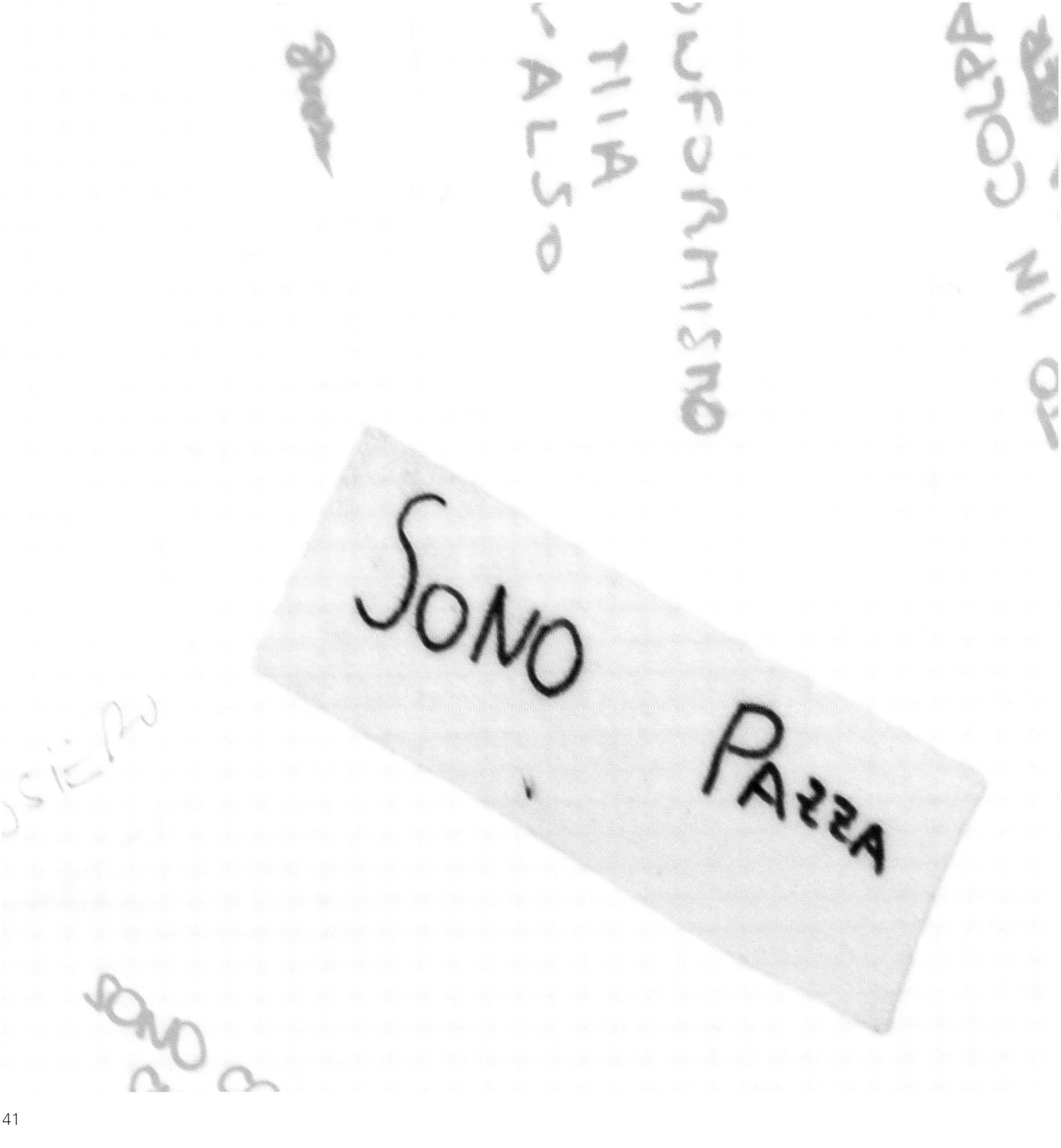
SONO PAZZA

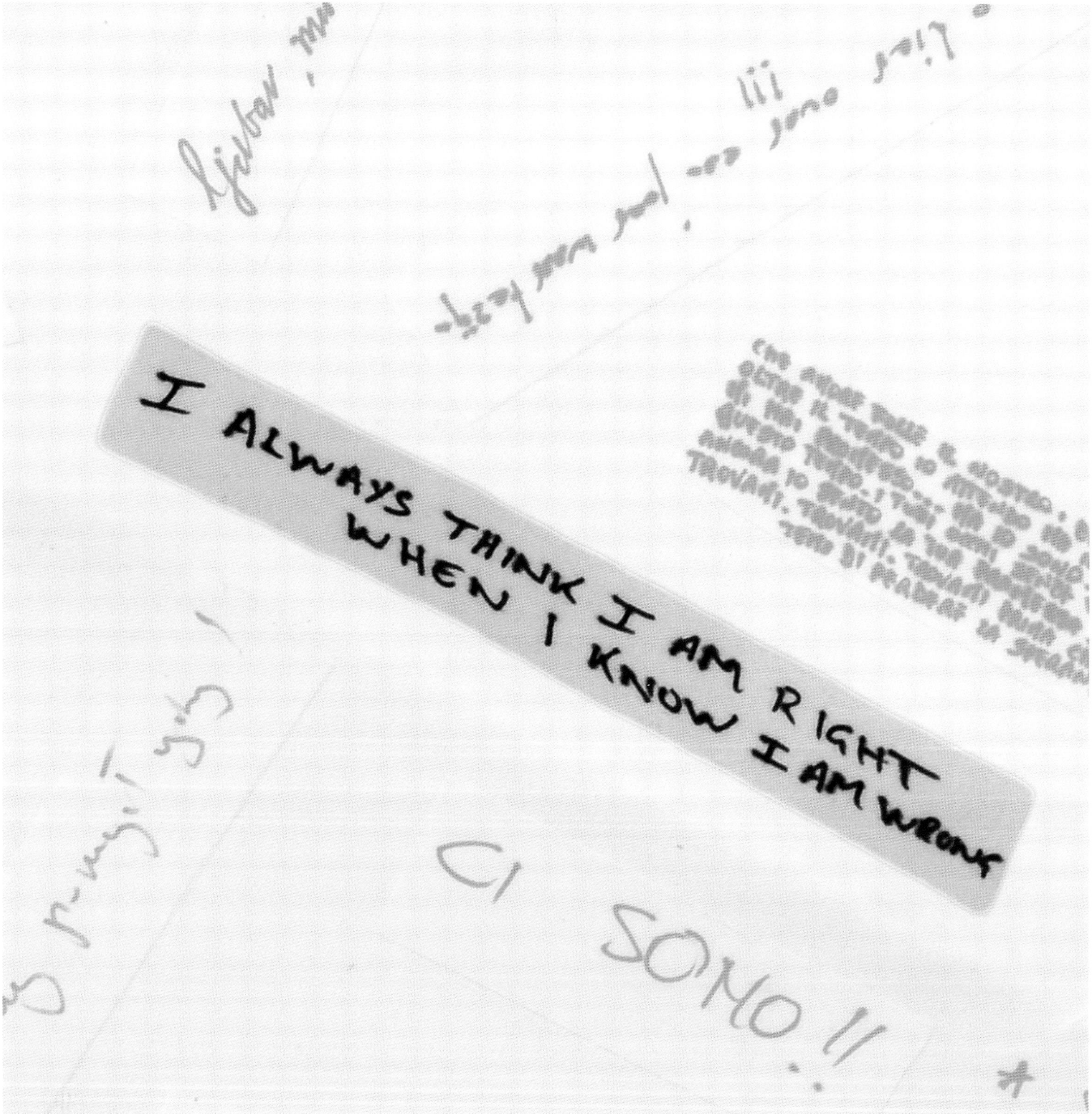
I ALWAYS THINK I AM RIGHT
WHEN I KNOW I AM WRONG
CI SONO !!

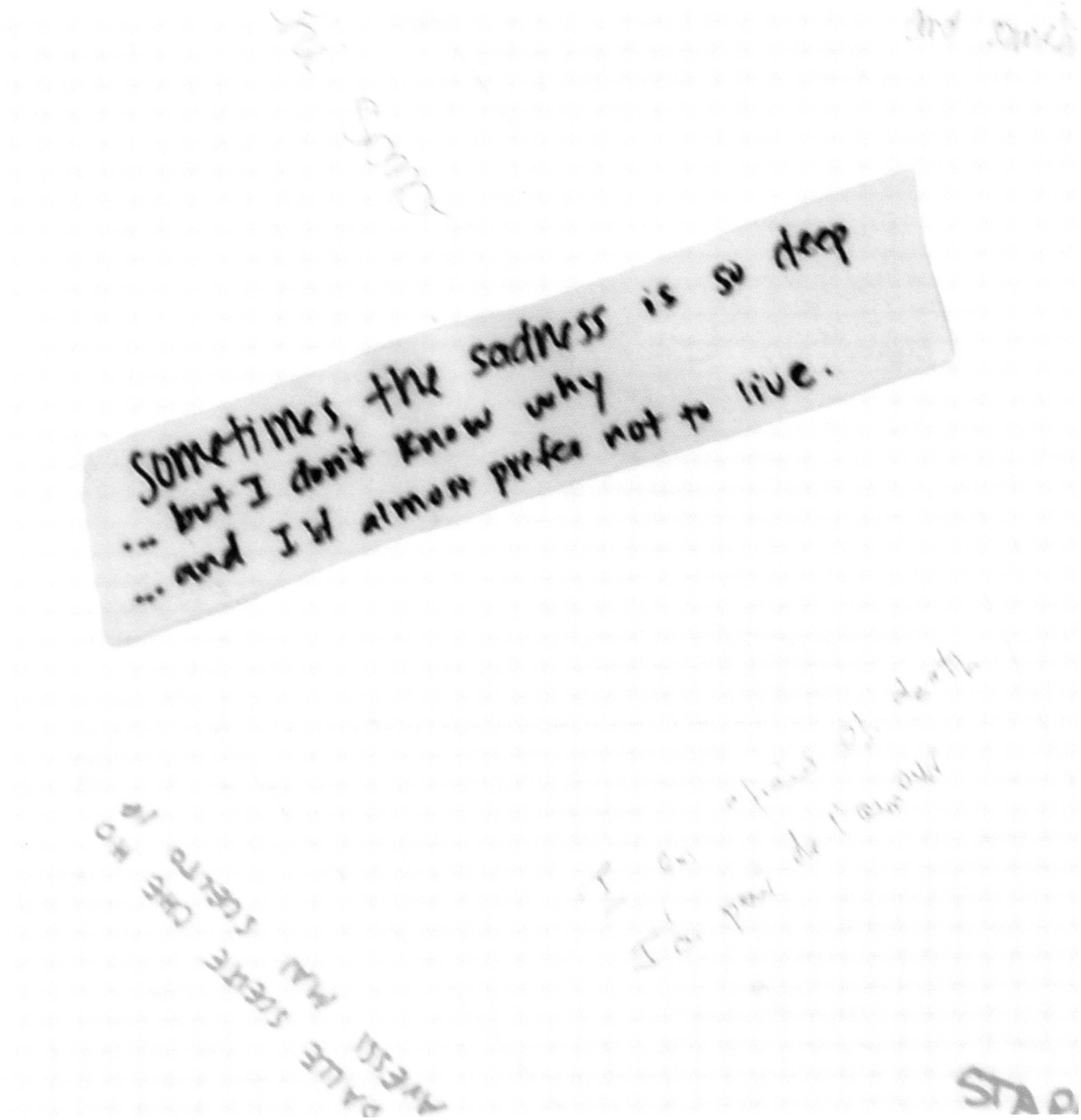
Sometimes the sadness is so deep
... but I don't know why
... and I'd almost prefer not to live.

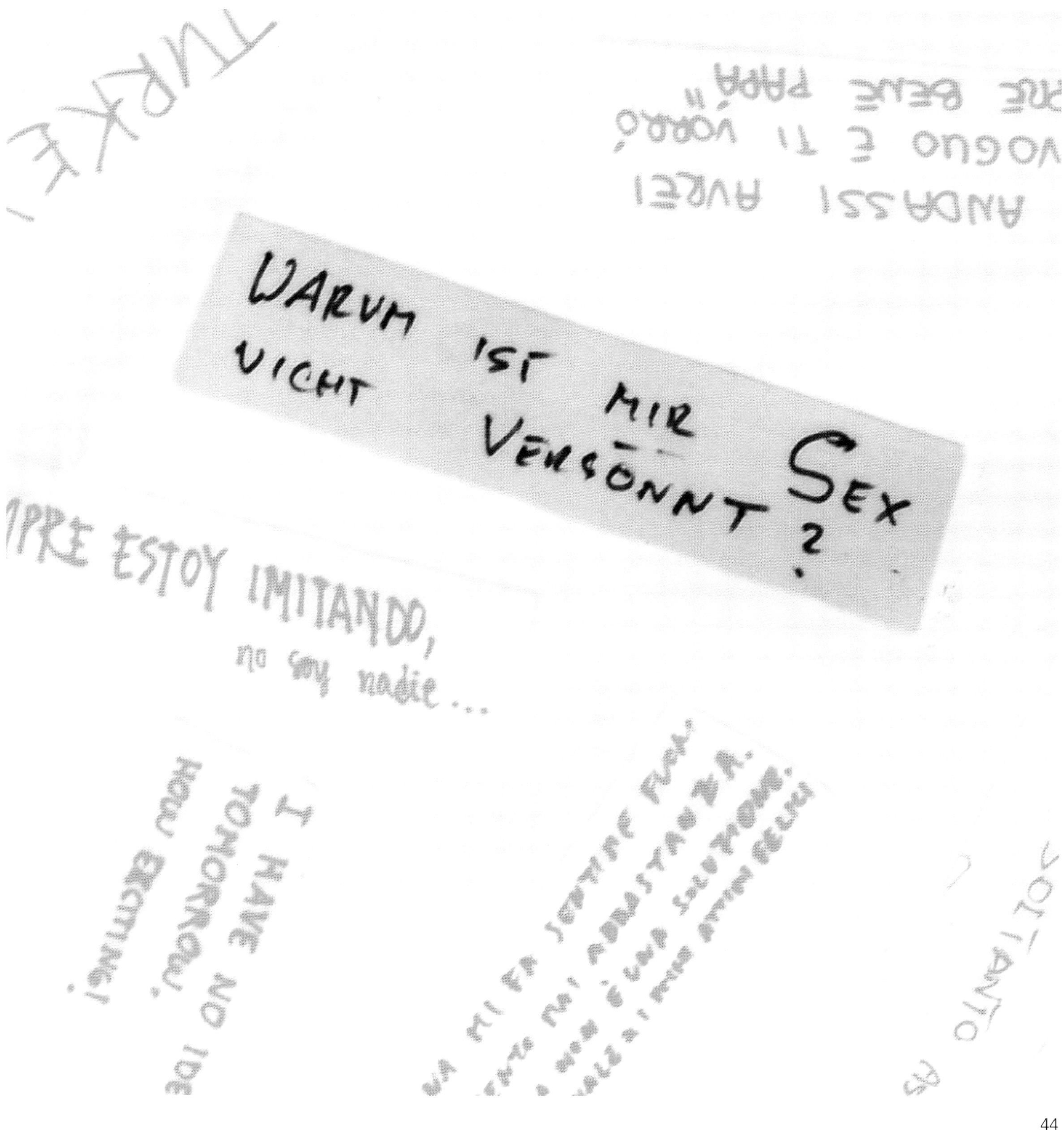
WARUM IST MIR SEX NICHT VERSÖNNT?
PRE ESTOY IMITANDO,
no soy nadie...

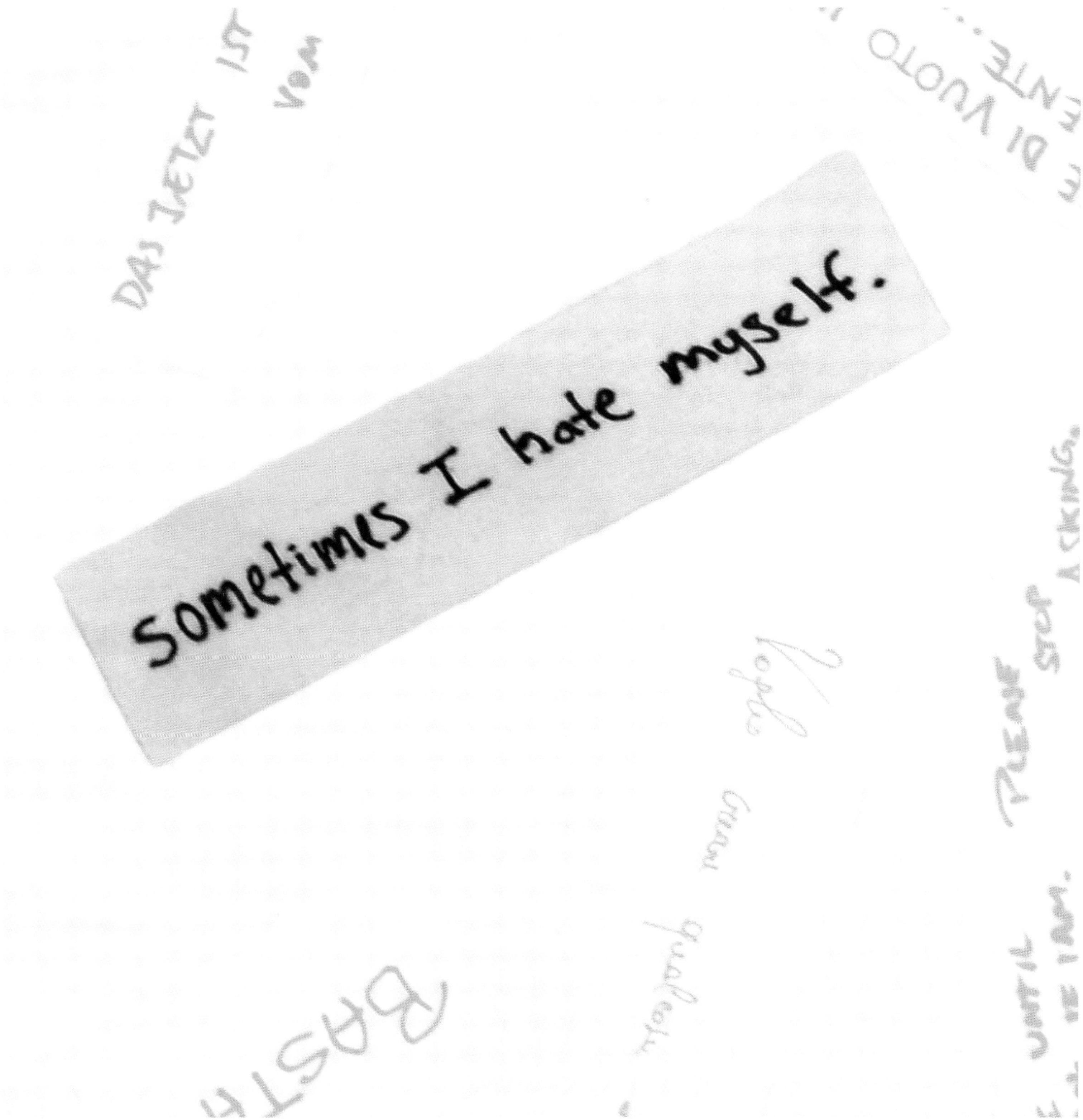
Sometimes I hate myself.
PLEASE STOP ASKING.

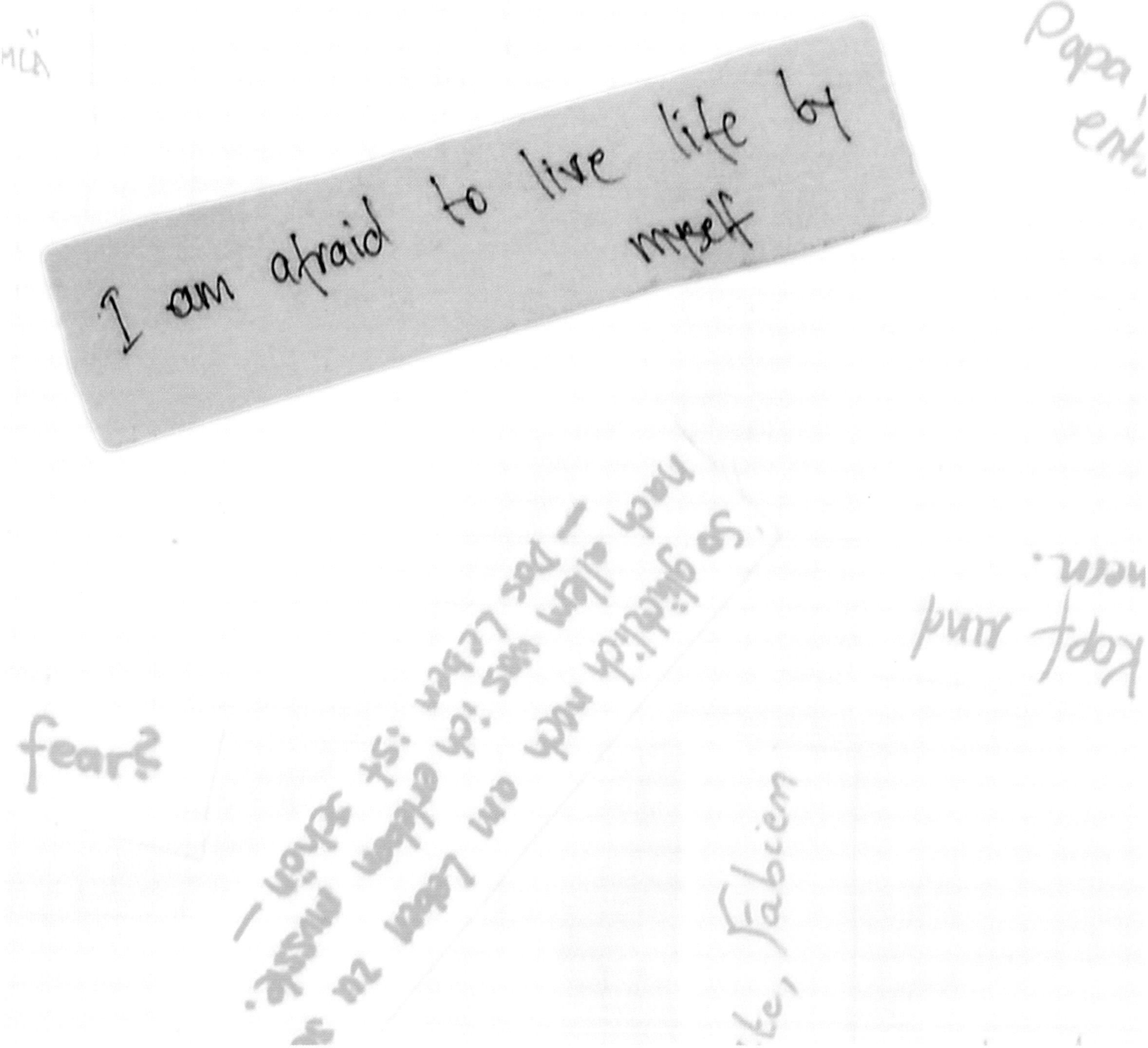
I am afraid to live life by myself
fear?

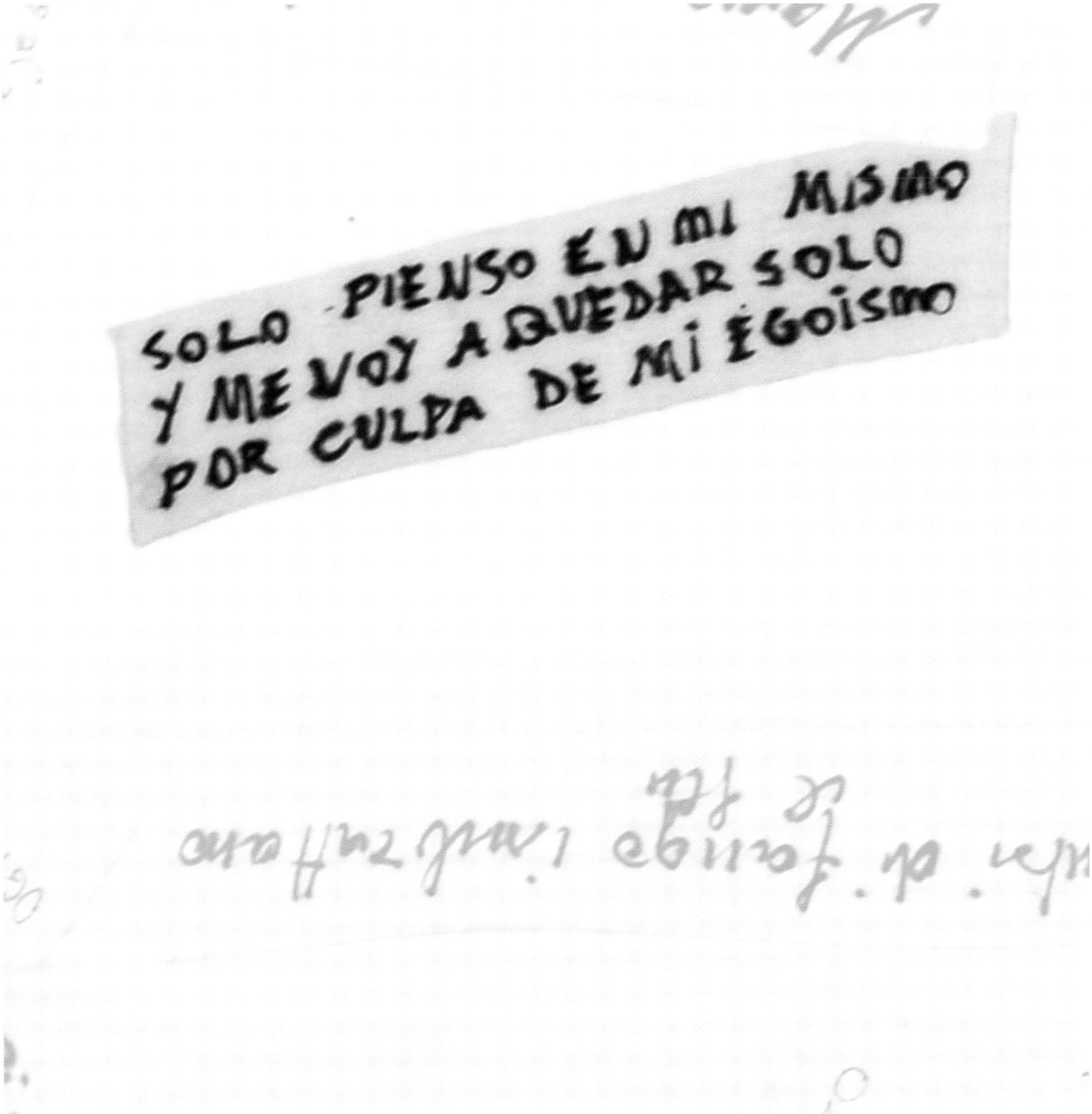
SOLO PIENSO EN MI MISMO
Y ME VOY A QUEDAR SOLO
POR CULPA DE MI EGOISMO

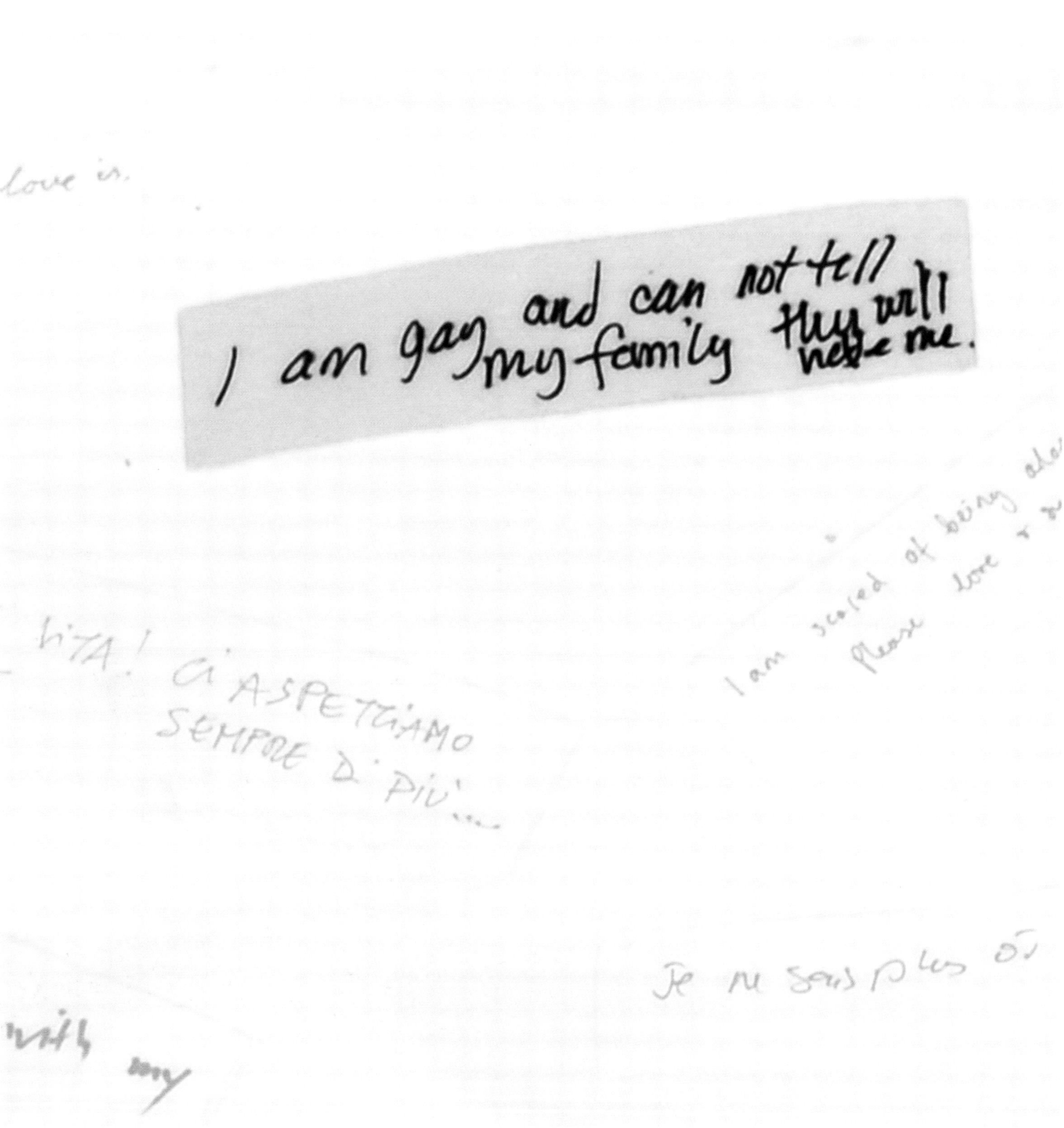
love is.
I am gay and can not tell my family they will
VITA! CI ASPETTIAMO SEMPRE DI PIÙ...
I am scared of being
Please love
with my

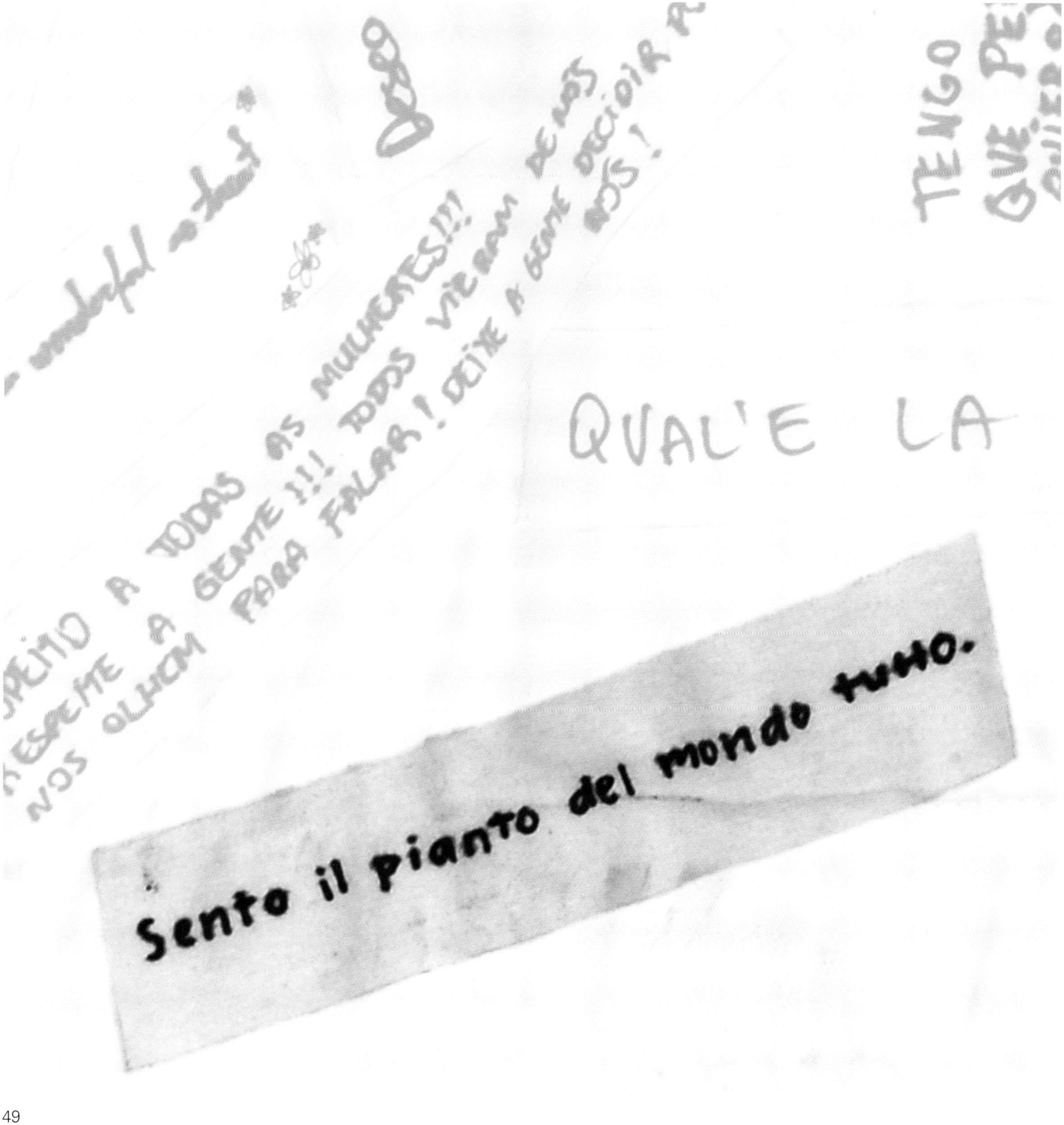
TENGO
QUAL'E LA
A TODAS AS MULHERES!!!
A GENTE!!! TODOS VIERAM DE NÓS
NOS OLHEM PARA FALAR! DEIXE A GENTE DECIDIR
NÓS!
Sento il pianto del mondo tutto.

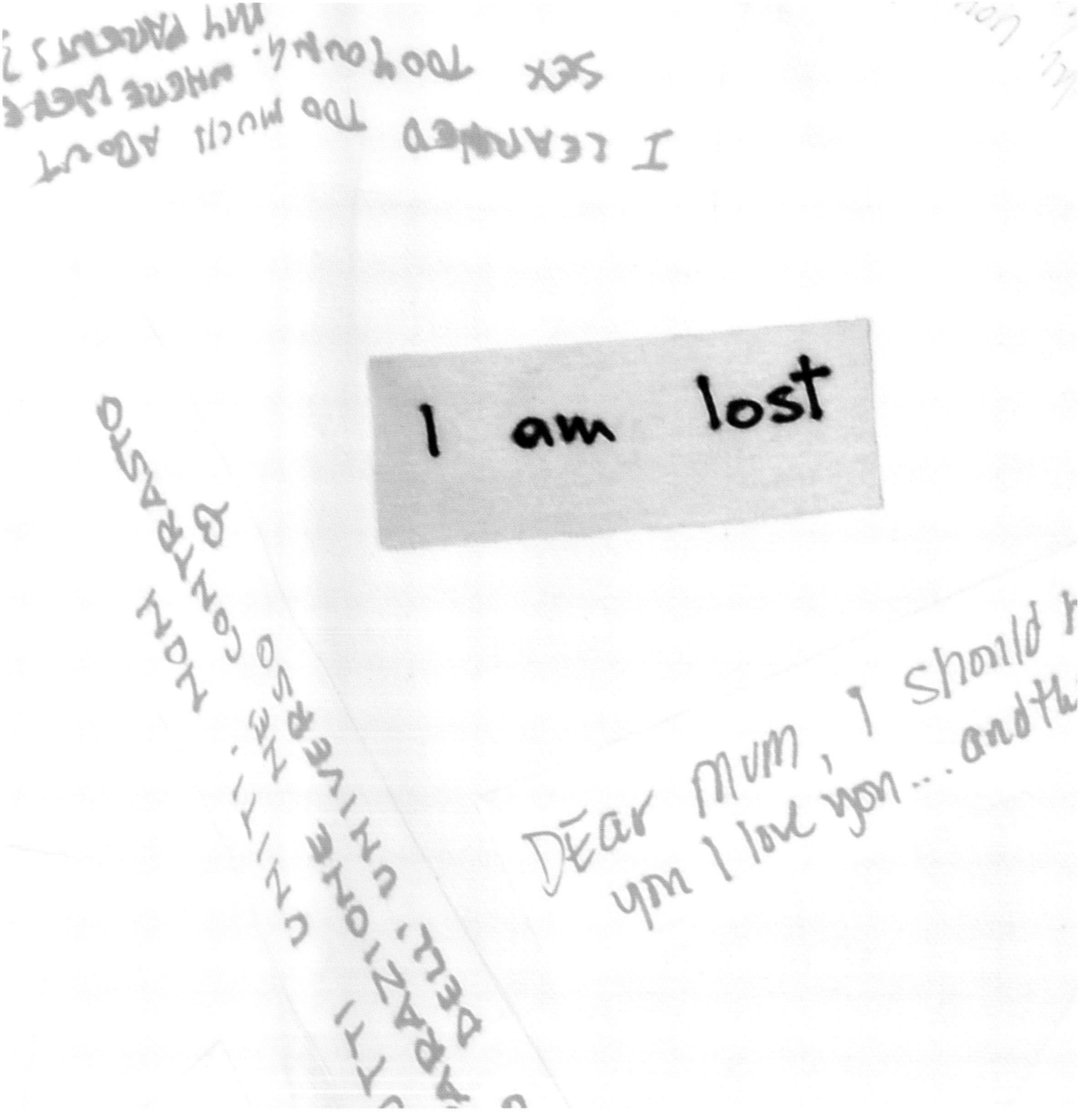
I LEARNED TOO MUCH ABOUT
SEX TOO YOUNG. WHERE WERE
MY PARENTS?
I am lost
DEAR Mum, I should
you I love you... and

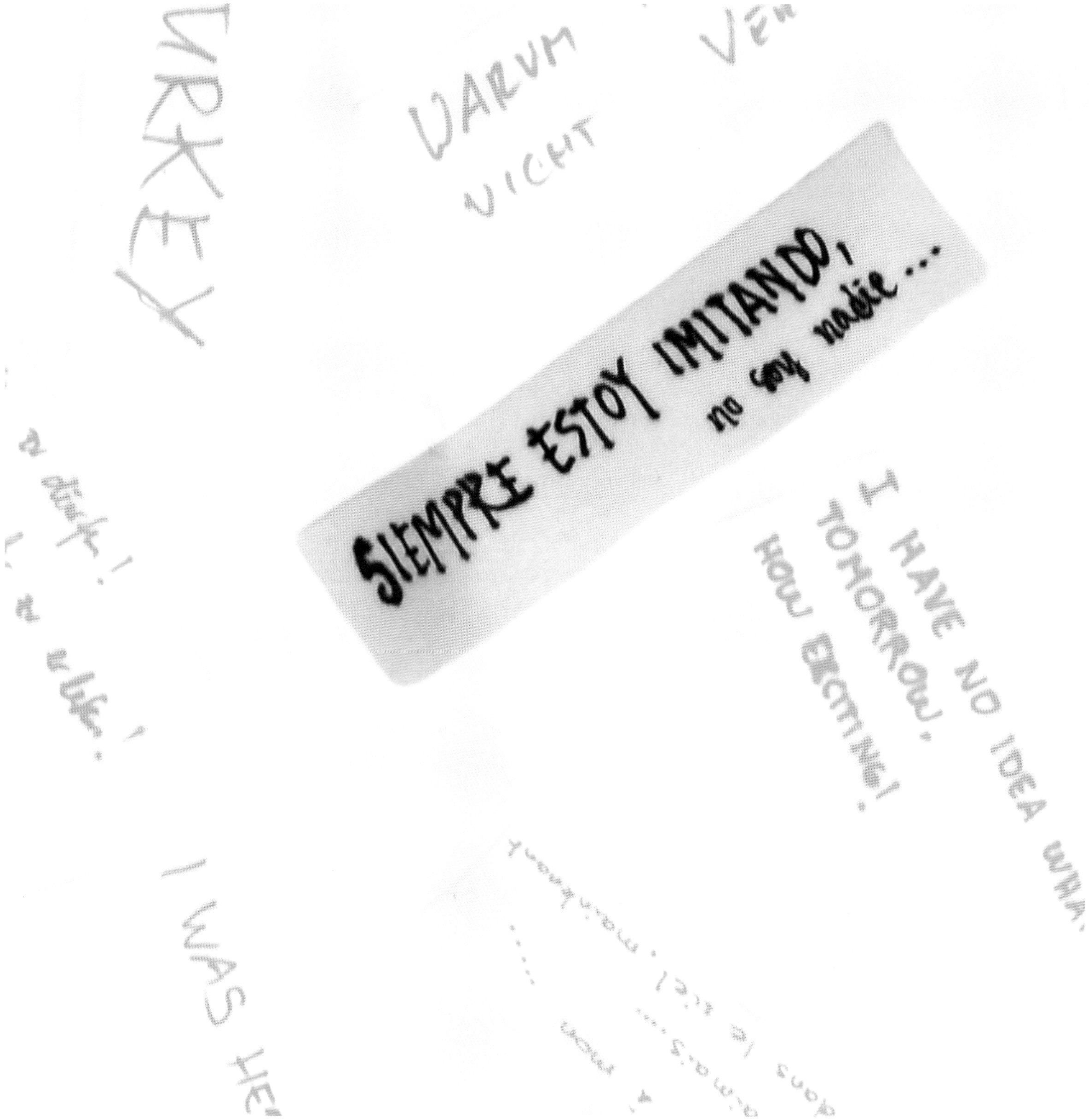
SIEMPRE ESTOY IMITANDO,
no soy nadie ...
WARUM
NICHT
I HAVE NO IDEA
TOMORROW,
HOW EXCITING!
I WAS

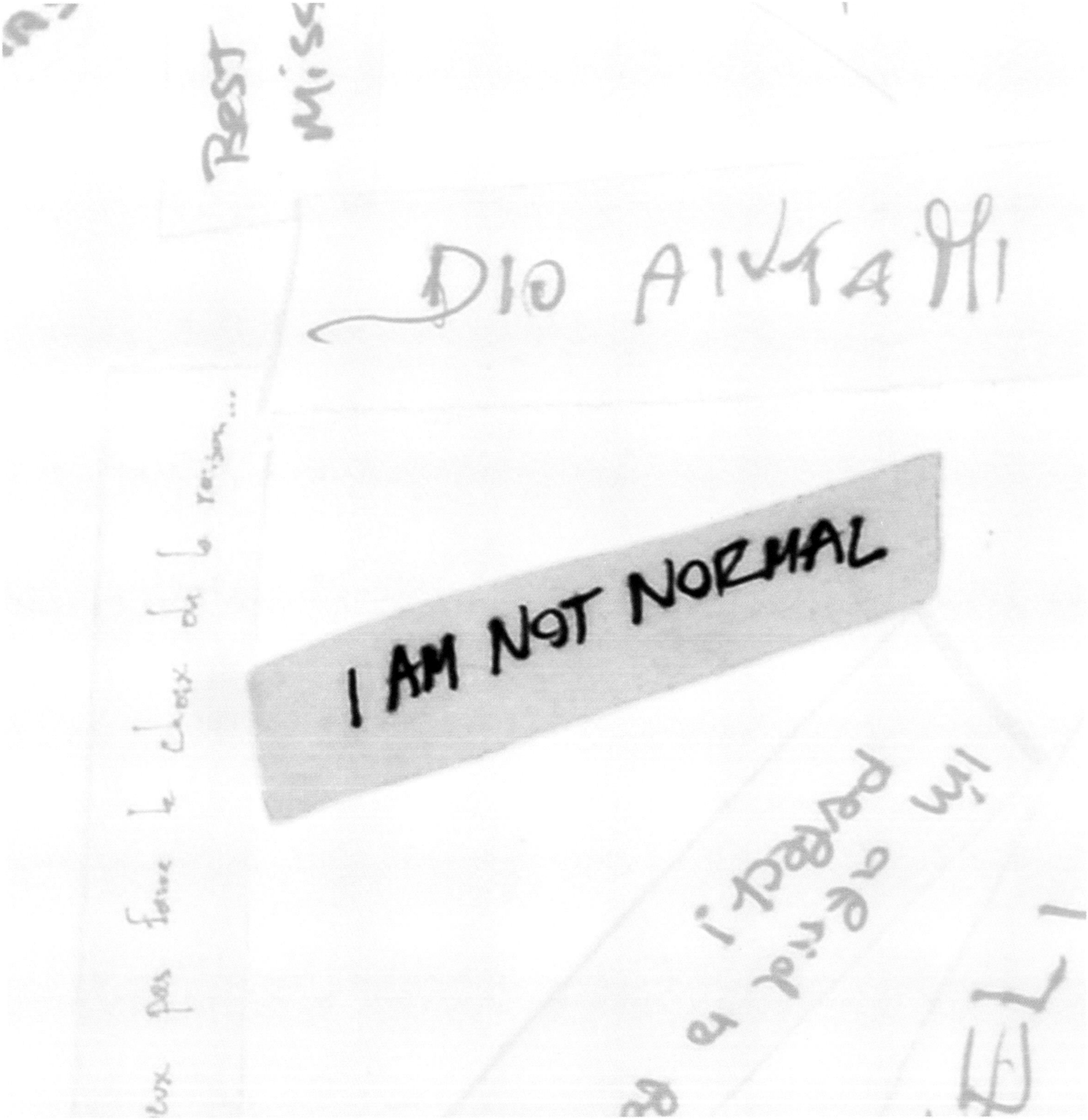
DIO AIUTAMI
I AM NOT NORMAL

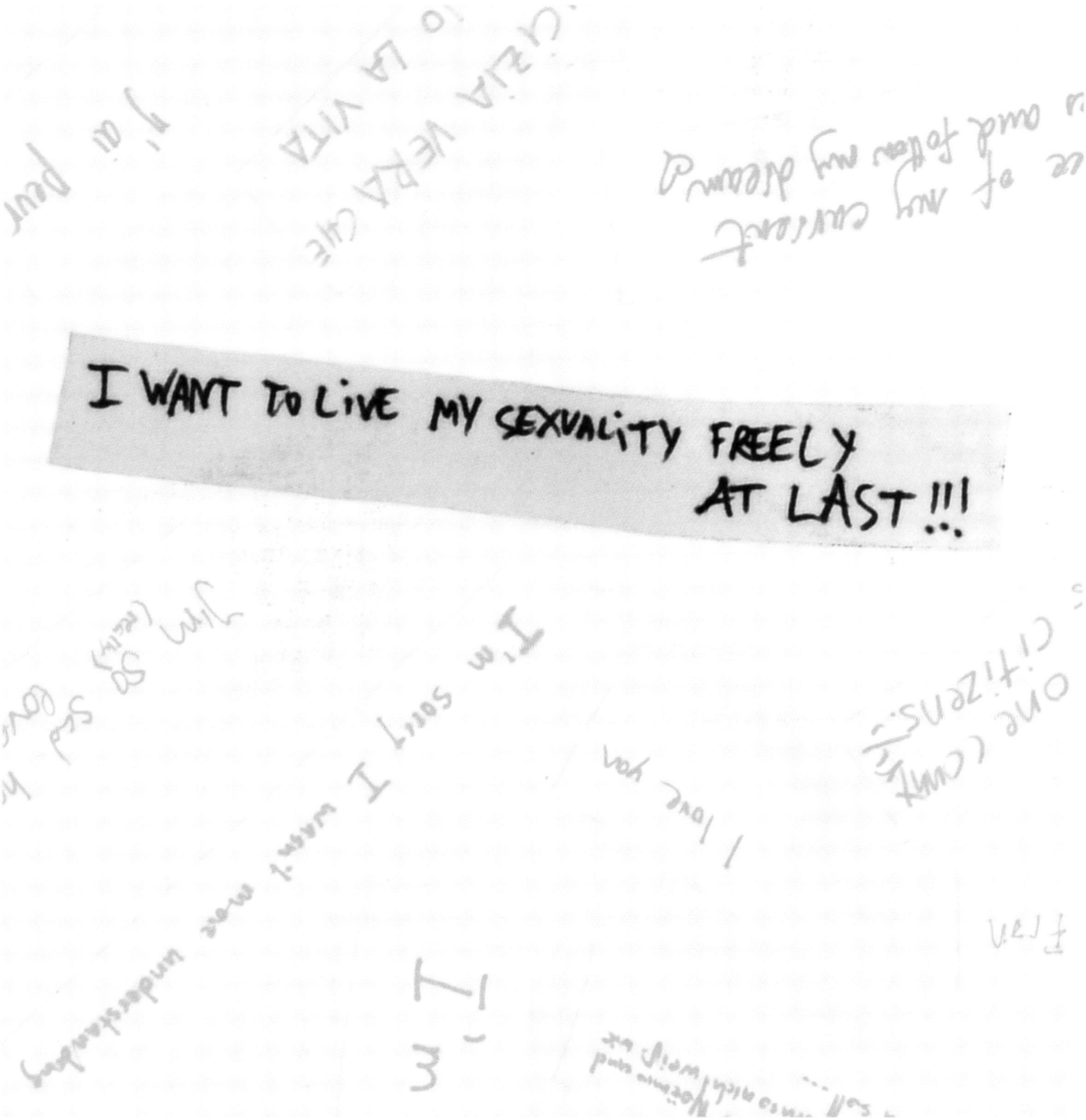
I WANT TO LIVE MY SEXUALITY FREELY
AT LAST!!!

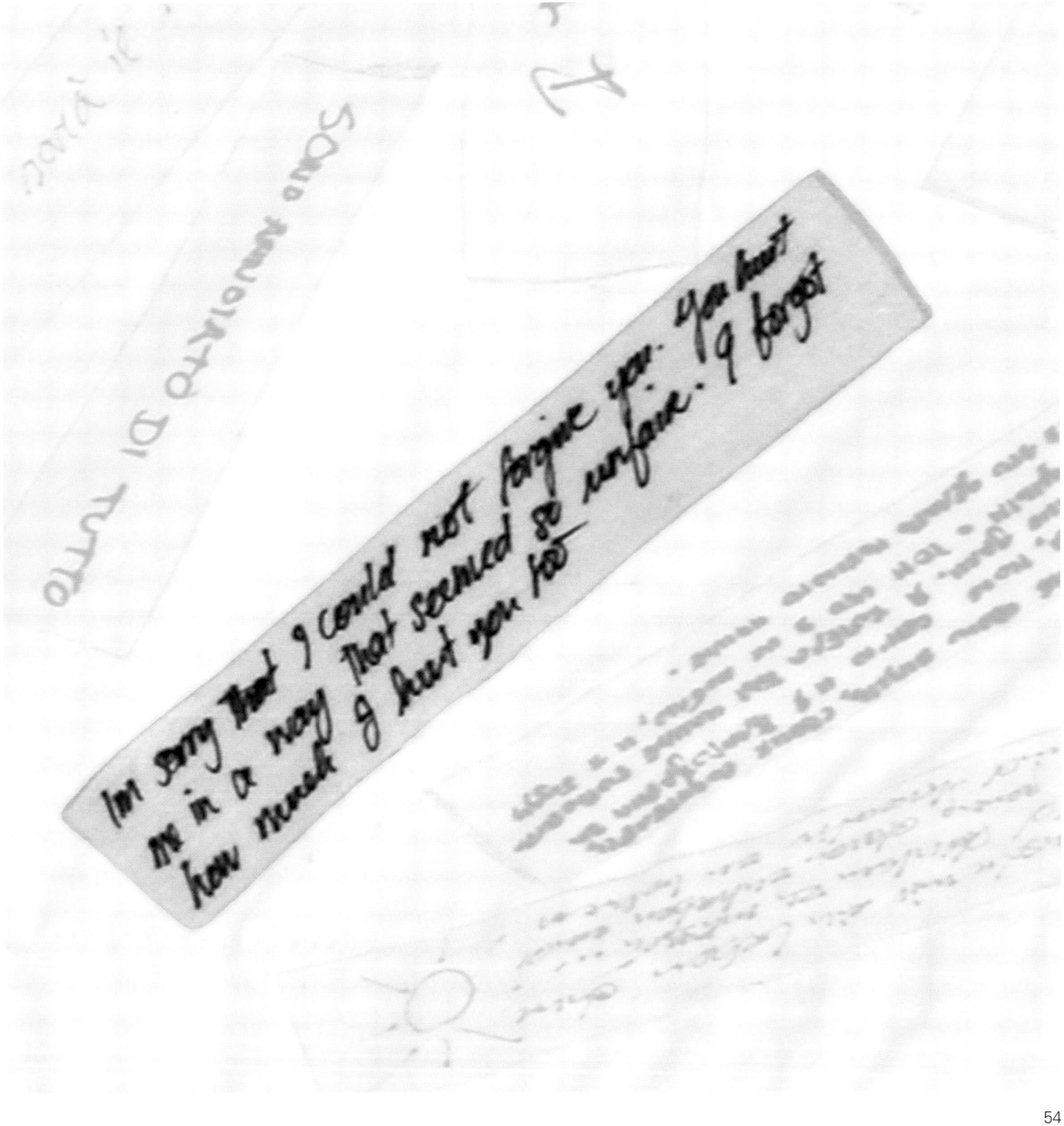
I'm sorry that I could not forgive you. You hurt
me in a way that seemed so unfair. I forgot
how much I hurt you too

inside the silence
SEI UN PESSIMO PADRE.

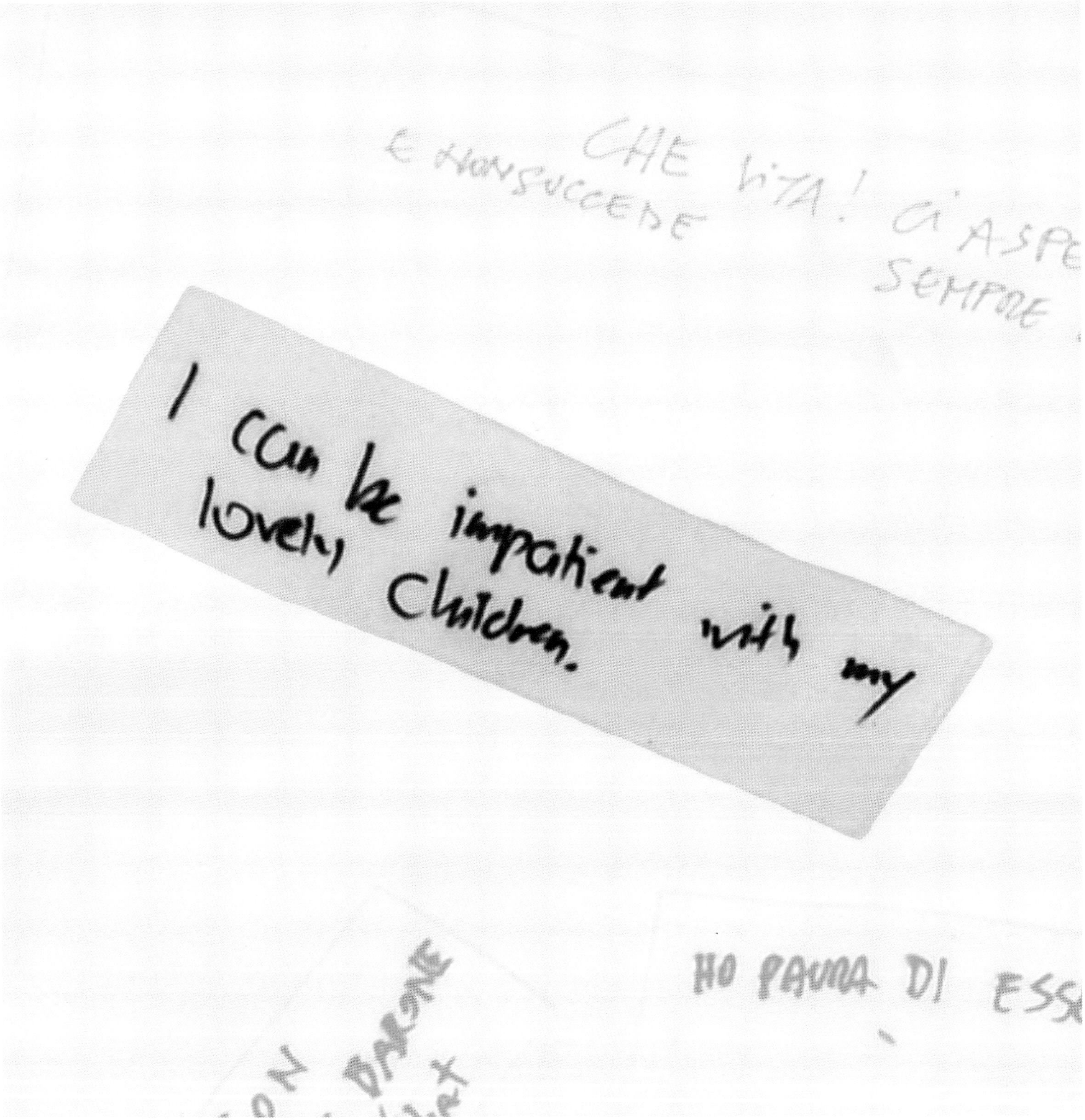
CHE VITA!
E NON SUCCEDE
I can be impatient with my lovely children.
HO PAURA DI

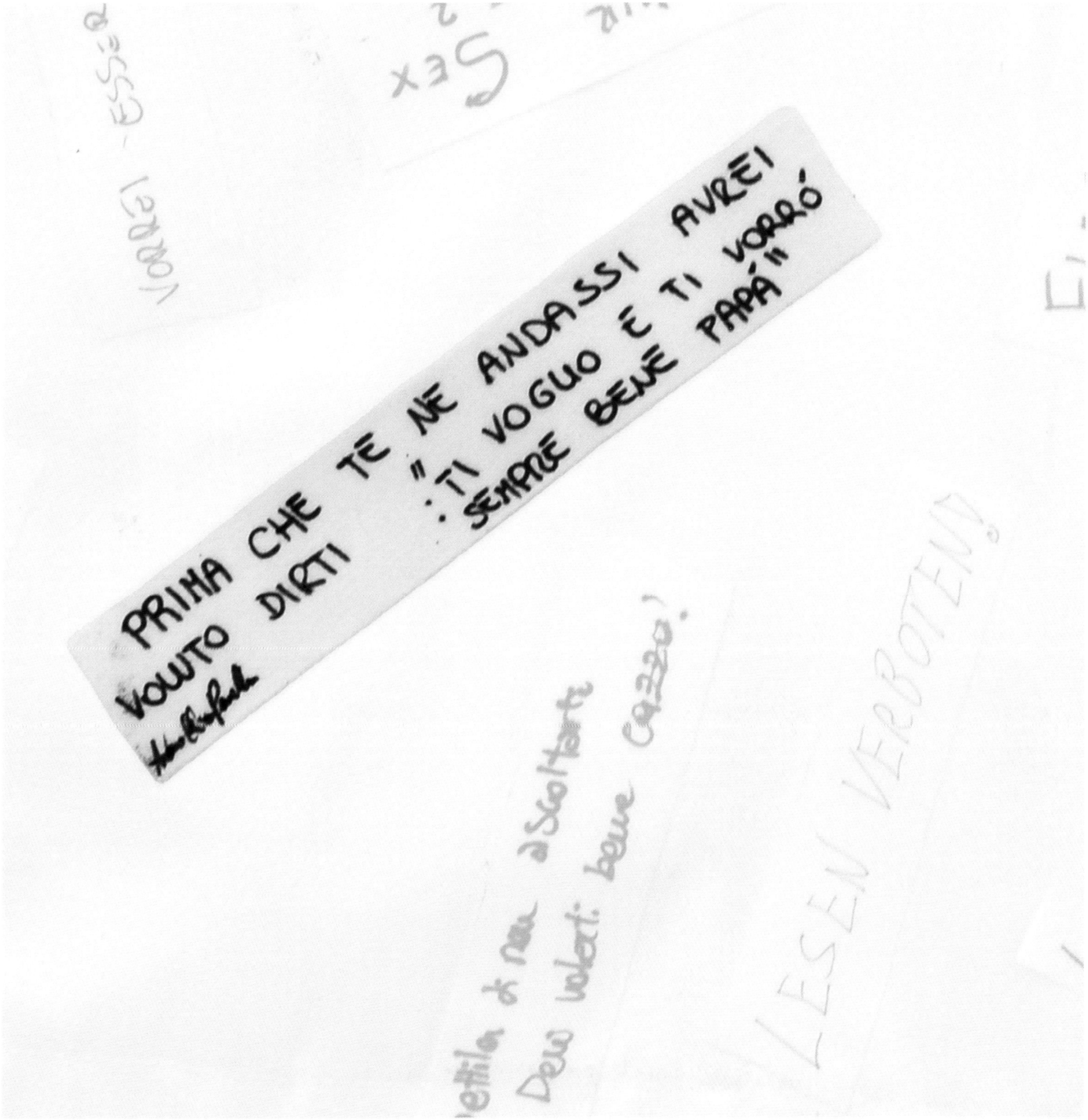
PRIMA CHE TE NE ANDASSI AVREI
VOLUTO DIRTI: "TI VOGLIO E TI VORRÓ
SEMPRE BENE PAPÁ"
SEX
LESEN VERBOTEN!

I COULD KILL
NOTHING REALLY MATTERS
AND I'M OKAY WITH THAT.
doesn't
me
little girl blue...

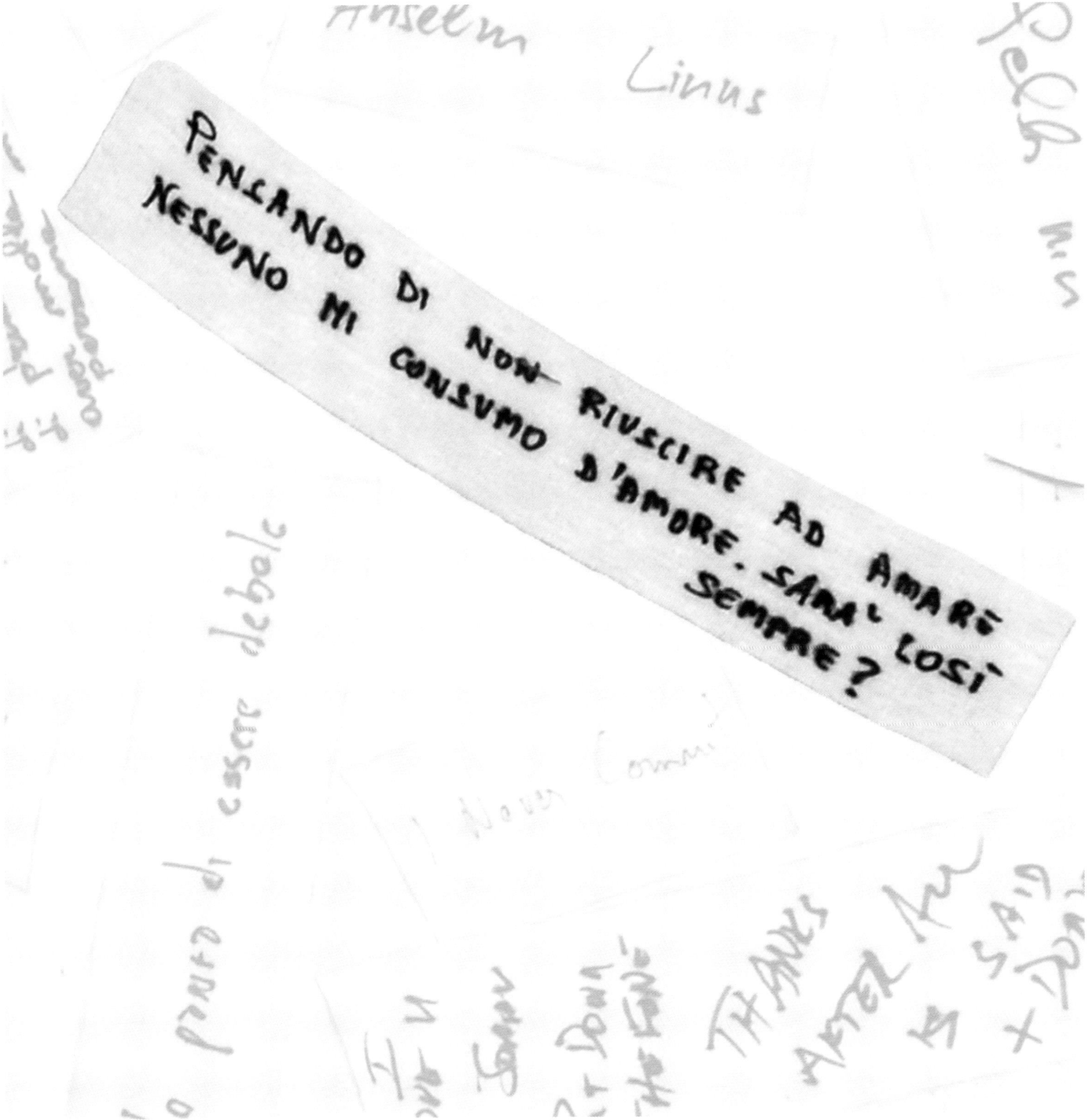
Anselm
Linus
PENSANDO DI NON RIUSCIRE AD AMARE
NESSUNO MI CONSUMO D'AMORE. SARÀ COSÌ
SEMPRE?

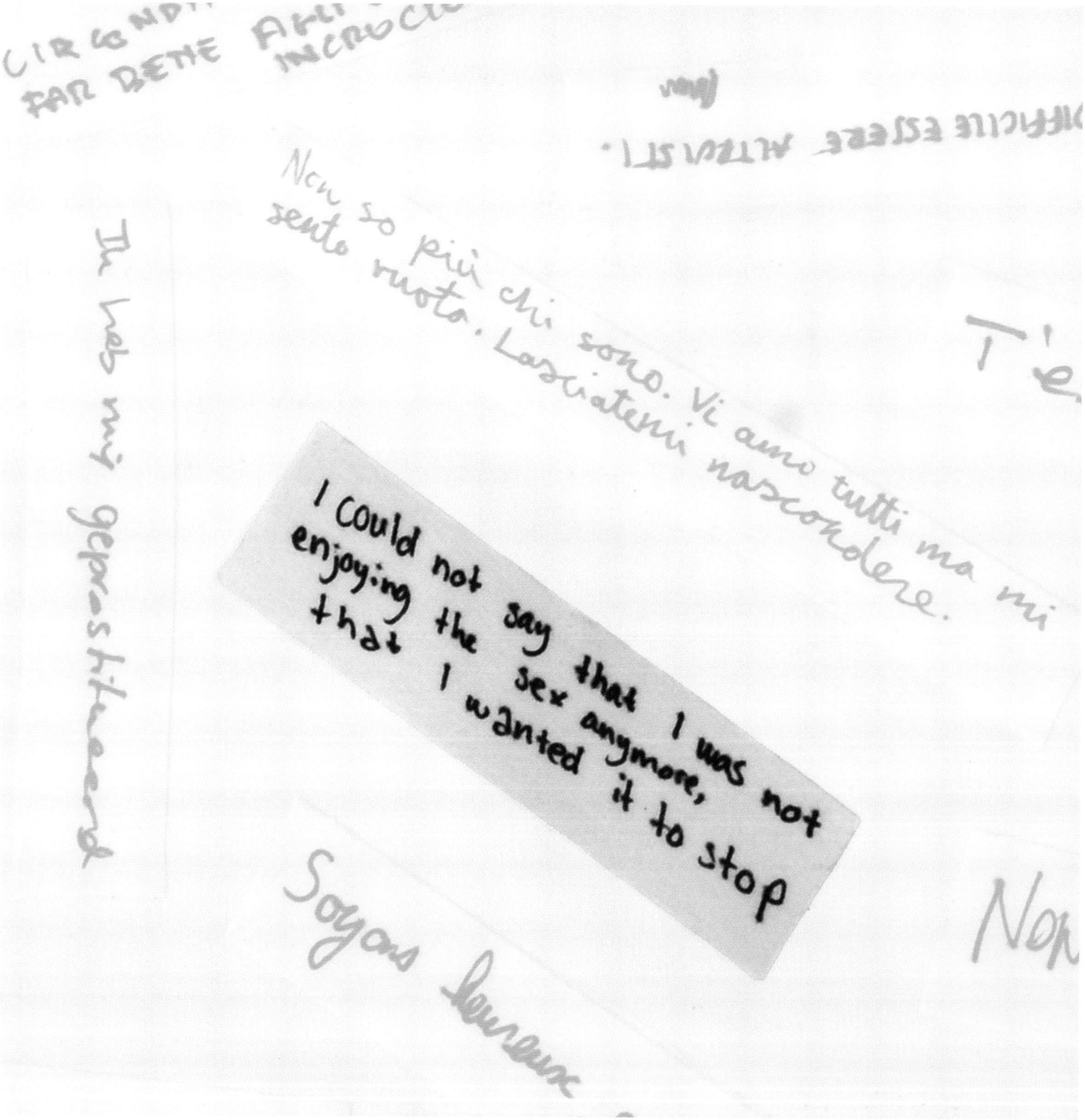
Non so più chi sono. Vi amo tutti ma mi
sento vuota. Lasciatemi nascondere.
Ik heb mij geprostitueerd
I could not say that I was not
enjoying the sex anymore,
that I wanted it to stop

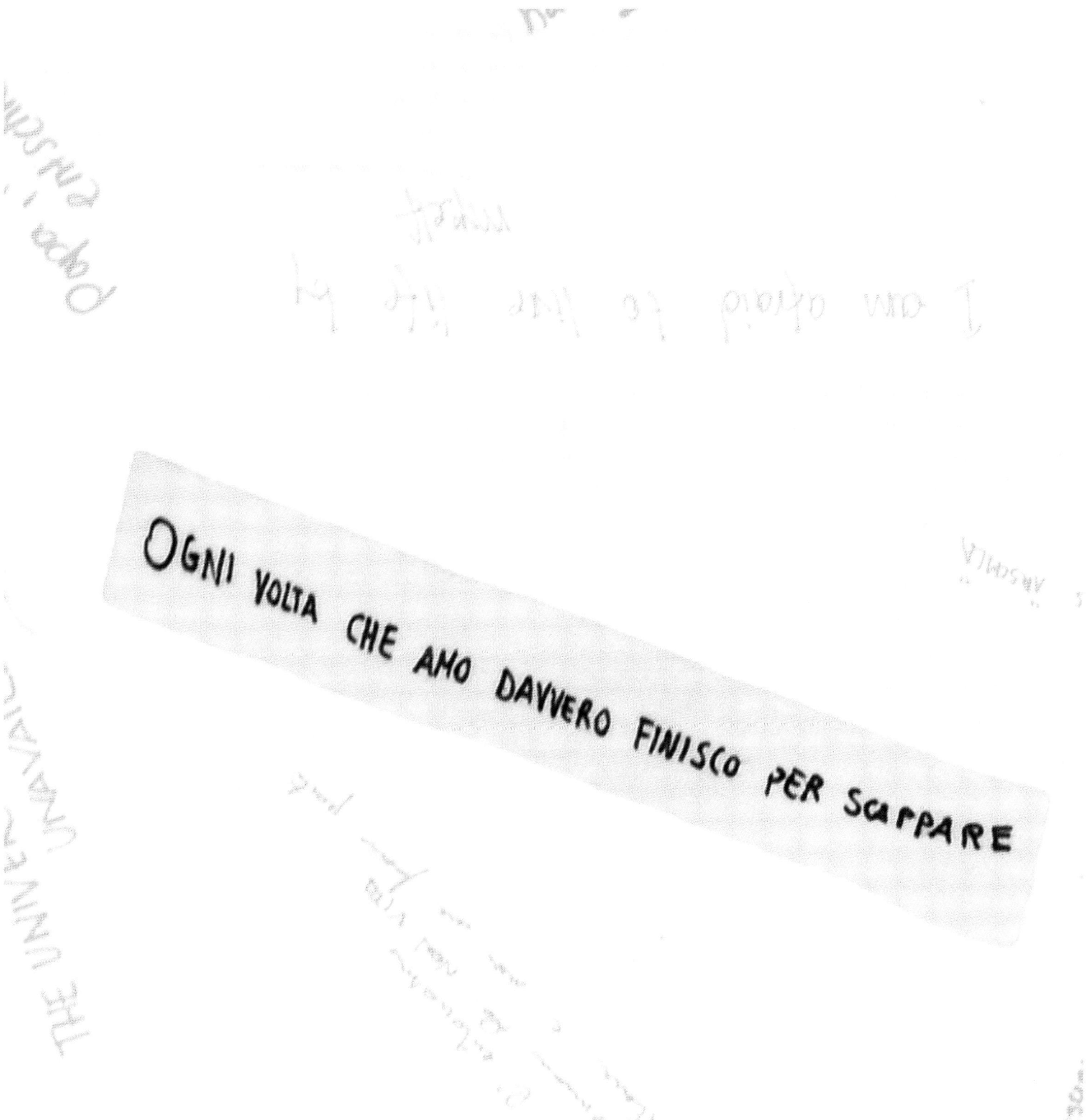
OGNI VOLTA CHE AMO DAVVERO FINISCO PER SCAPPARE

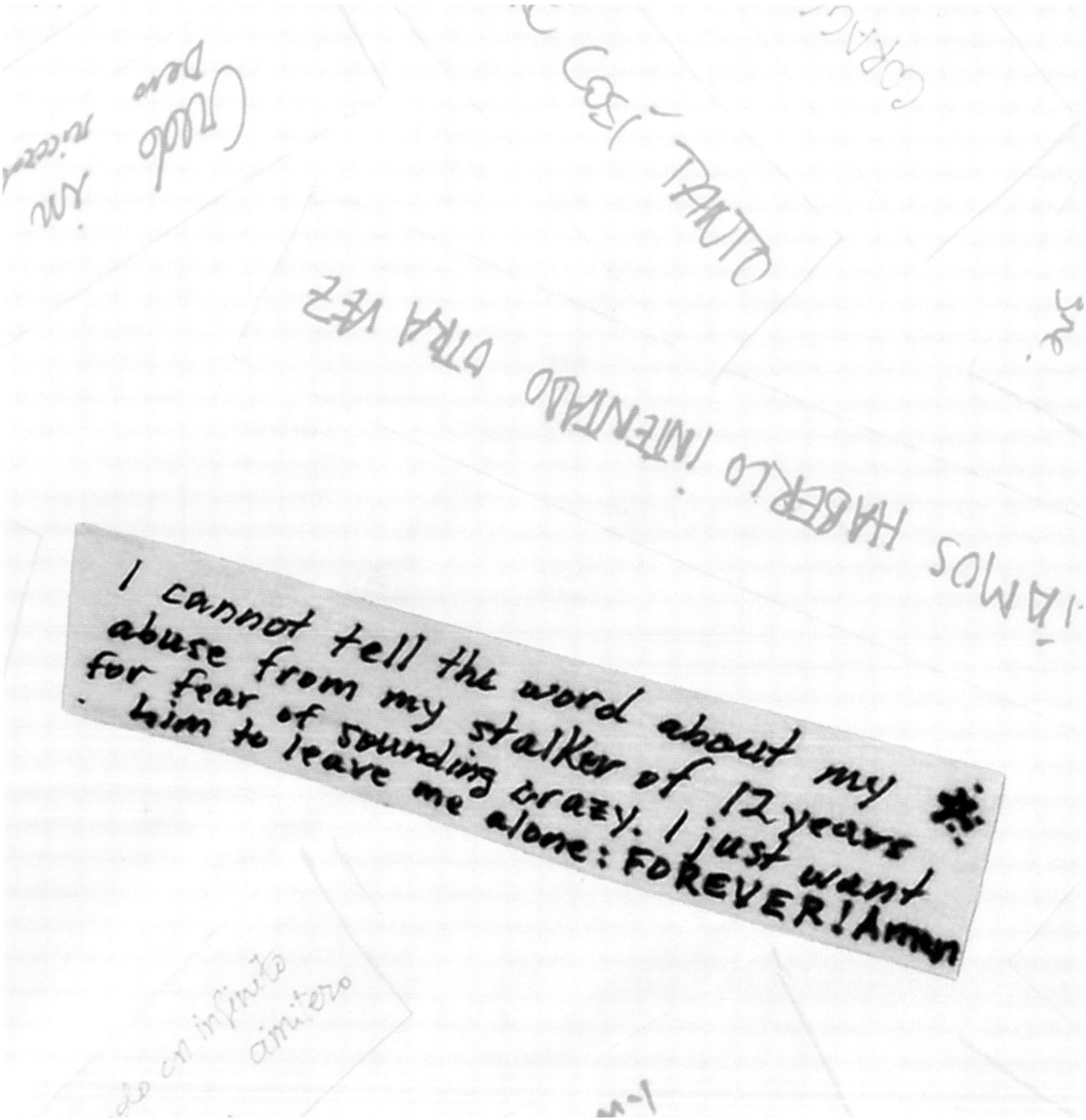
COSÌ TANTO
HABERLO INTENTADO OTRA VEZ
I cannot tell the word about my
abuse from my stalker of 12 years
for fear of sounding crazy. I just want
him to leave me alone: FOREVER! Amen

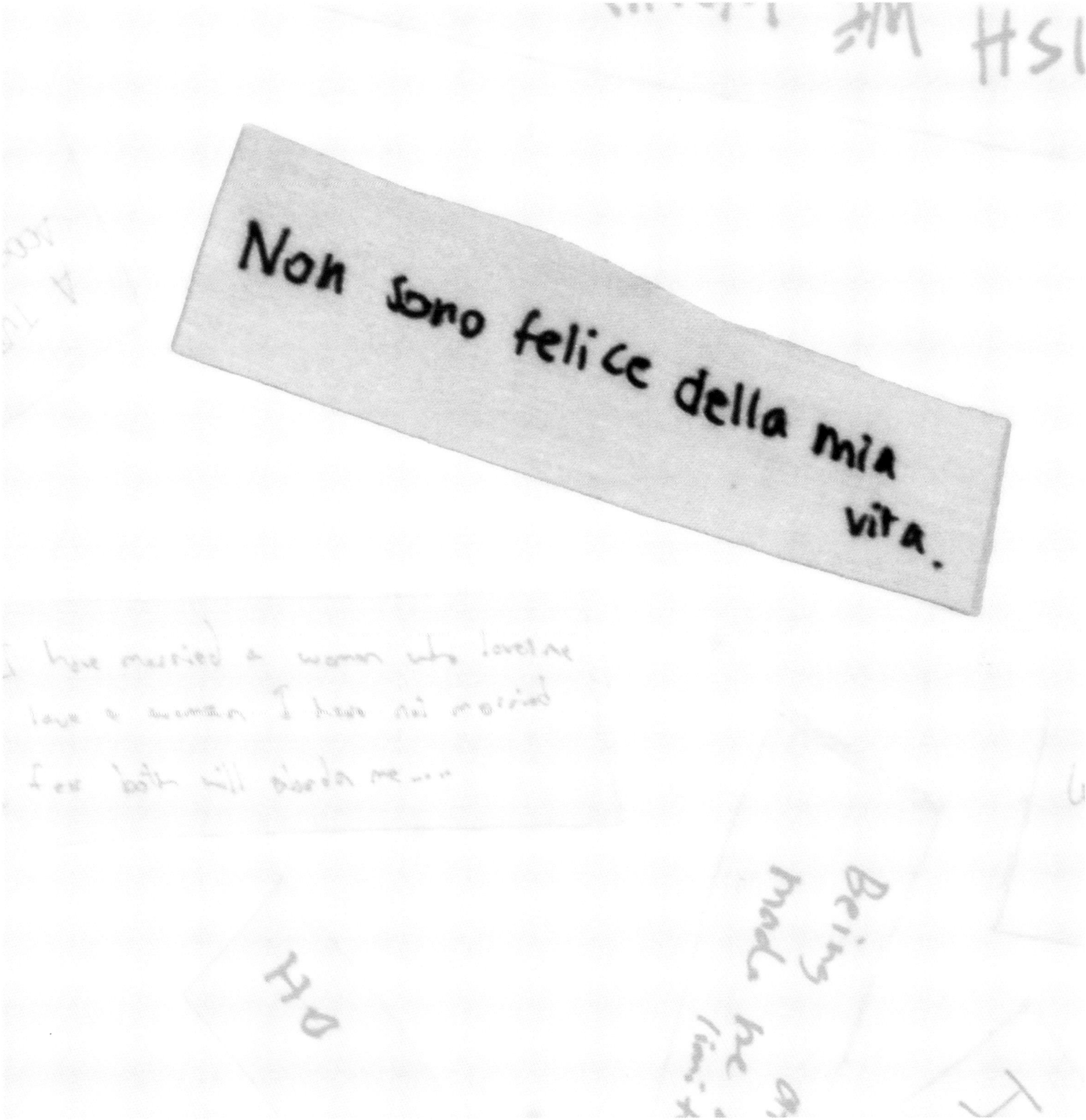
Non sono felice della mia vita.

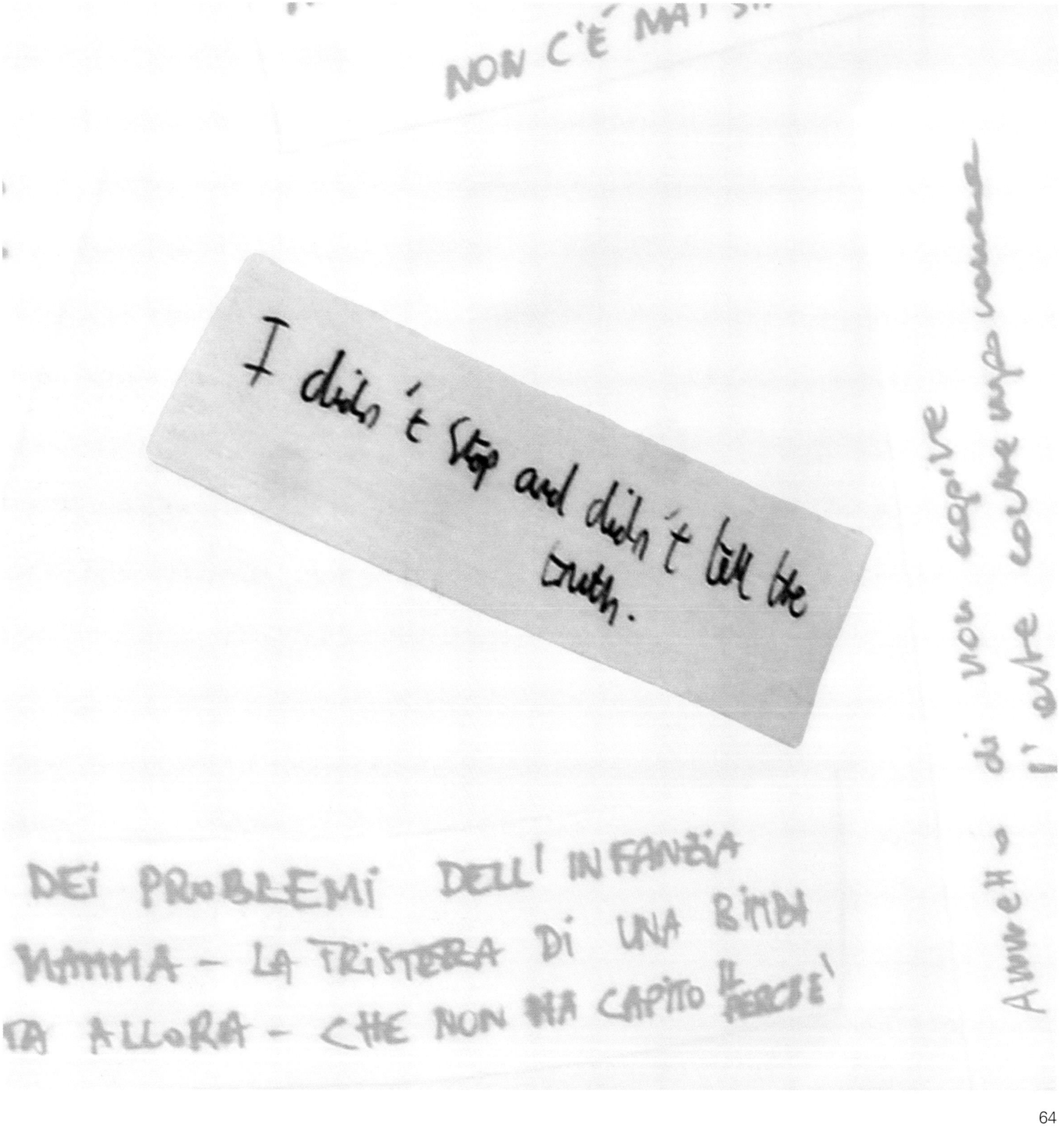
NON C'È
I didn't stop and didn't tell the truth.
DEI PROBLEMI DELL'INFANZIA
MAMMA - LA TRISTEZZA DI UNA BIMBA
DA ALLORA - CHE NON HA CAPITO IL PERCHE'

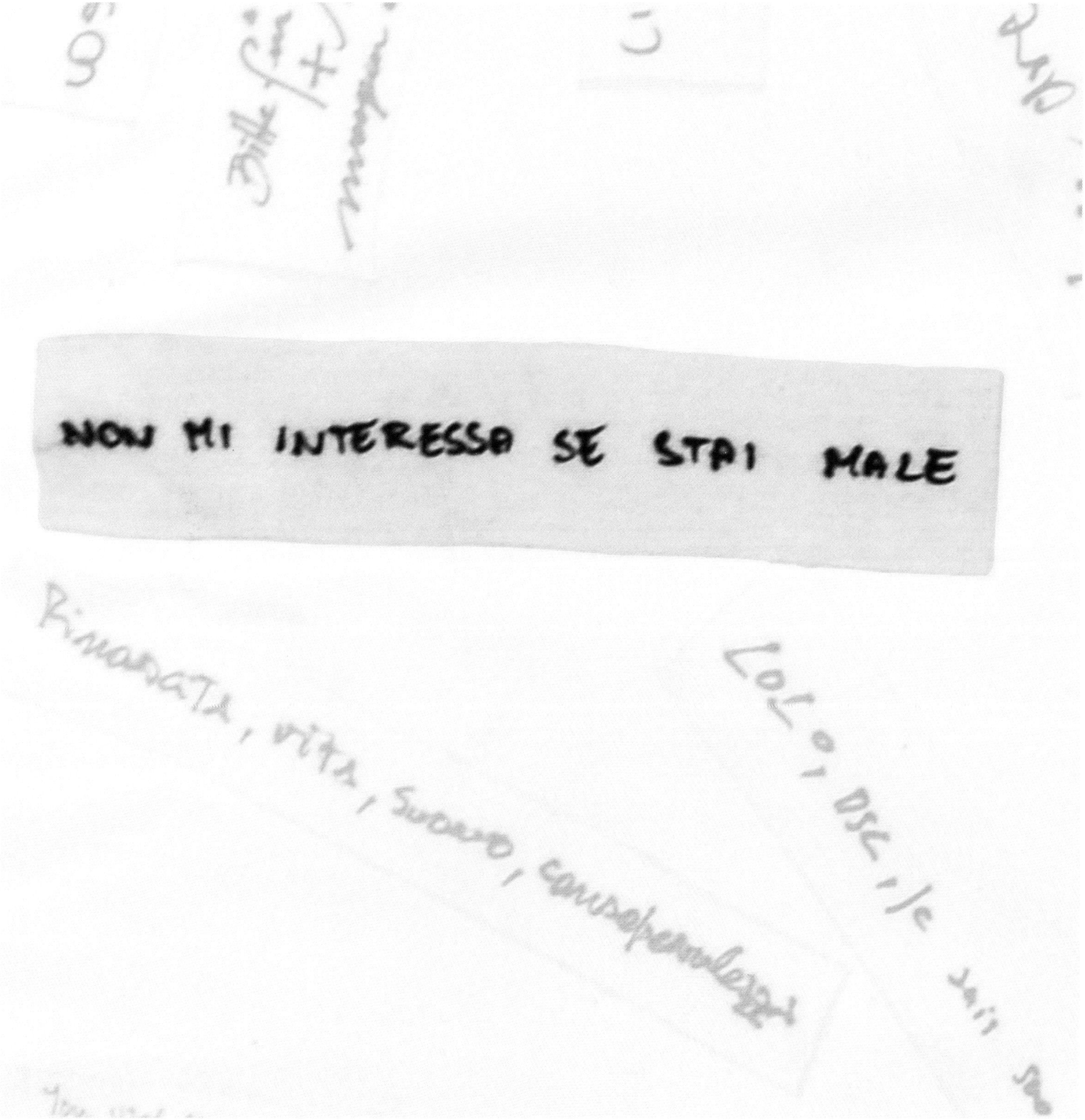
NON MI INTERESSA SE STAI MALE

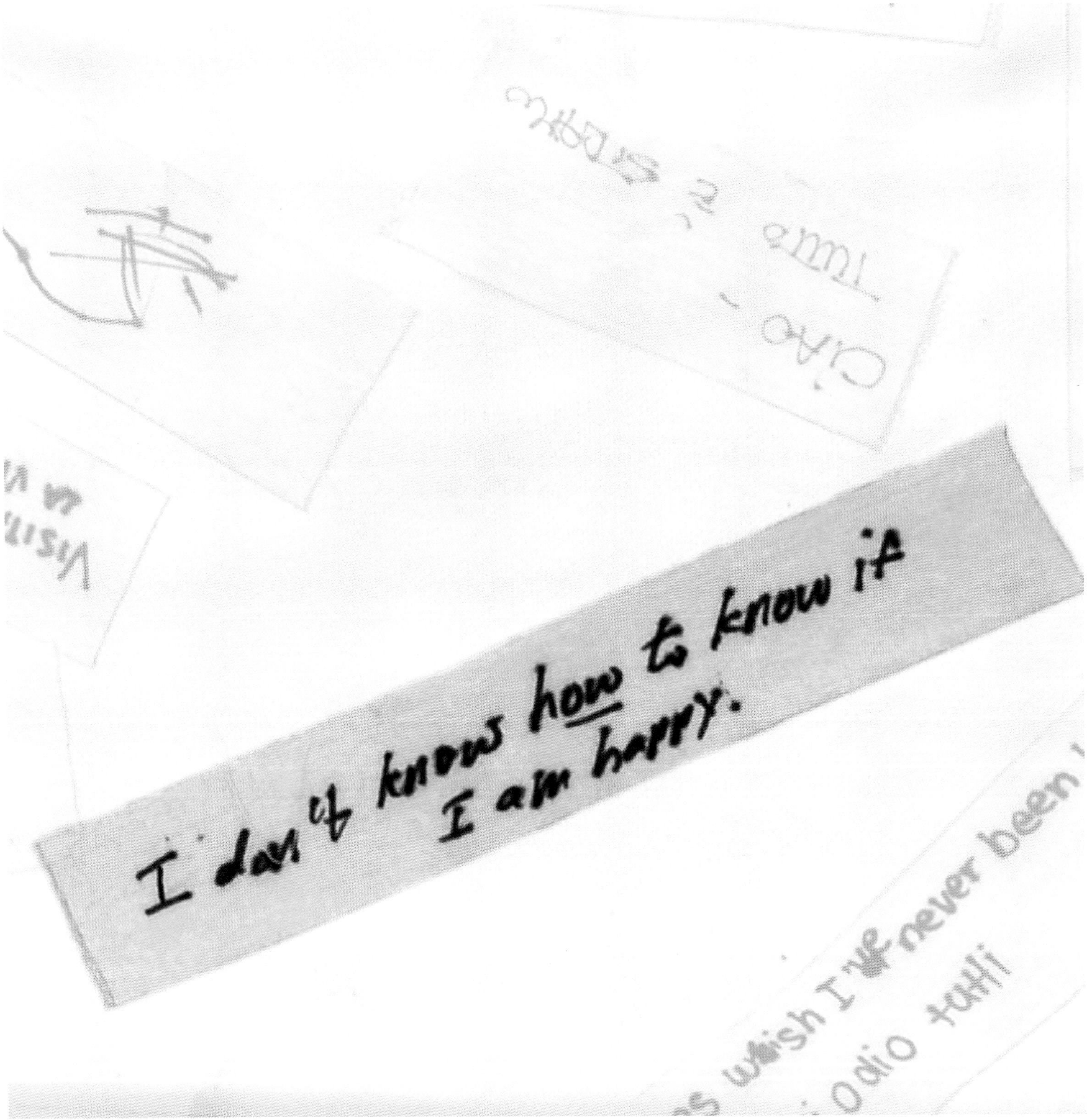
I don't know how to know if
I am happy.

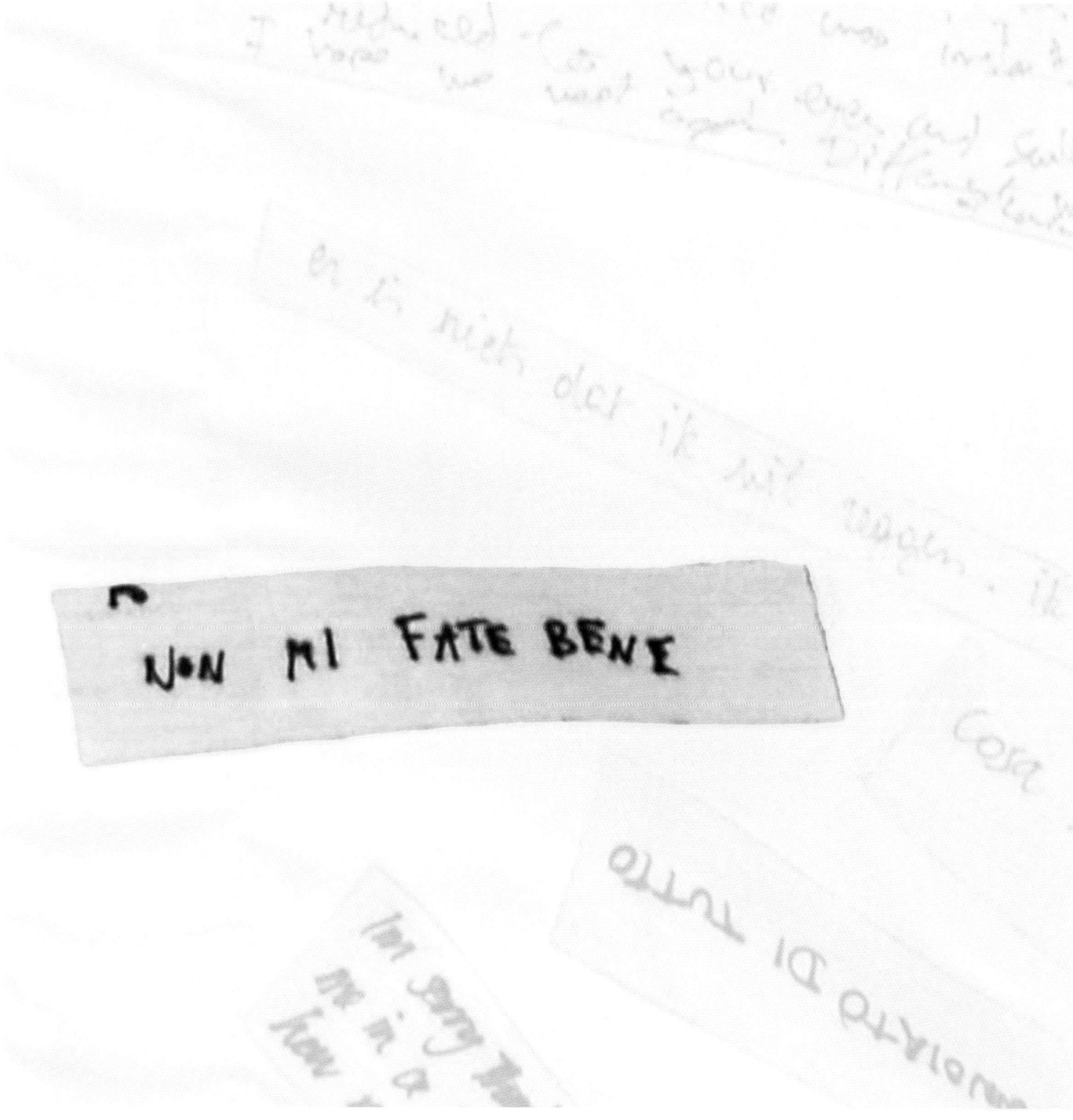
NON MI FATE BENE
Cosa

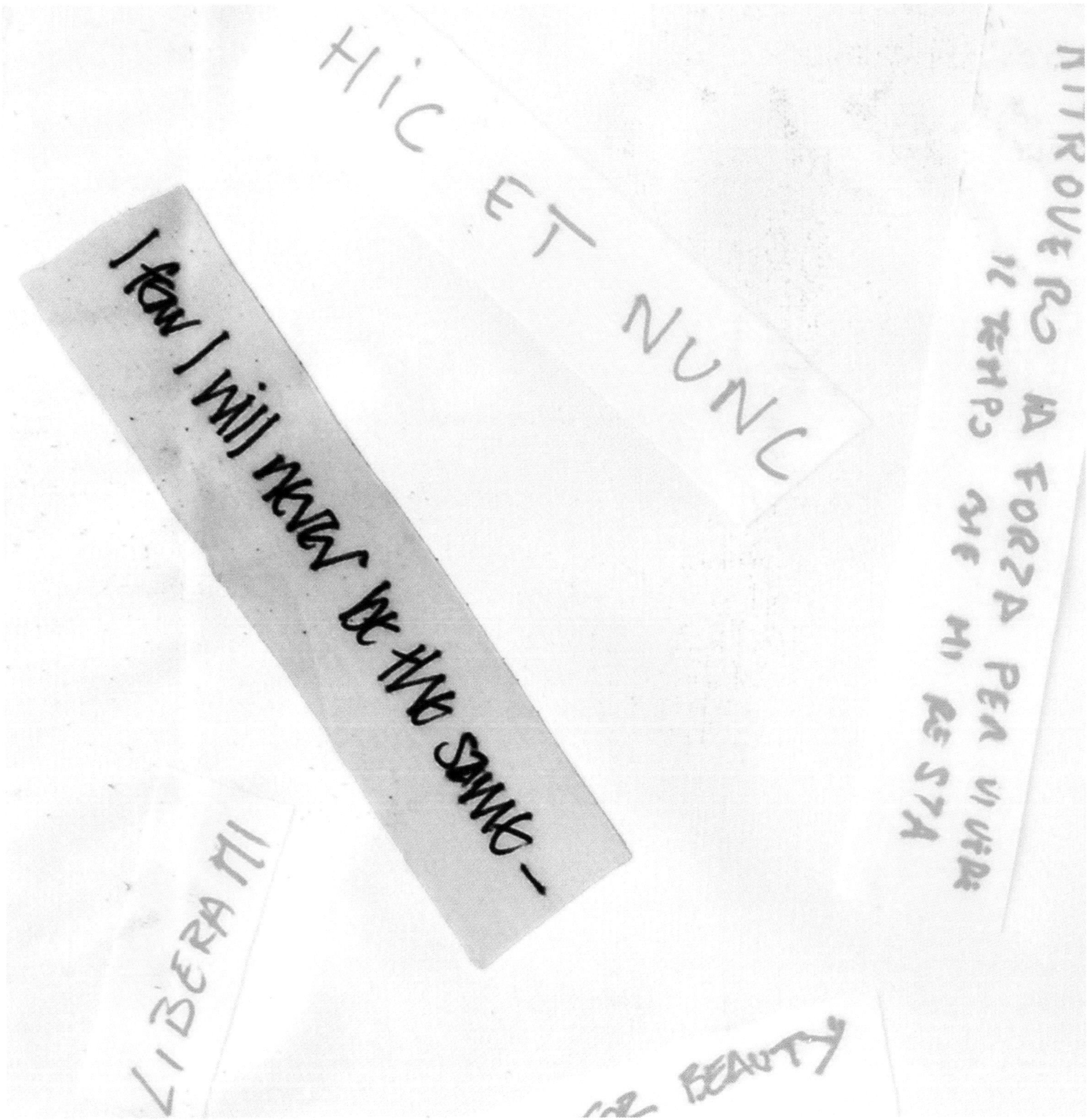
HIC ET NUNC
I fear I will never be the same -
ITROVERò LA FORZA PER VIVERE
IL TEMPO CHE MI RESTA
LIBERAMI
BEAUTY

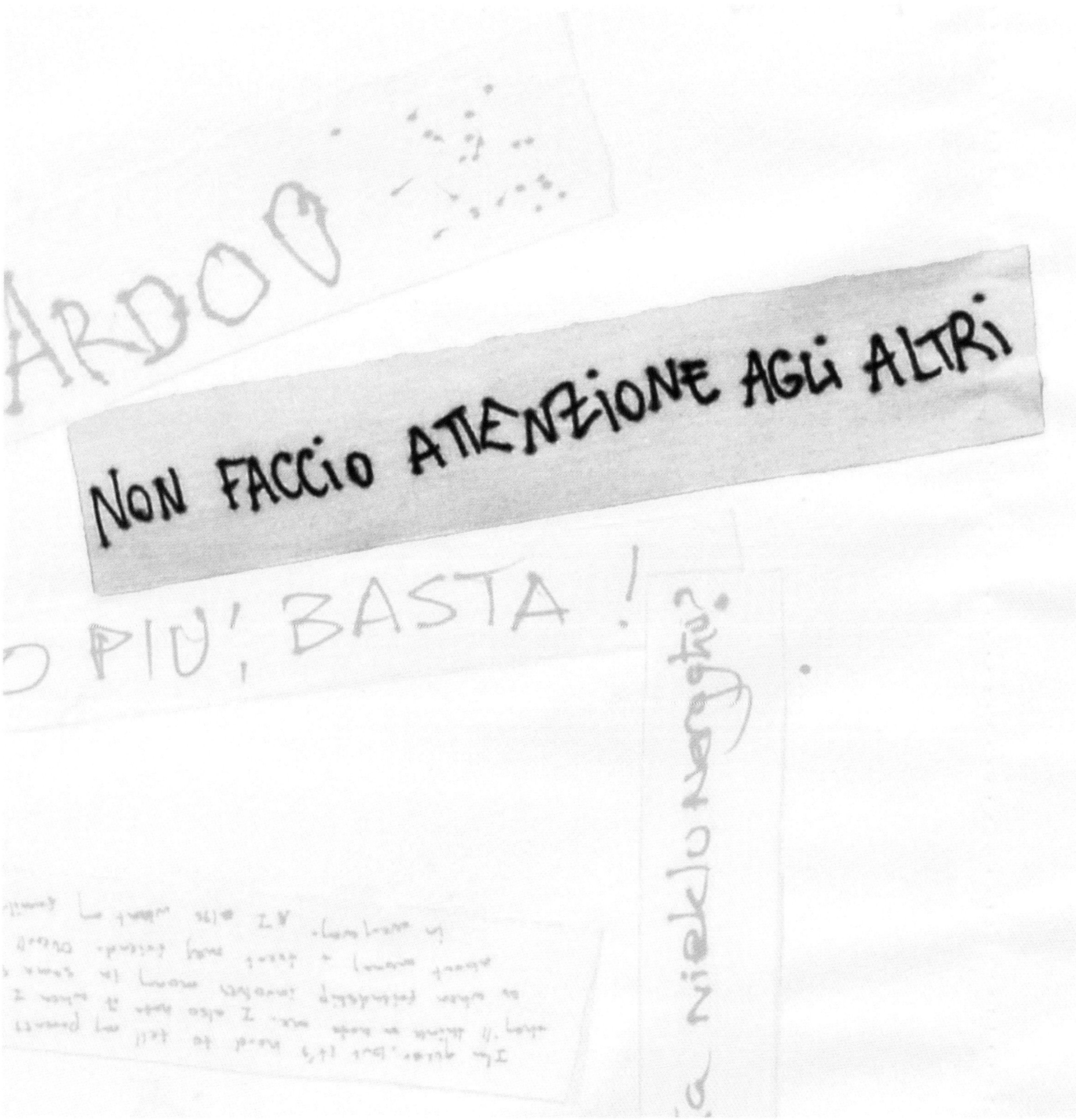
ARDOO
NON FACCIO ATTENZIONE AGLI ALTRI
O PIU', BASTA!

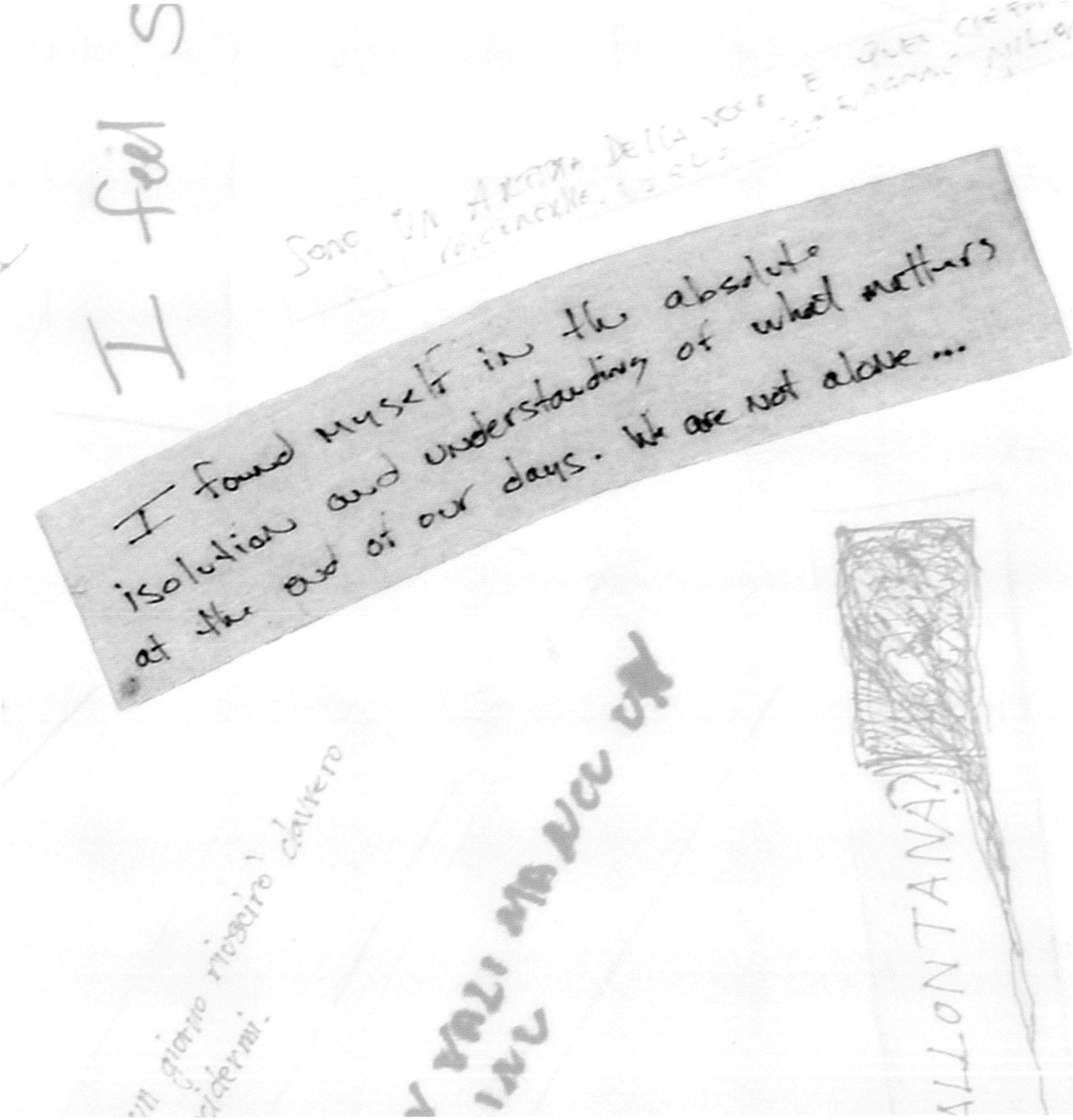
I feel S
I found myself in the absolute
isolation and understanding of what matters
at the end of our days. We are not alone...
un giorno riuscirò davvero
ALLONTANA!

NON AVEVO IL CORAGGIO DI
DIRE CHE AVEVO PAURA

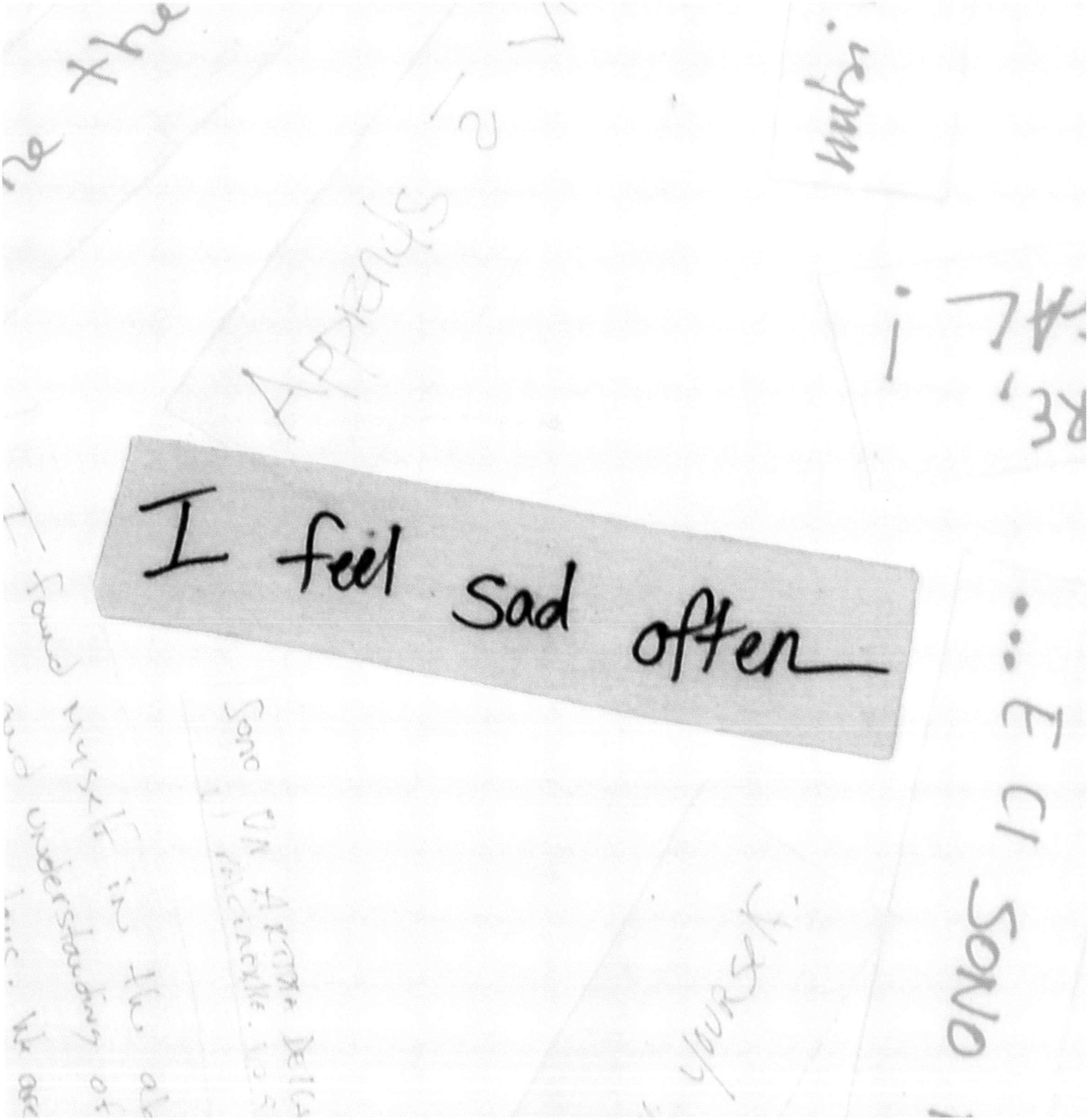
I feel sad often
... E CI SONO

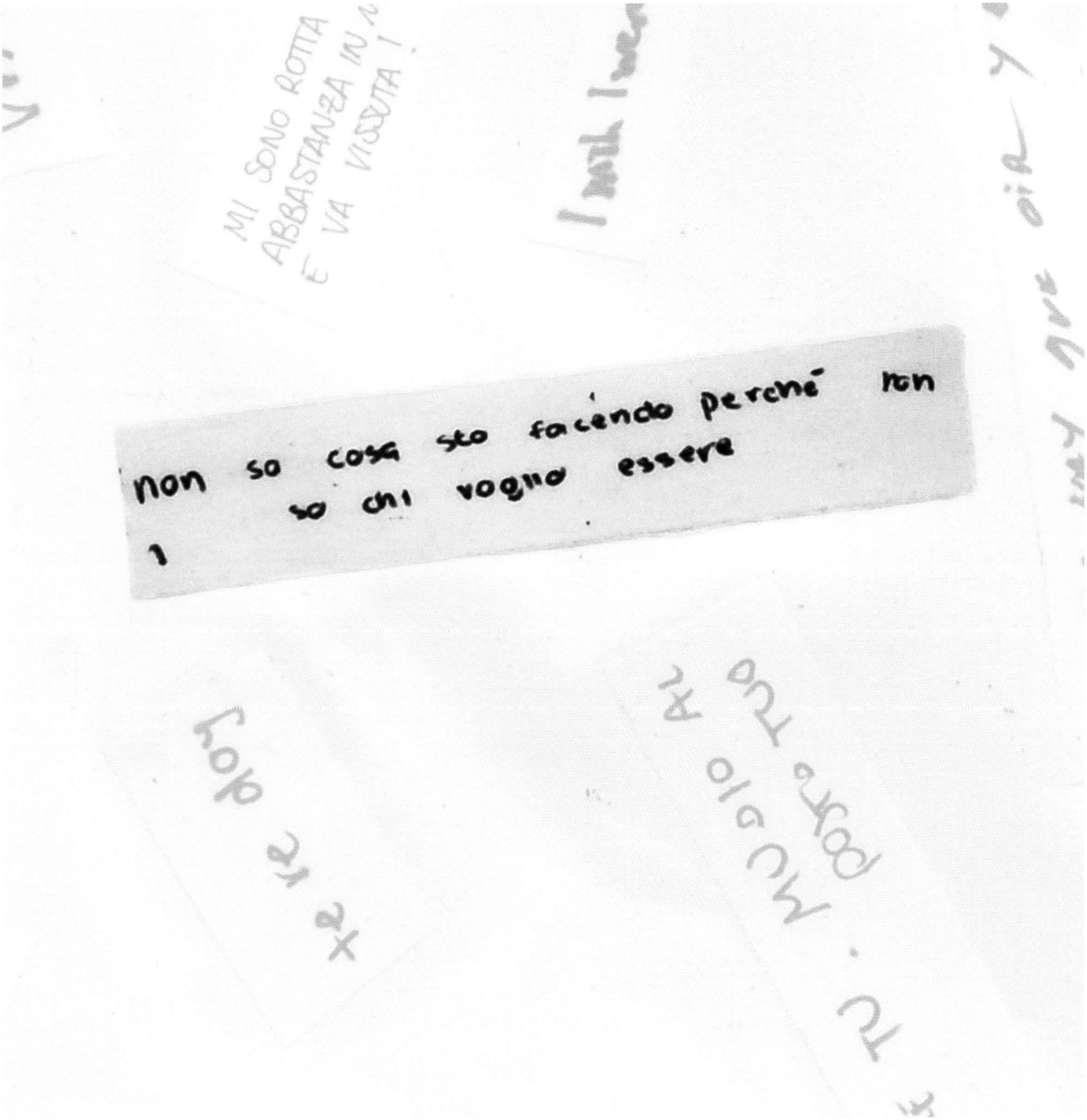
MI SONO ROTTA
ABBASTANZA IN
È VA VISSUTA !
non so cosa sto facendo perché non
so chi voglio essere

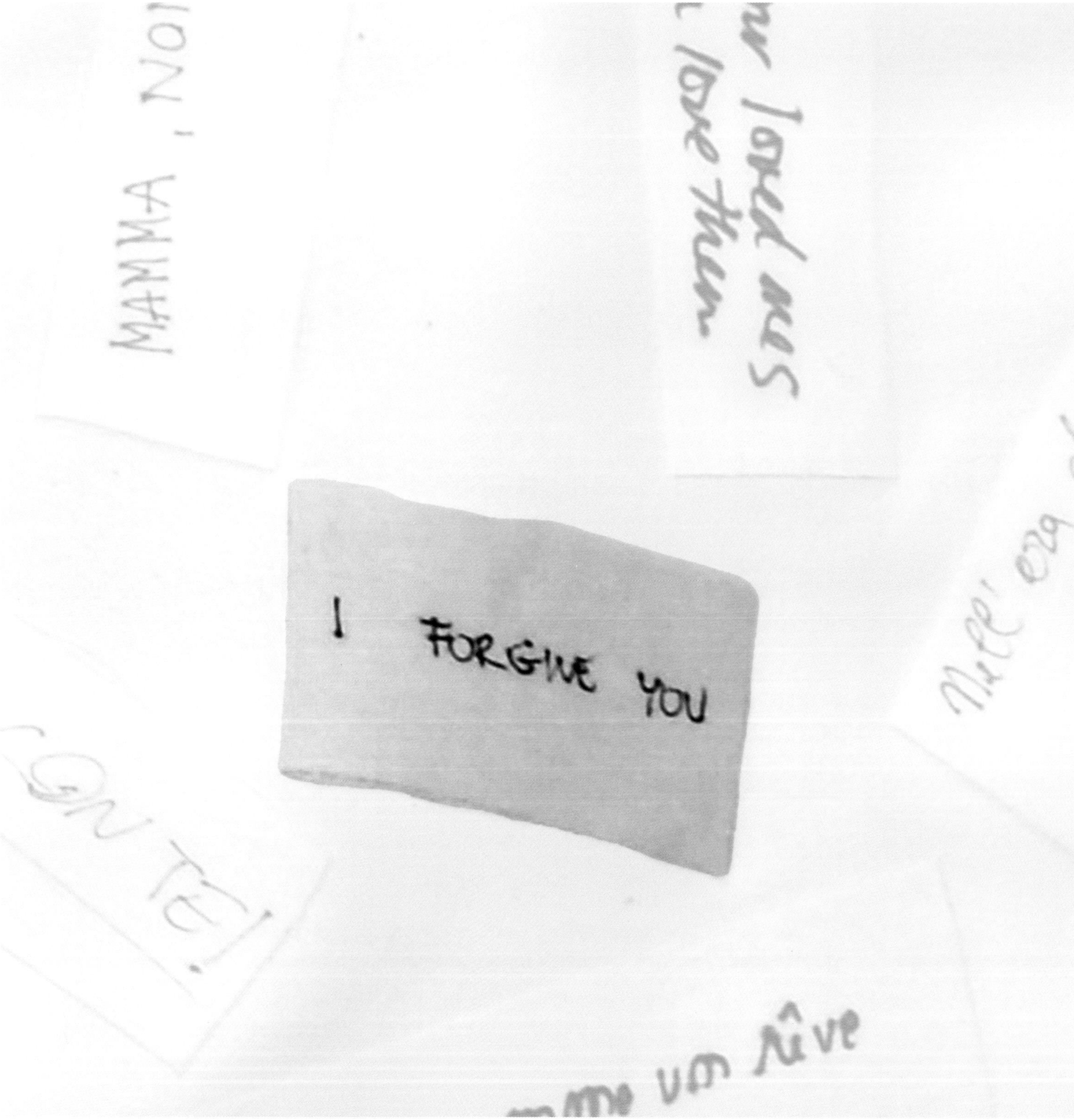
I FORGIVE YOU
MAMMA, NO

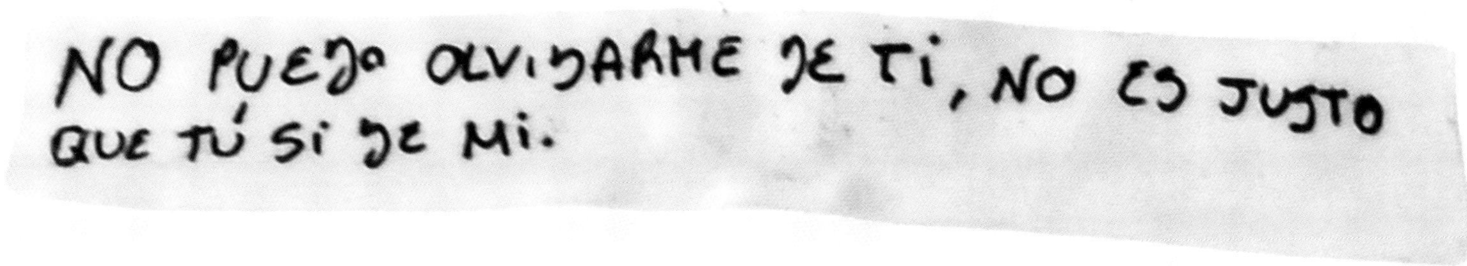
NO PUEDO OLVIDARME DE TI, NO ES JUSTO
QUE TÚ SI DE MI.

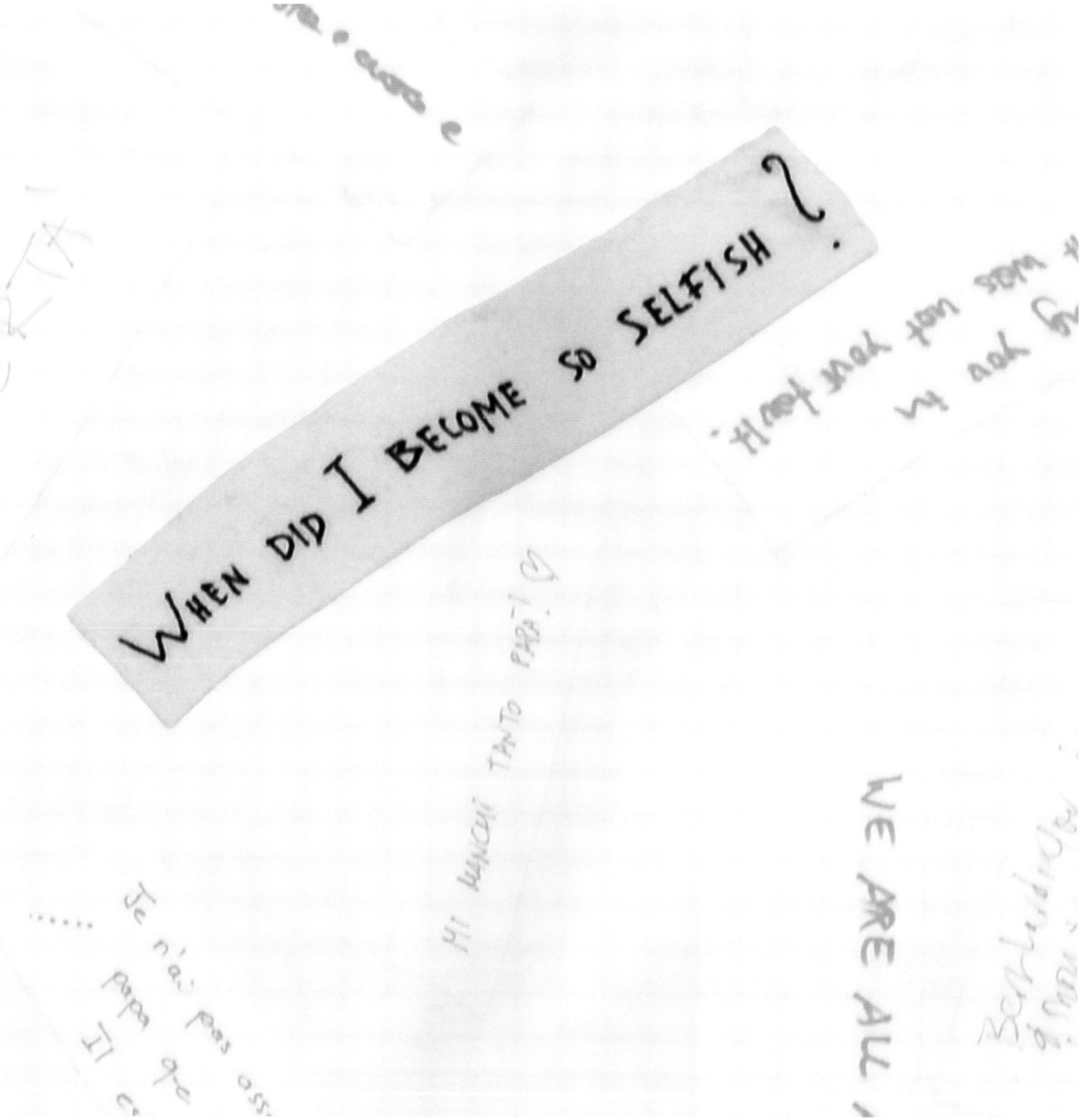
WHEN DID I BECOME SO SELFISH ?
MI MANCHI TANTO PAPÀ!
WE ARE ALL

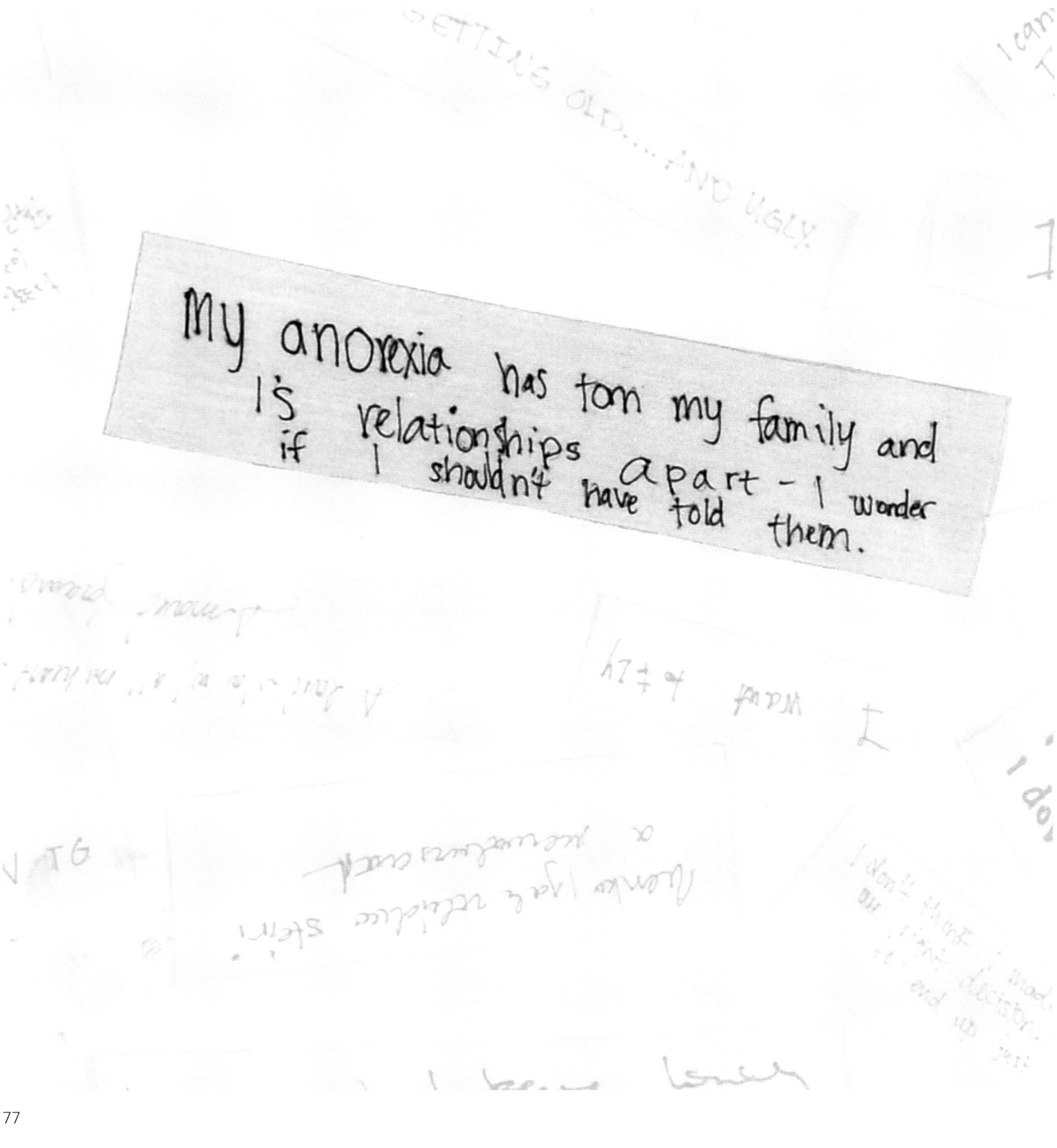
GETTING OLD....AND UGLY
My anorexia has torn my family and I's relationships apart - I wonder if I shouldn't have told them.

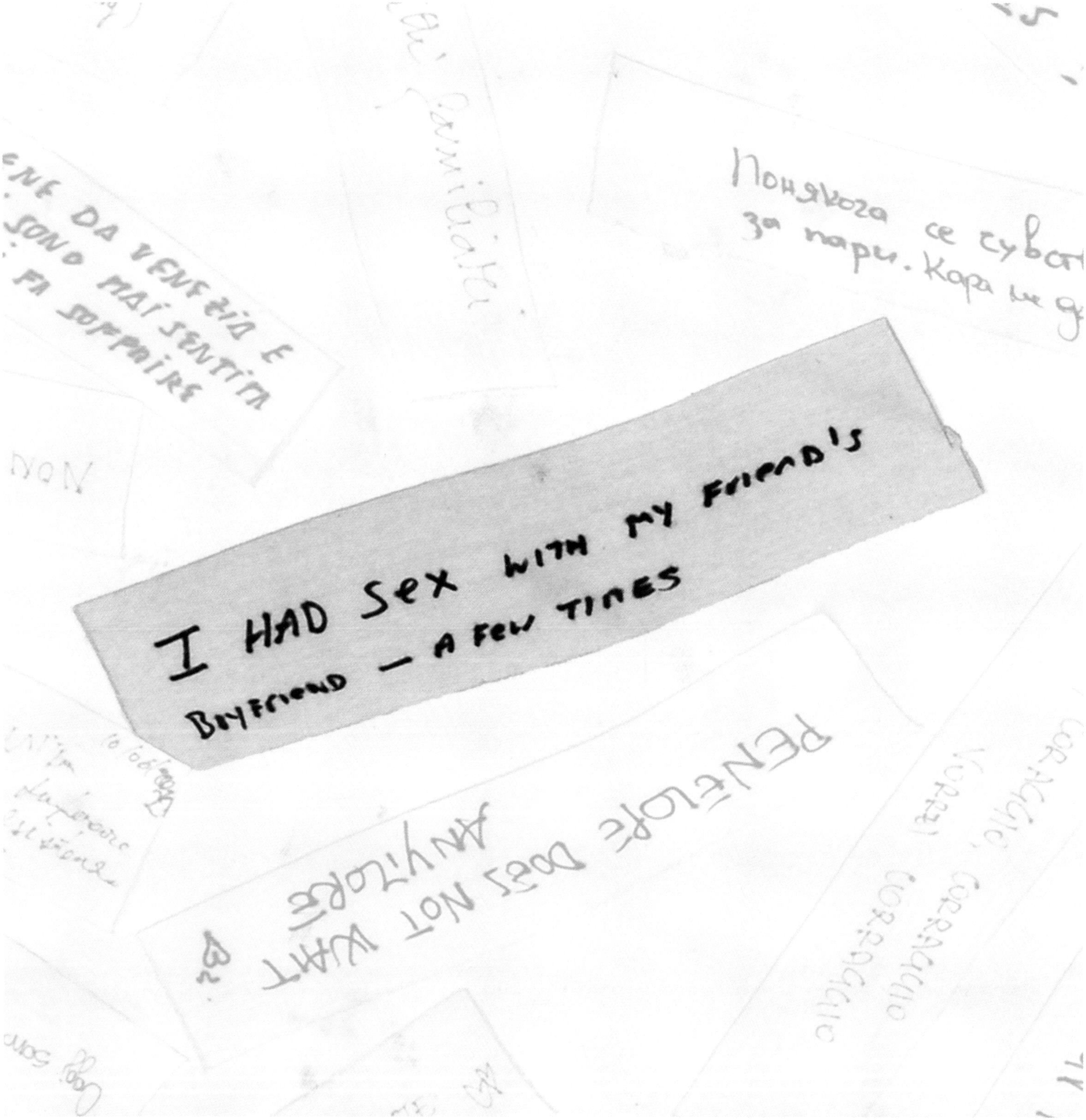
I HAD SEX WITH MY FRIEND'S
BOYFRIEND — A FEW TIMES

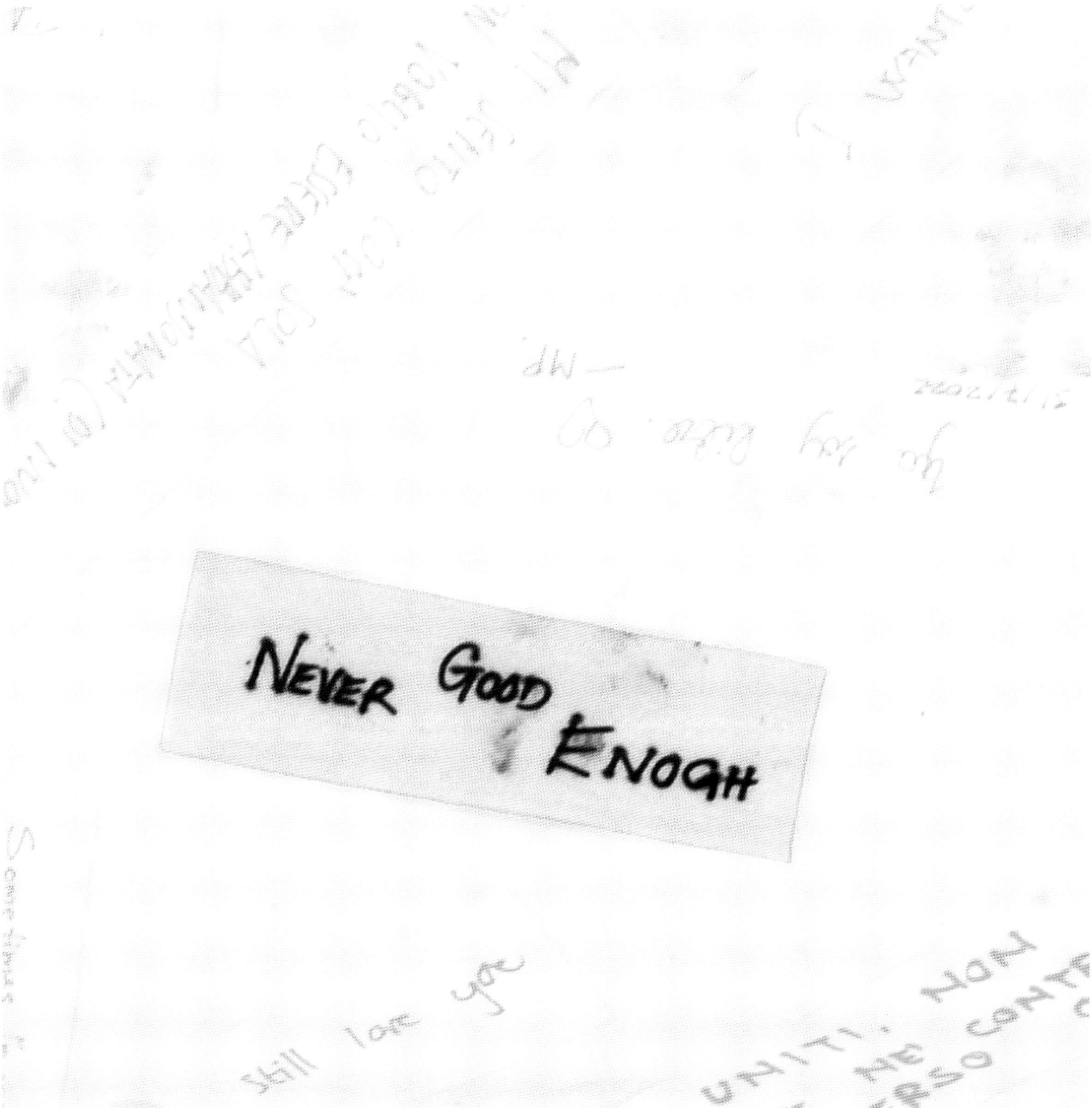
NEVER GOOD
ENOGH

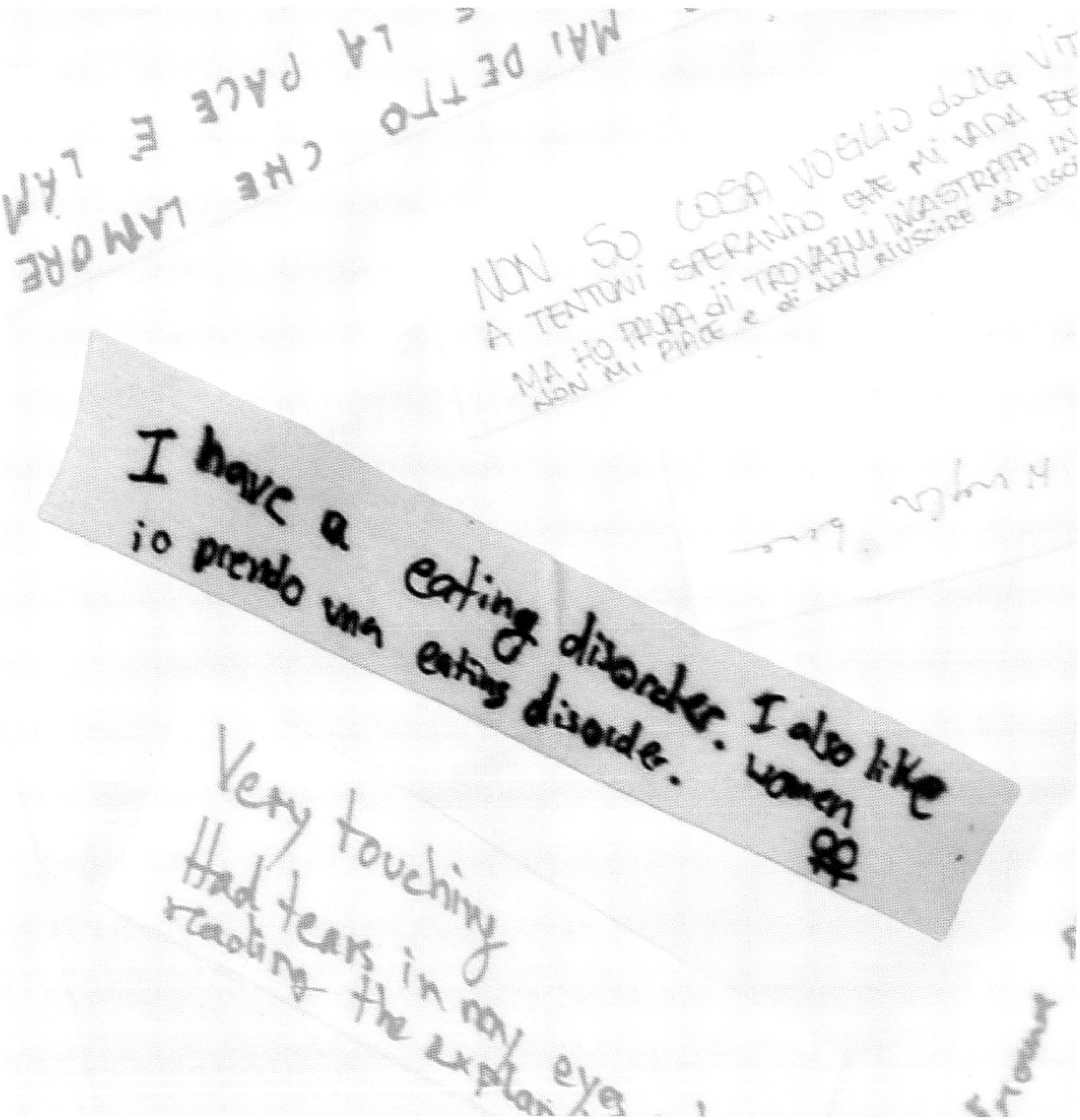
I have a eating disorder. I also like women
io prendo una eating disorde.
Very touching
Had tears in my eyes
NON SO COSA VOGLIO dalla VIT
A TENTONI SPERANDO CHE MI VADA BE
MA HO PAURA di TROVARMI INCASTRATA IN
NON MI PIACE e di NON RIUSCIRE AD USC

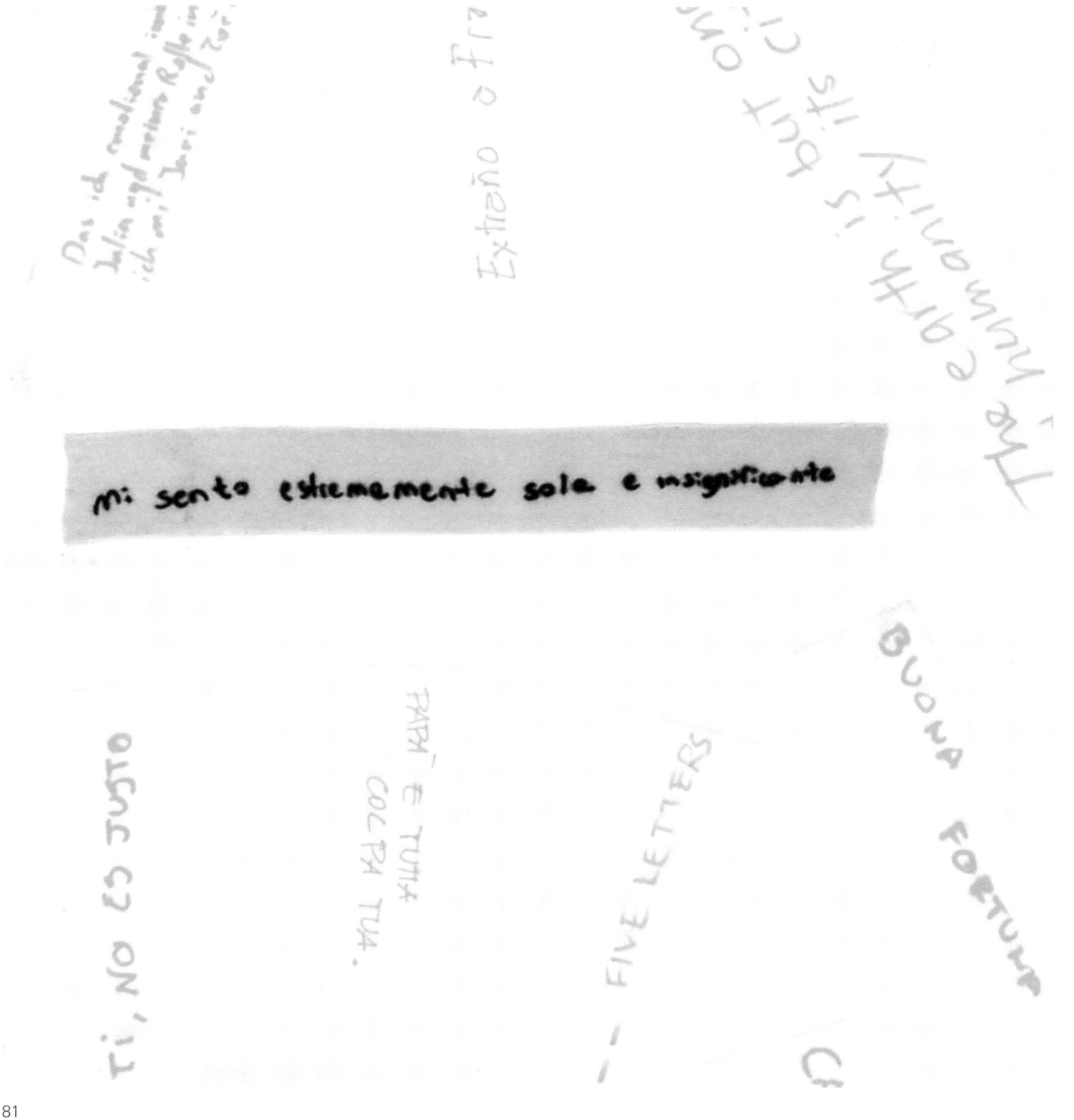
mi sento estremamente sola e insignificante
Extraño a Fra
PAPÀ È TUTTA COLPA TUA.
FIVE LETTERS

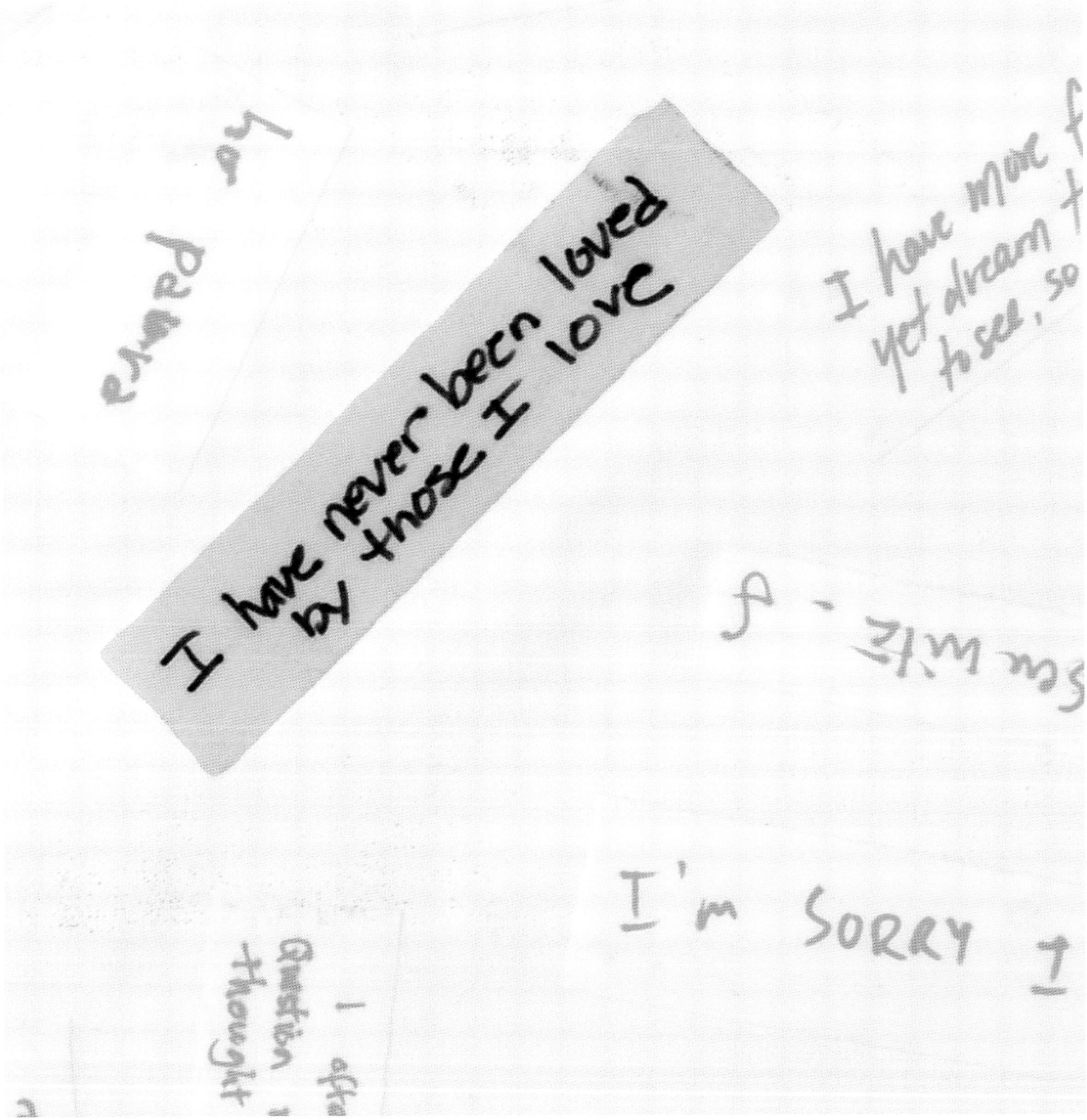
I have never been loved
by those I love
I have more
yet dream
to see, so
I'm SORRY
Question
thought

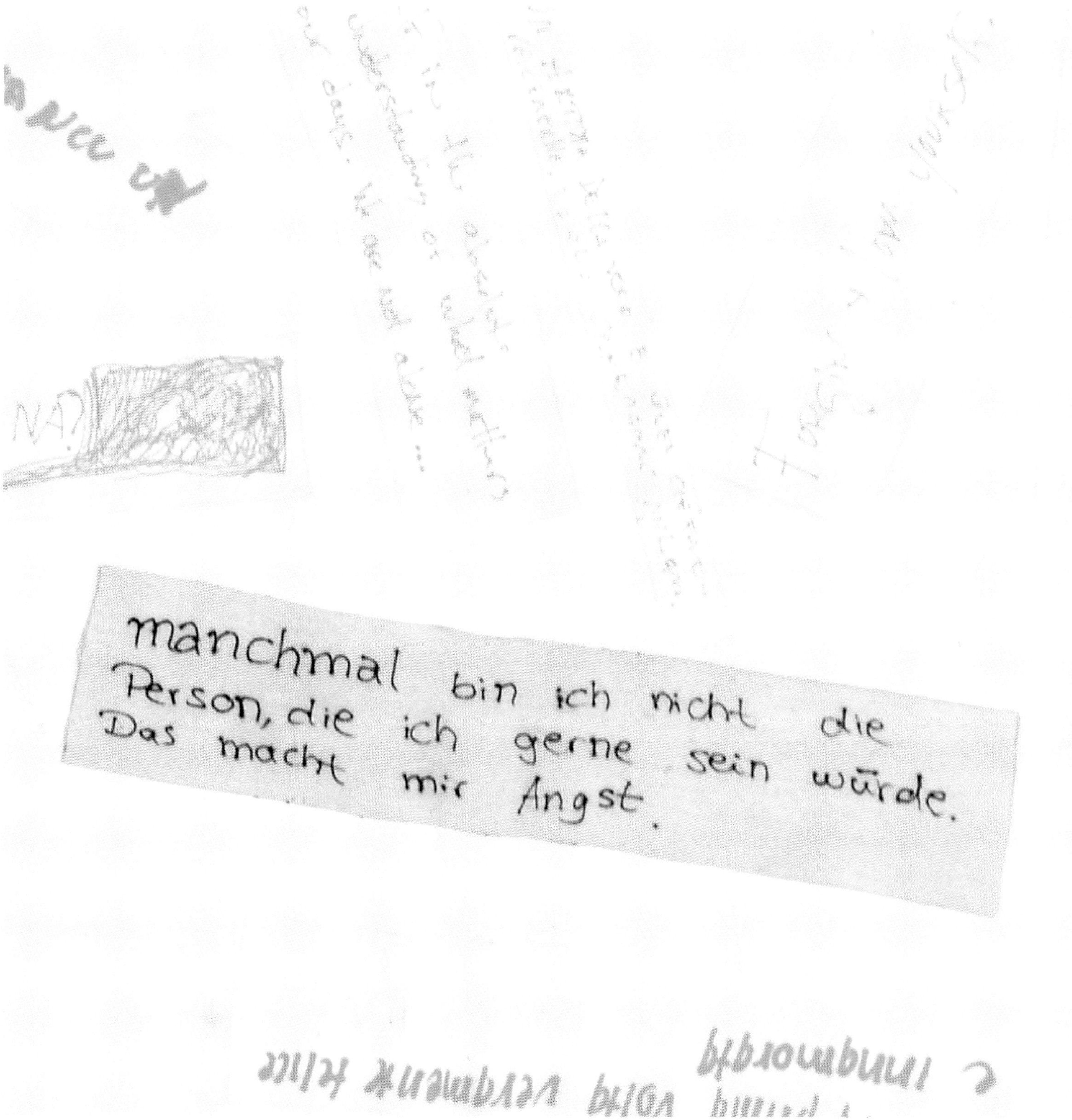
manchmal bin ich nicht die
Person, die ich gerne sein würde.
Das macht mir Angst.

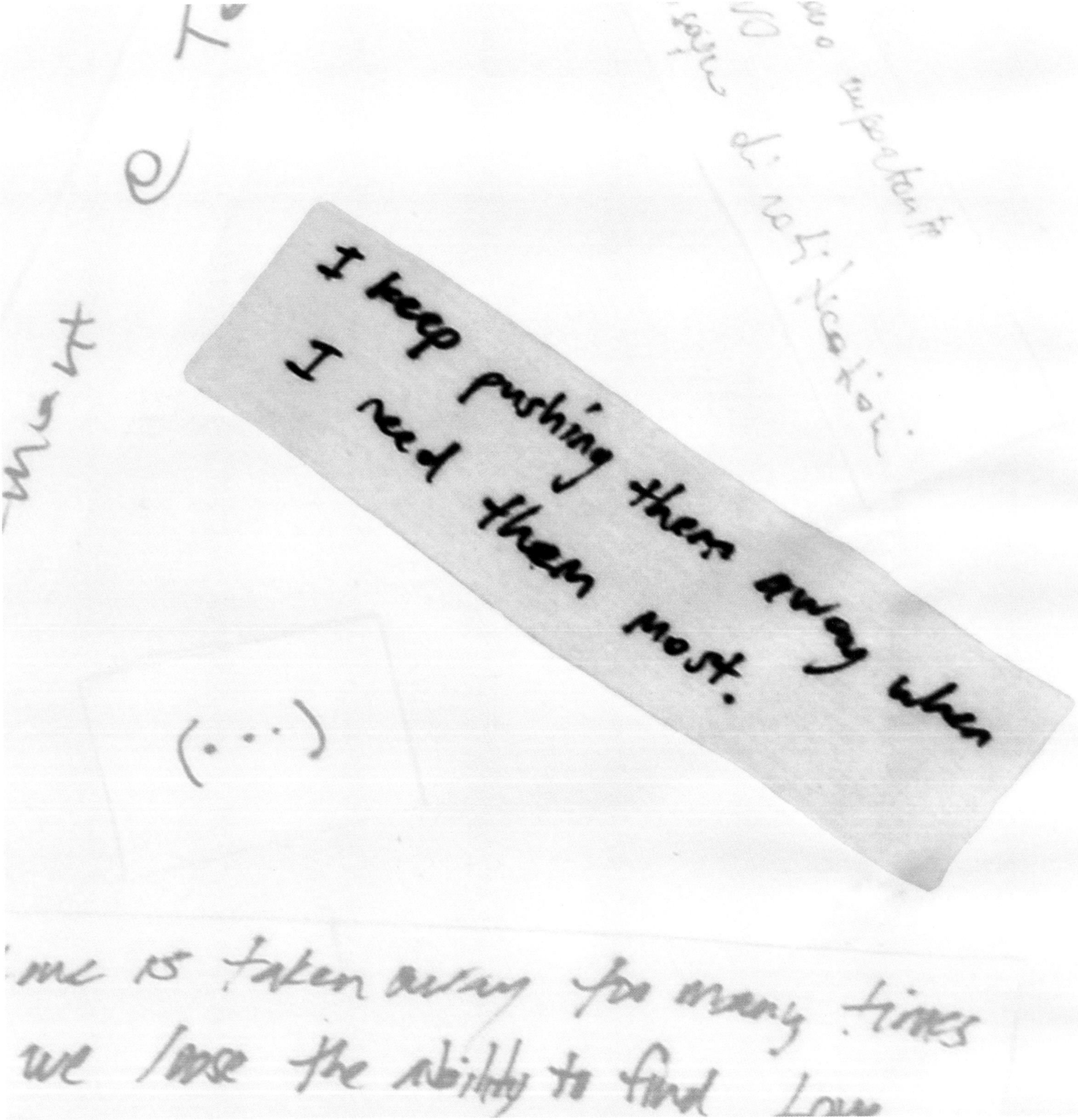
I keep pushing them away when
I need them most.

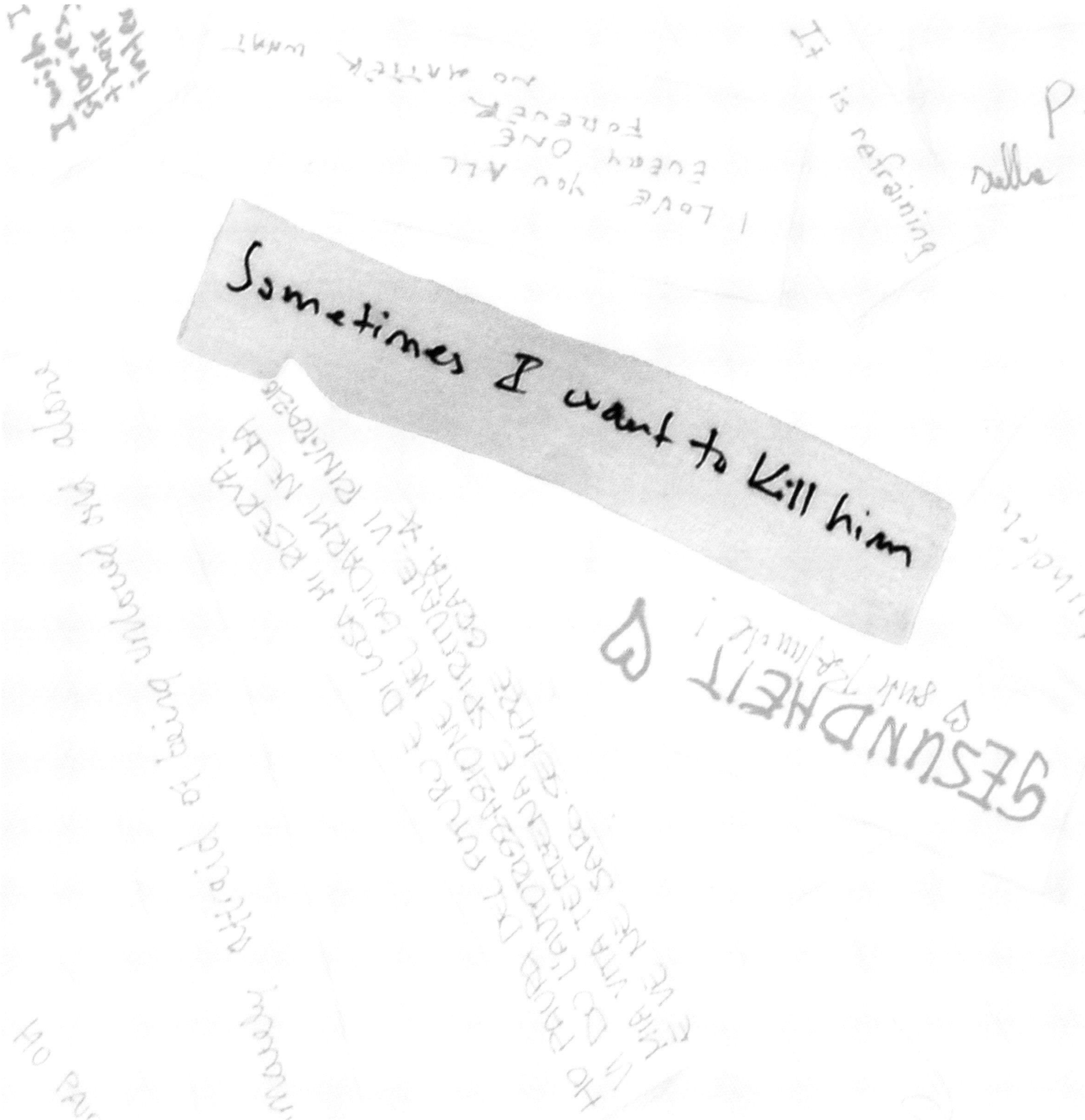
Sometimes I want to kill him

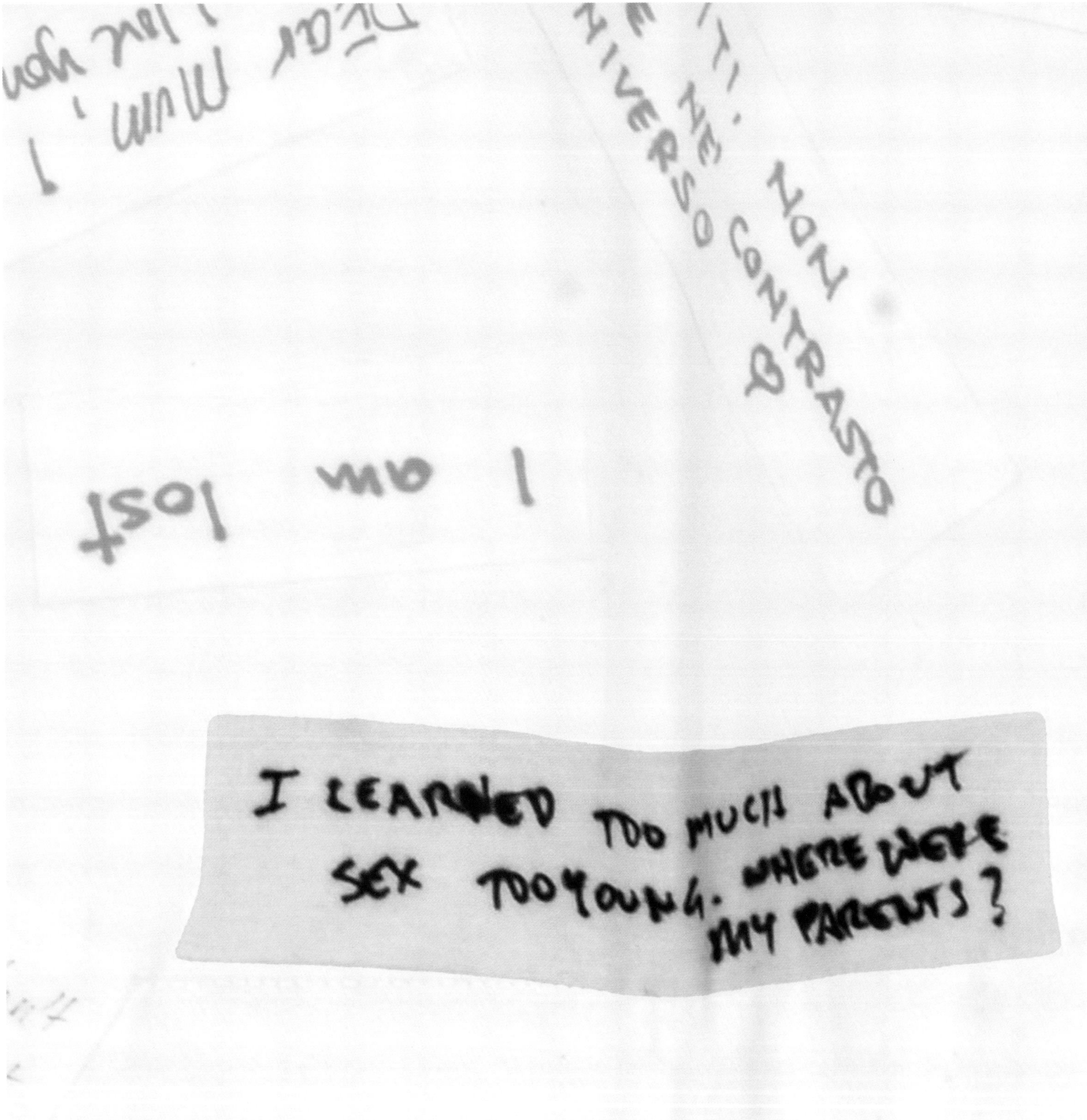
I LEARNED TOO MUCH ABOUT SEX TOO YOUNG. WHERE WERE MY PARENTS?
I am lost
Dear Mum, I love you

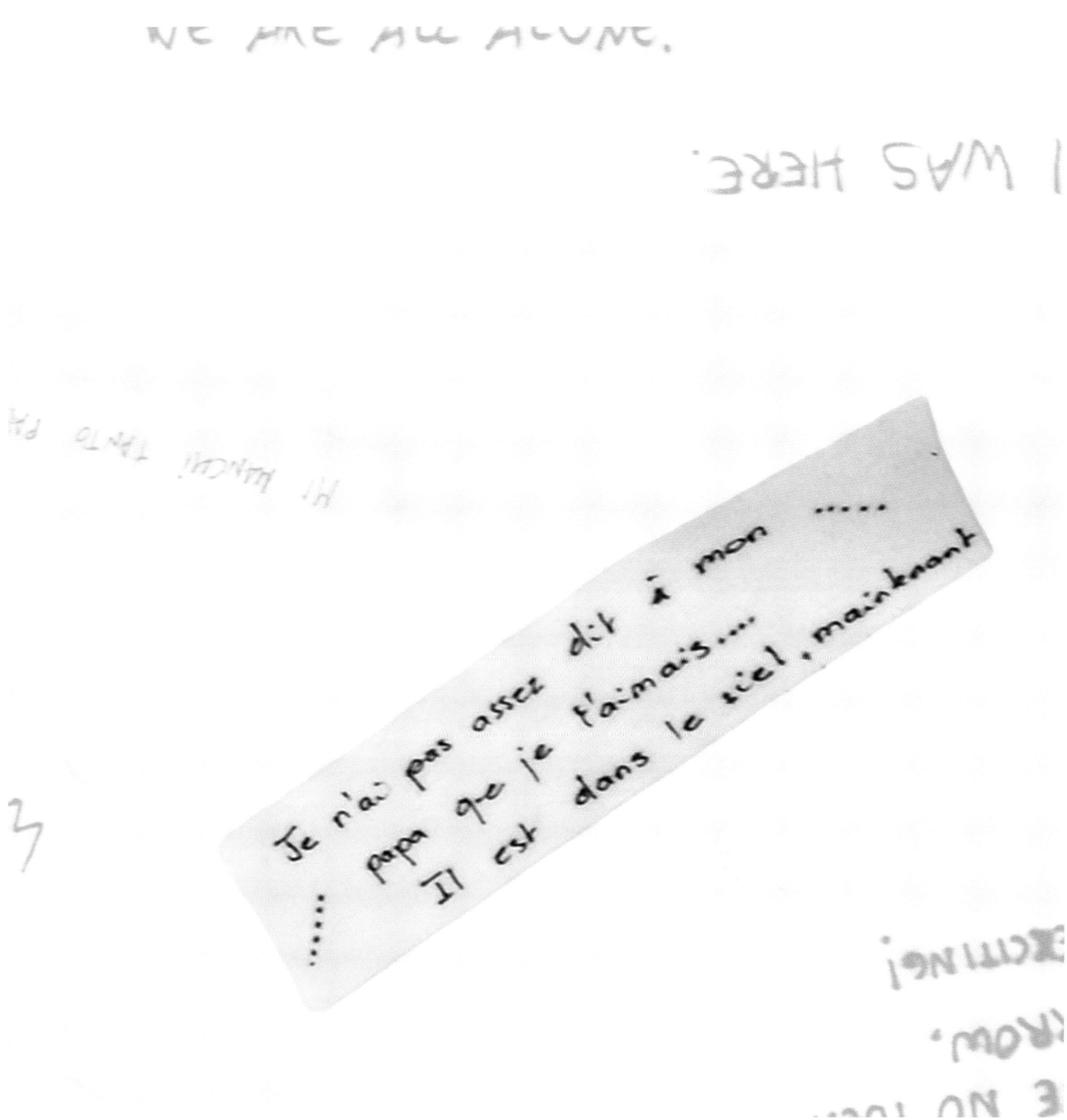
Je n'ai pas assez dit à mon .....
papa que je t'aimais....
Il est dans le ciel, maintenant
.....

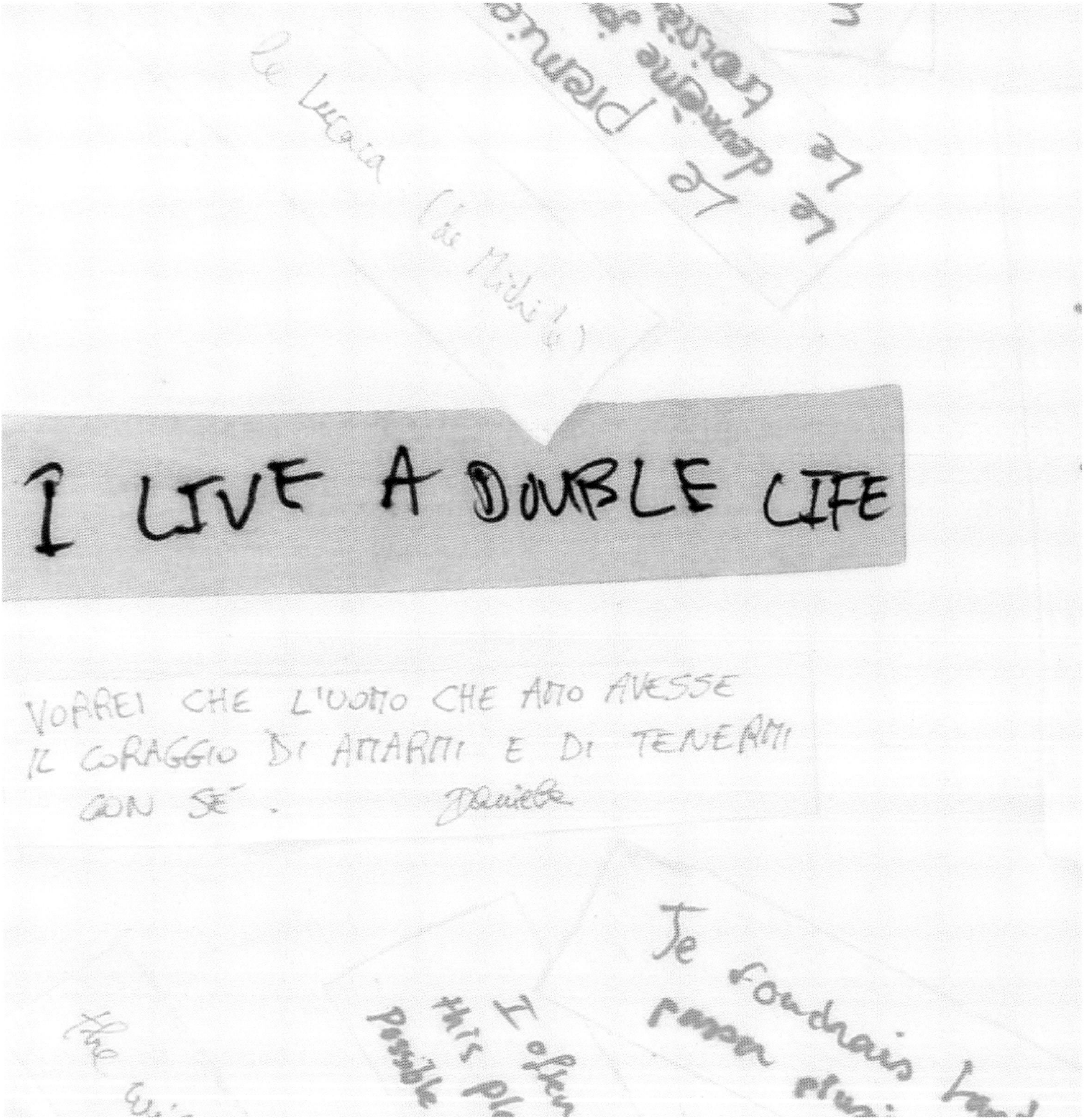
I LIVE A DOUBLE LIFE
VORREI CHE L'UOMO CHE AMO AVESSE
IL CORAGGIO DI AMARMI E DI TENERMI
CON SÉ.
Daniela

Ich bin so leer im Kopf und kann mich oft nicht erinnern.

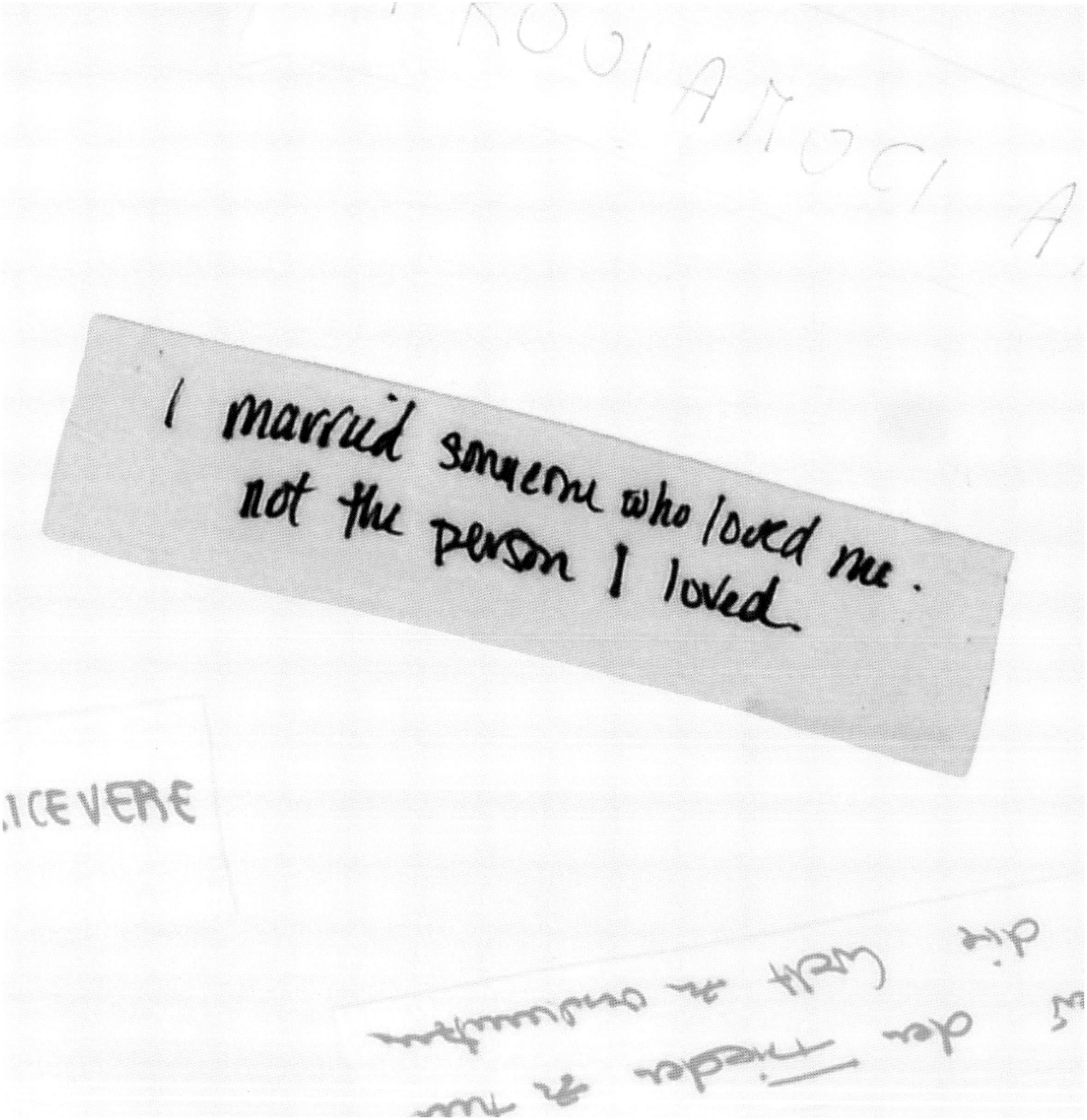
I married someone who loved me.
not the person I loved.

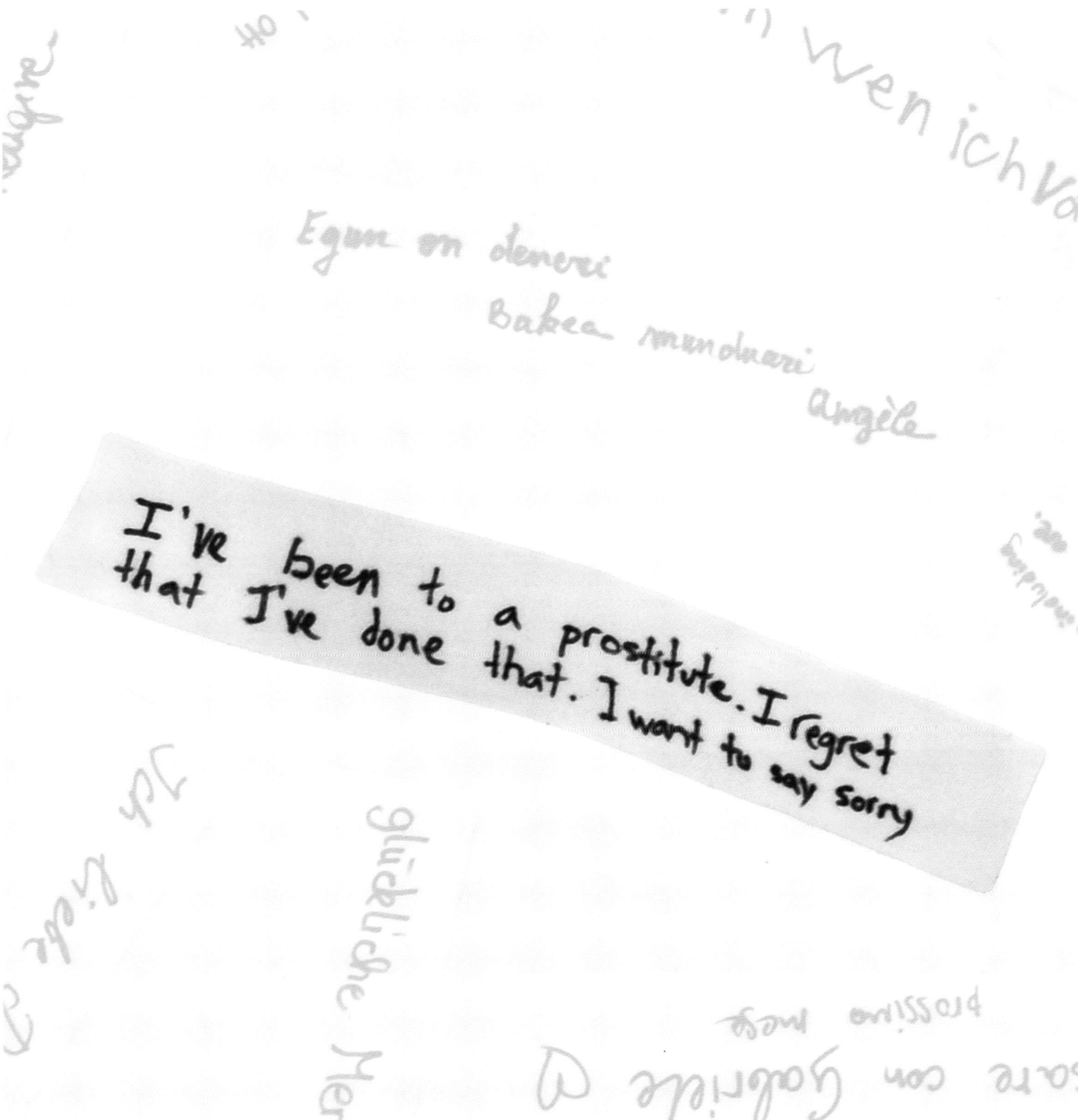

I've been to a prostitute. I regret that I've done that. I want to say sorry
Wen ichVa
Egun on denerei
Bakea munduari
Angèle

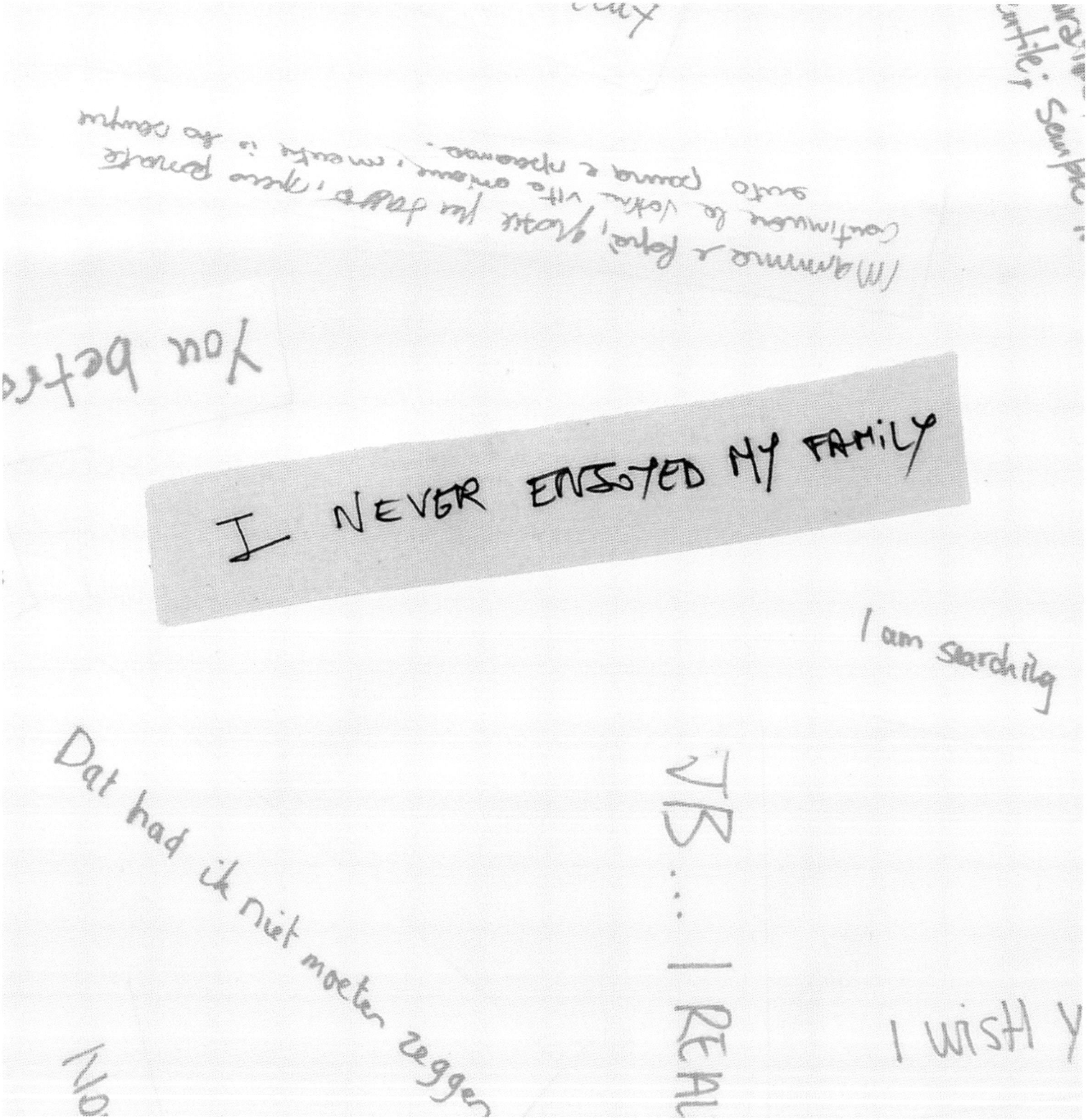
I NEVER ENJOYED MY FAMILY
I am searching
Dat had ik niet moeten zeggen
JB ... I REAL
I WISH Y

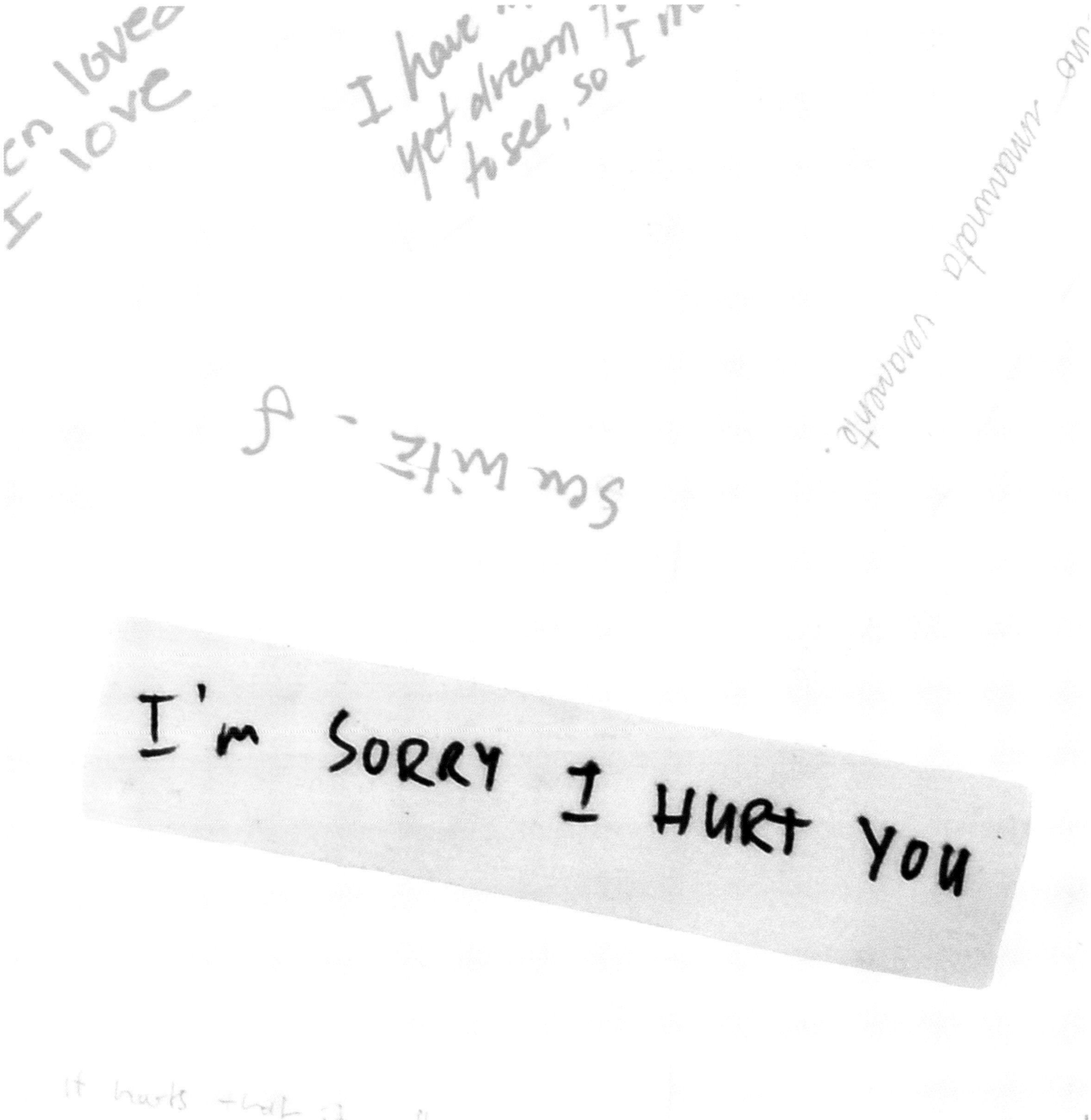
I'M SORRY I HURT YOU

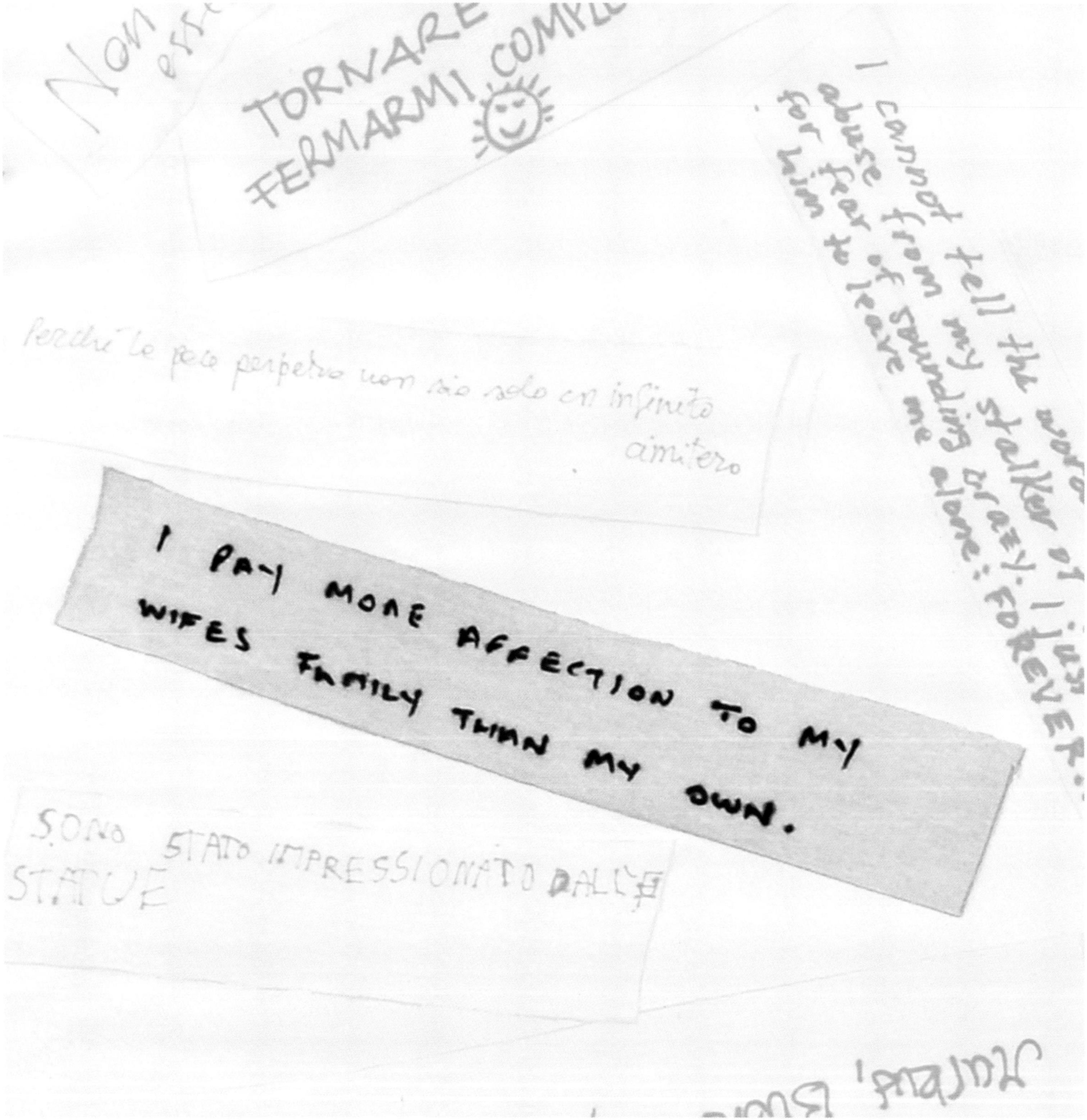
TORNARE
FERMARMI
I cannot tell the word
abuse from my stalker
for fear of sounding crazy.
him to leave me alone: FOREVER.
cimitero
I PAY MORE AFFECTION TO MY
WIFES FAMILY THAN MY OWN.
SONO STATO IMPRESSIONATO DALLE
STATUE

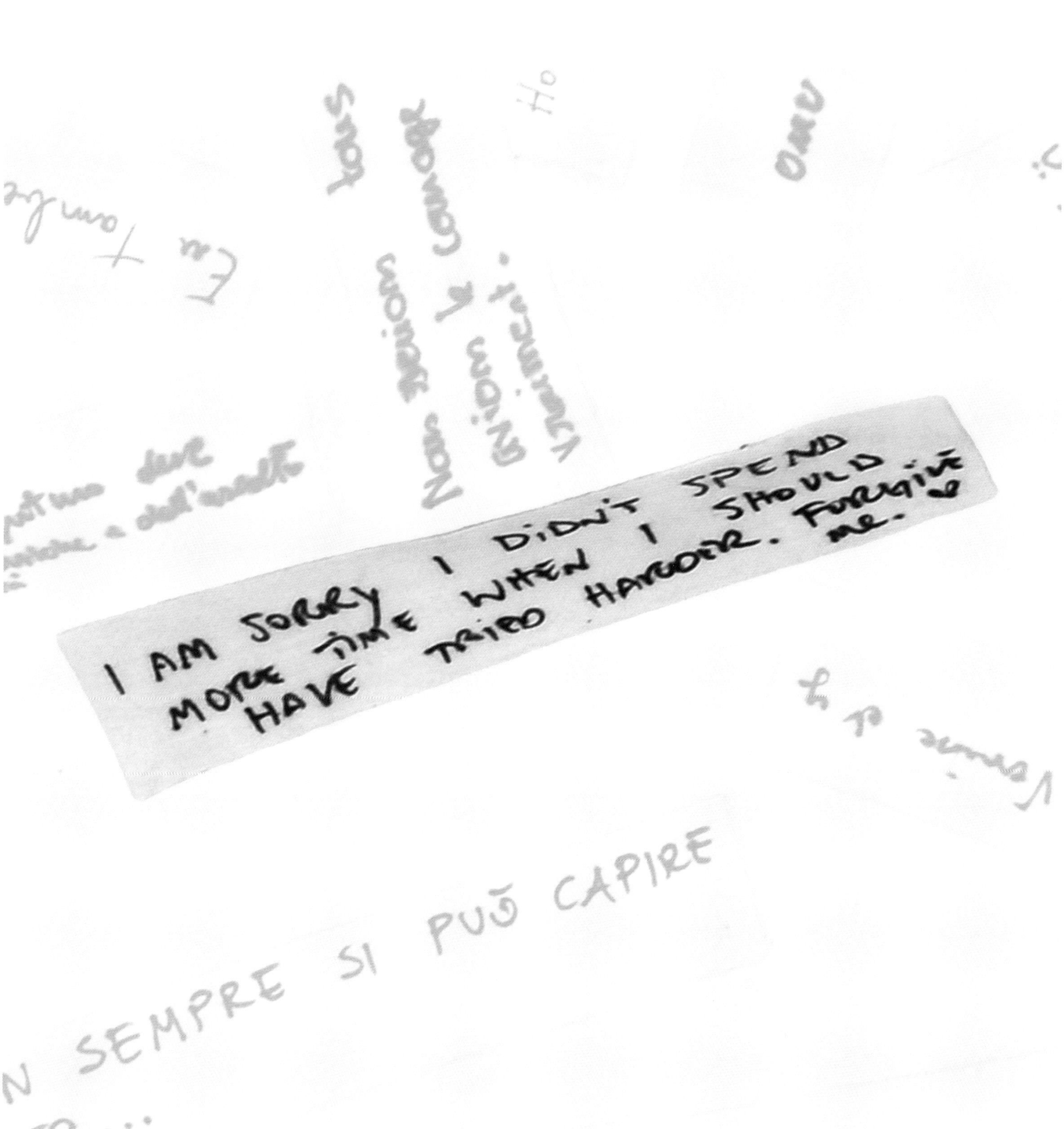
I AM SORRY I DIDN'T SPEND
MORE TIME WHEN I SHOULD
HAVE TRIED HARDER. FORGIVE
ME.
N SEMPRE SI PUÒ CAPIRE

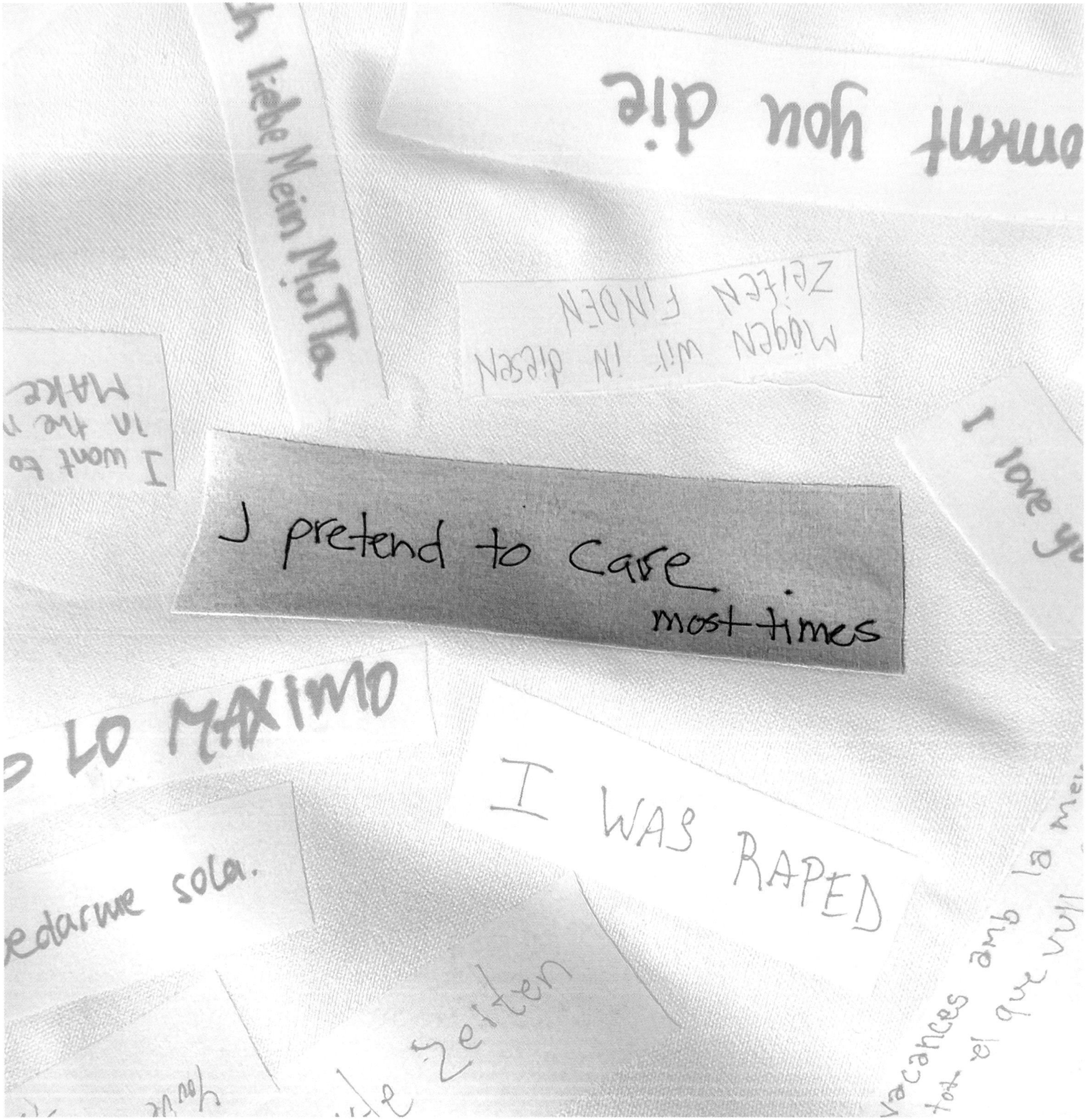
I pretend to care.
most times
I WAS RAPED
LO MAXIMO
edarme sola.
Mögen wir in diesen
Zeiten FINDEN

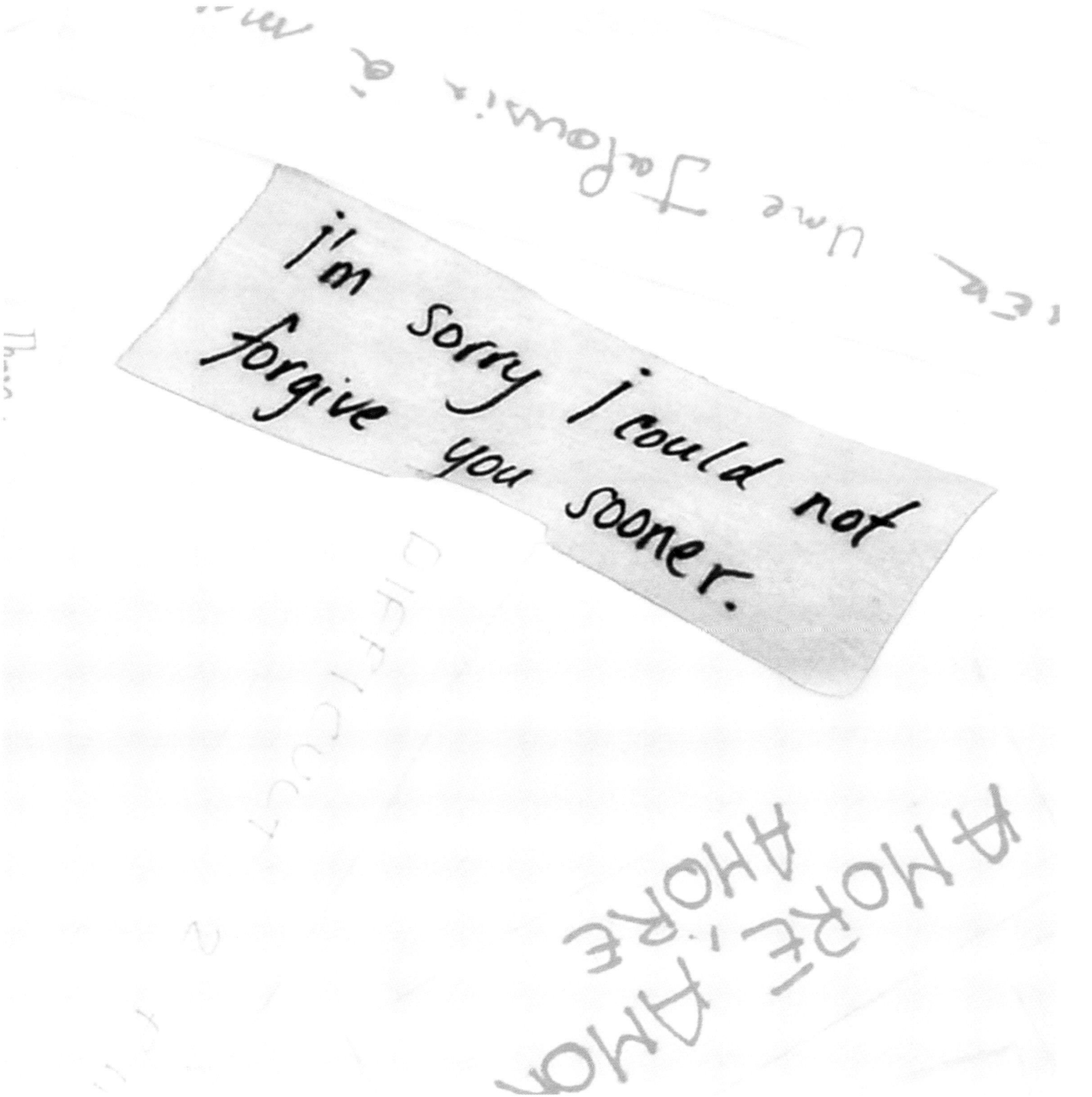
i'm sorry i could not
forgive you sooner.

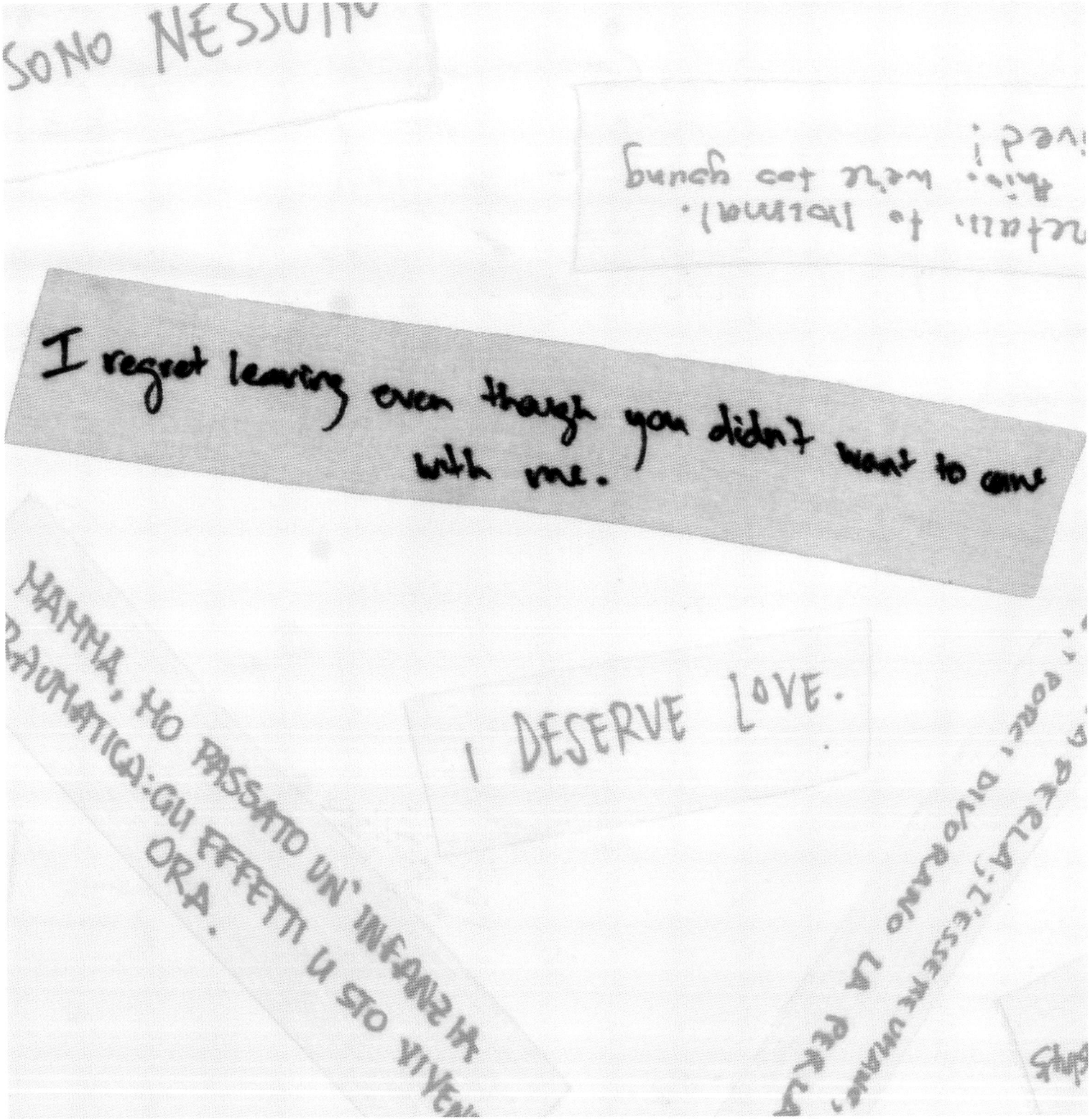
SONO NESSU
I regret leaving even though you didn't want to come with me.
I DESERVE LOVE.
MAMMA, HO PASSATO UN' INFANZIA
RAUMATICA: GLI EFFETTI LI STO VIVEN
ORA.

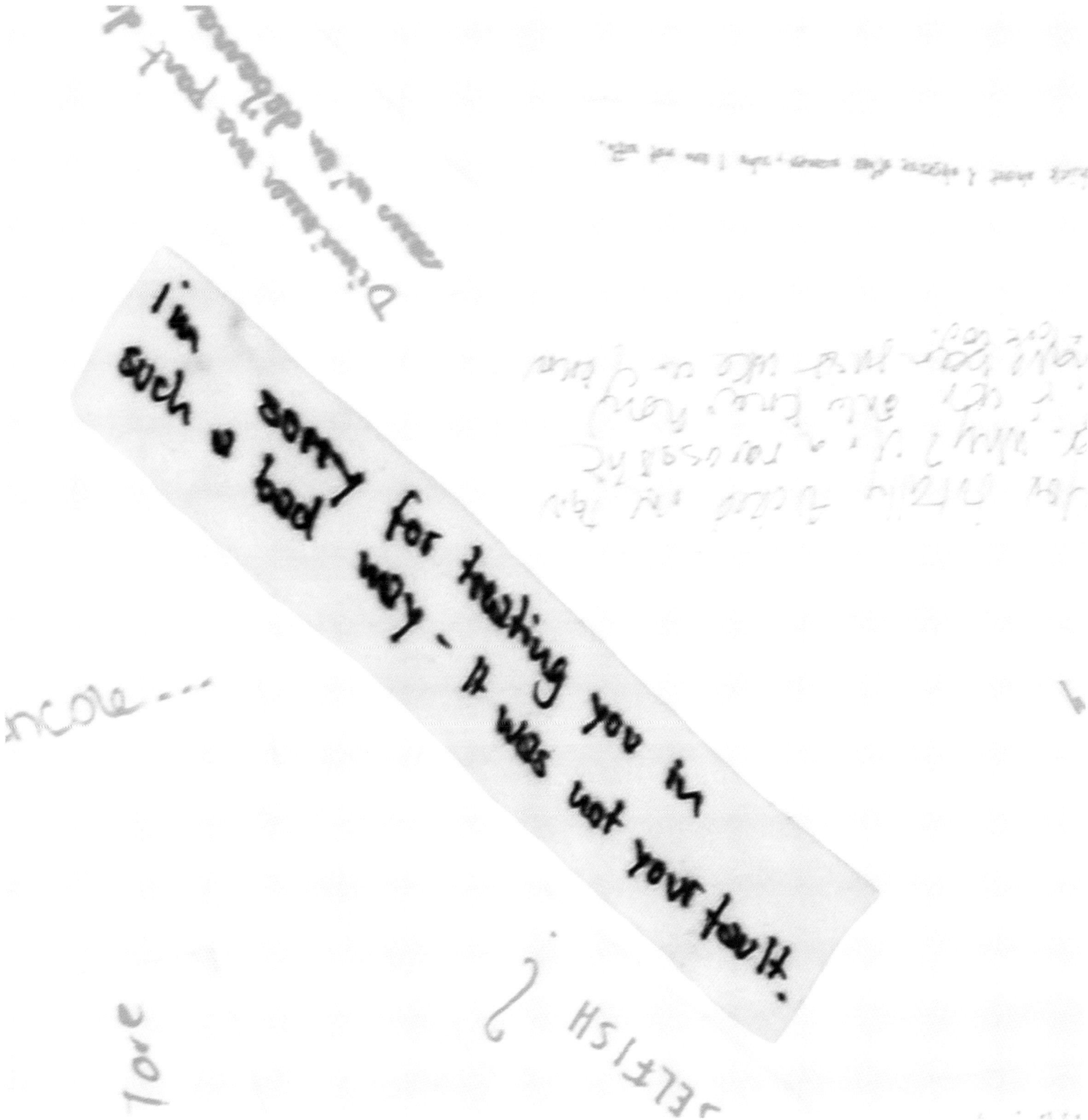
i'm sorry for treating you in
such a bad way - it was not your fault.

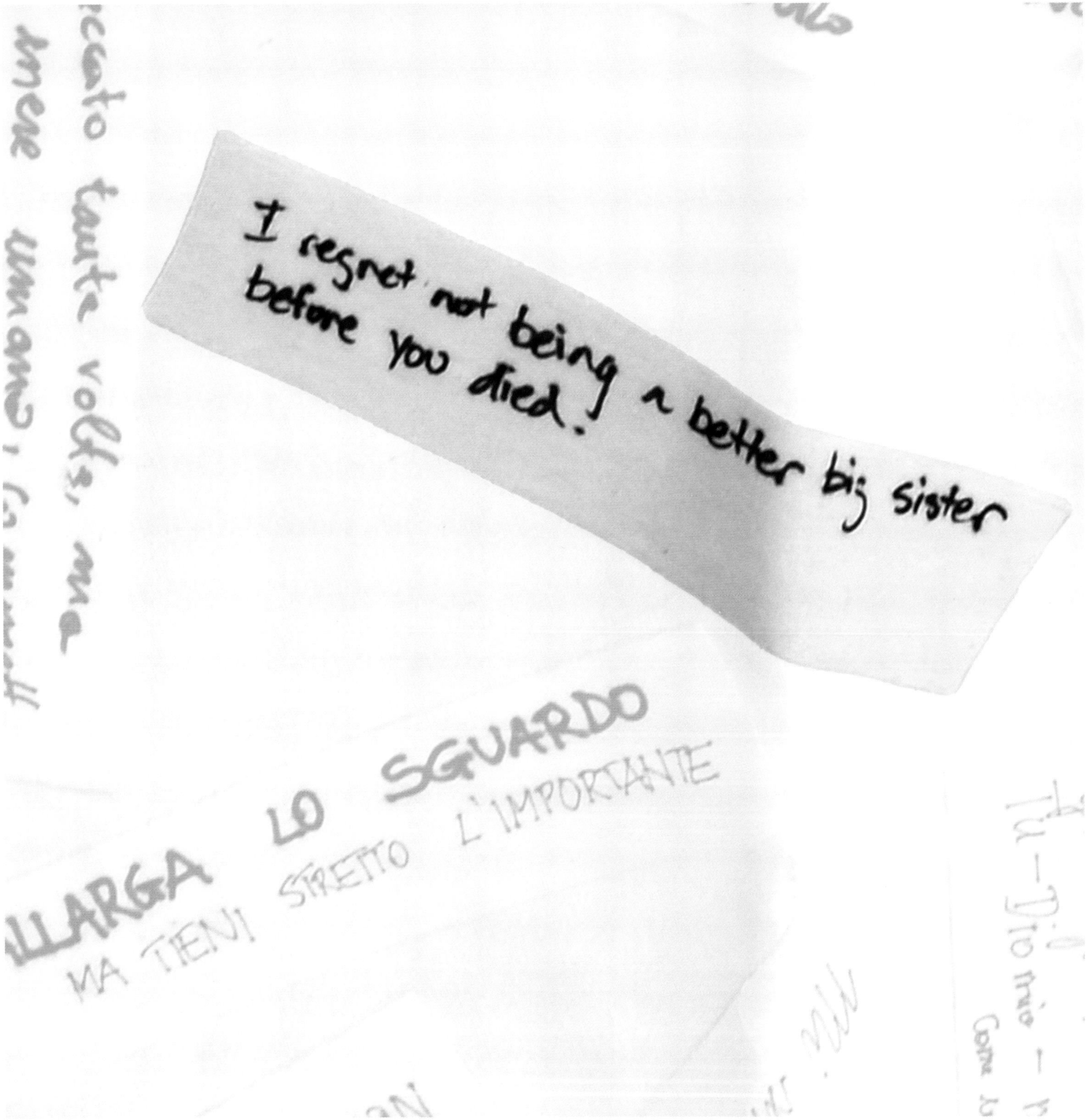
I regret not being a better big sister
before you died.
ALLARGA LO SGUARDO
MA TIENI STRETTO L'IMPORTANTE

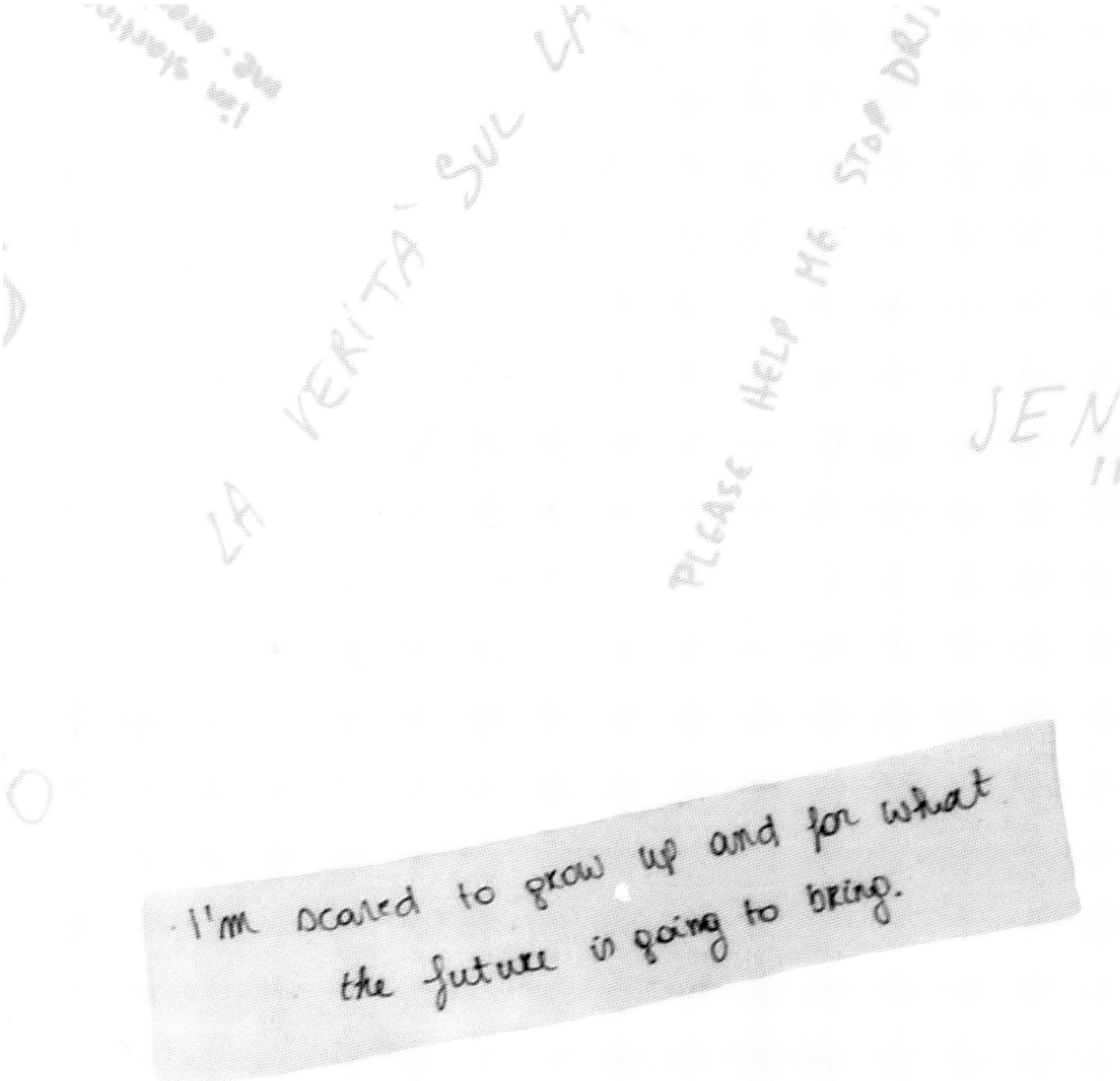
LA VERITA SUL
PLEASE HELP ME STOP
JEN
I'm scared to grow up and for what
the future is going to bring.

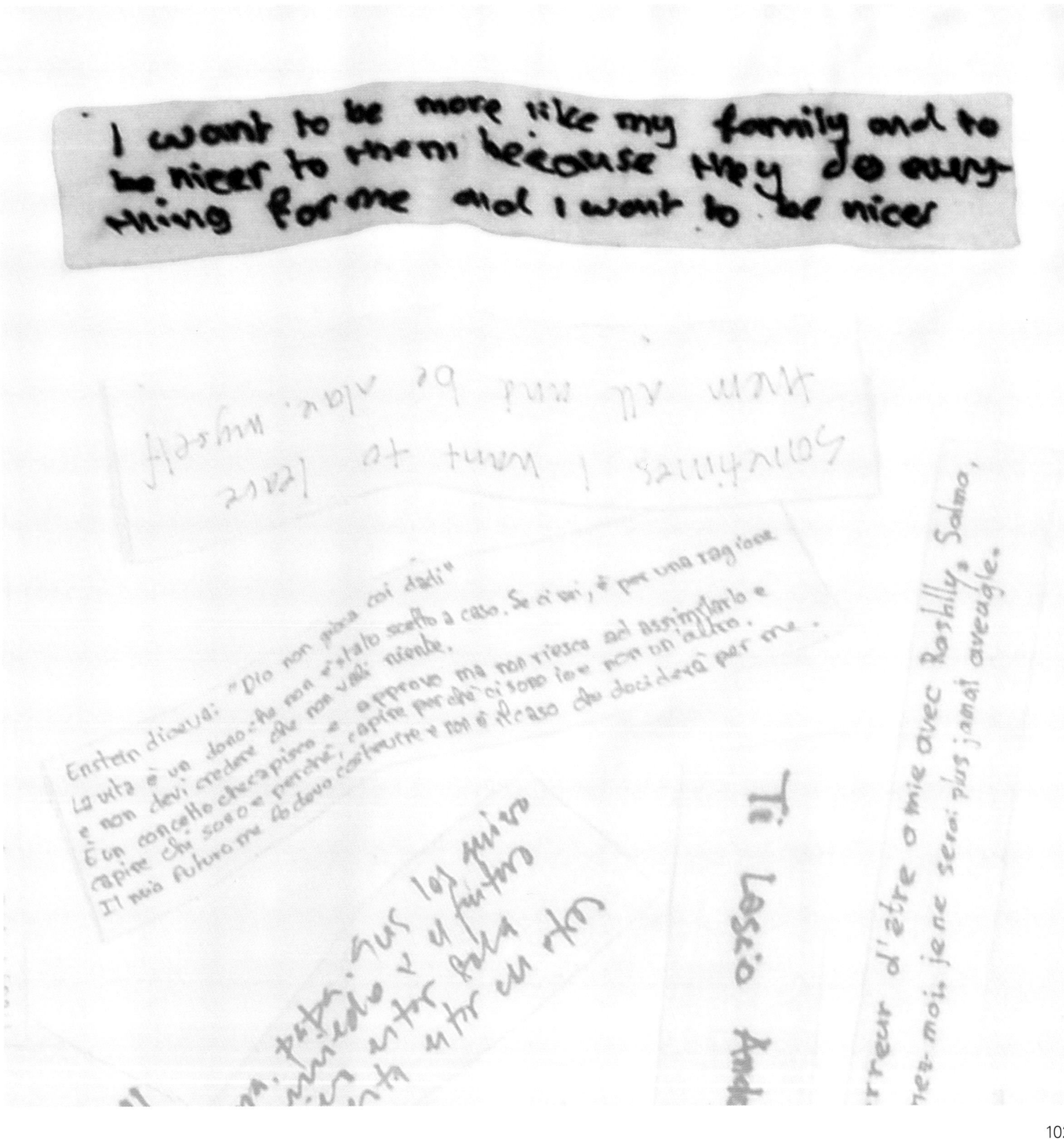
I want to be more like my family and to be nicer to them because they do every-thing for me and I want to be nicer
Enstein diceva: "Dio non gioca coi dadi"
La vita è un dono: che non è stato scelto a caso. Se ci sei, è per una ragione
e non devi credere che non vali niente.
È un concetto che capisco e approvo ma non riesco ad assimilarlo e
capire chi sono e perché, capire perché ci sono io e non un'altro.
Il mio futuro me lo devo costruire e non è il caso che deciderà per me.

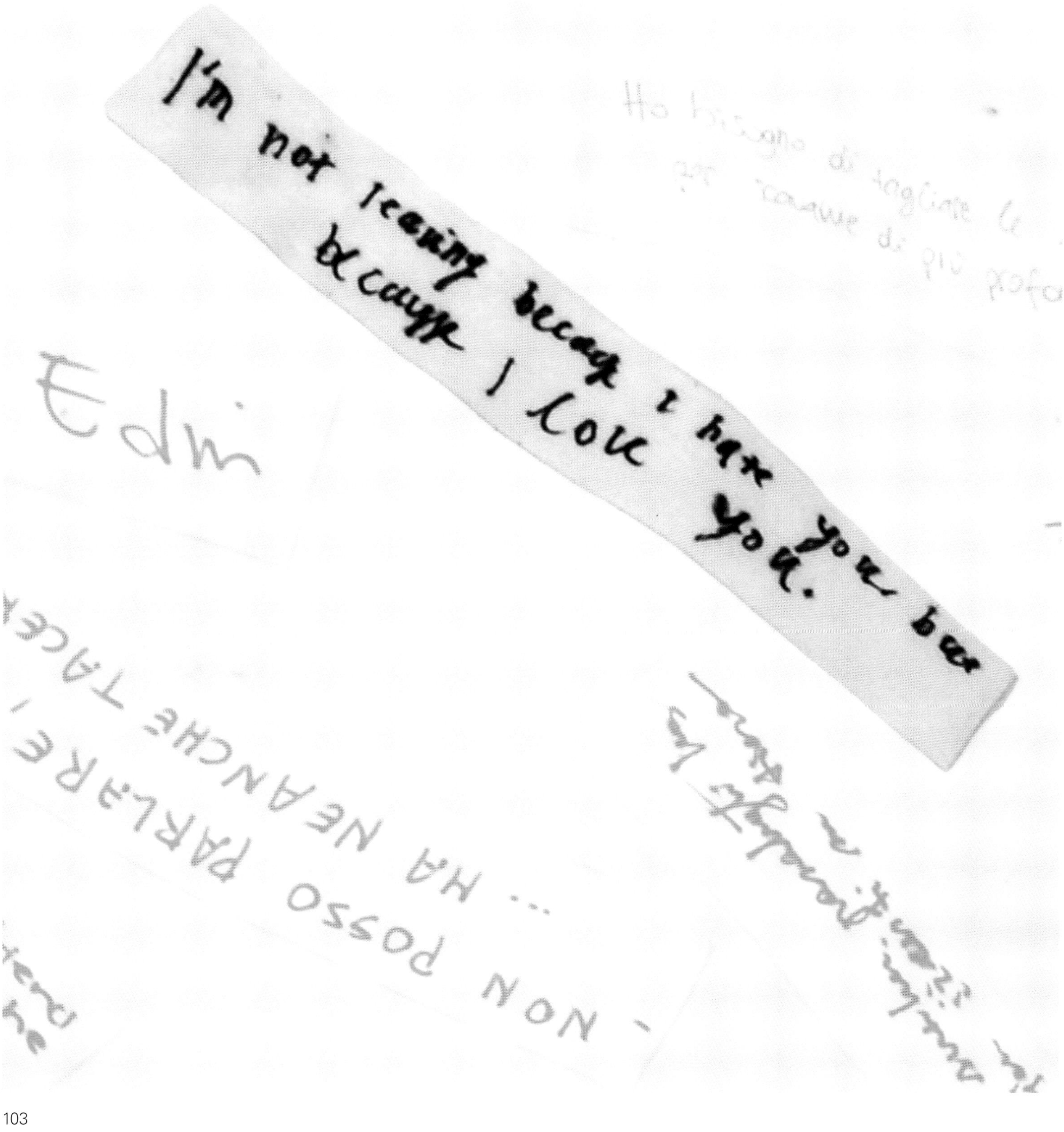
I'm not leaving because I hate you but
because I love you.
- NON POSSO PARLARE,
... HA NEANCHE

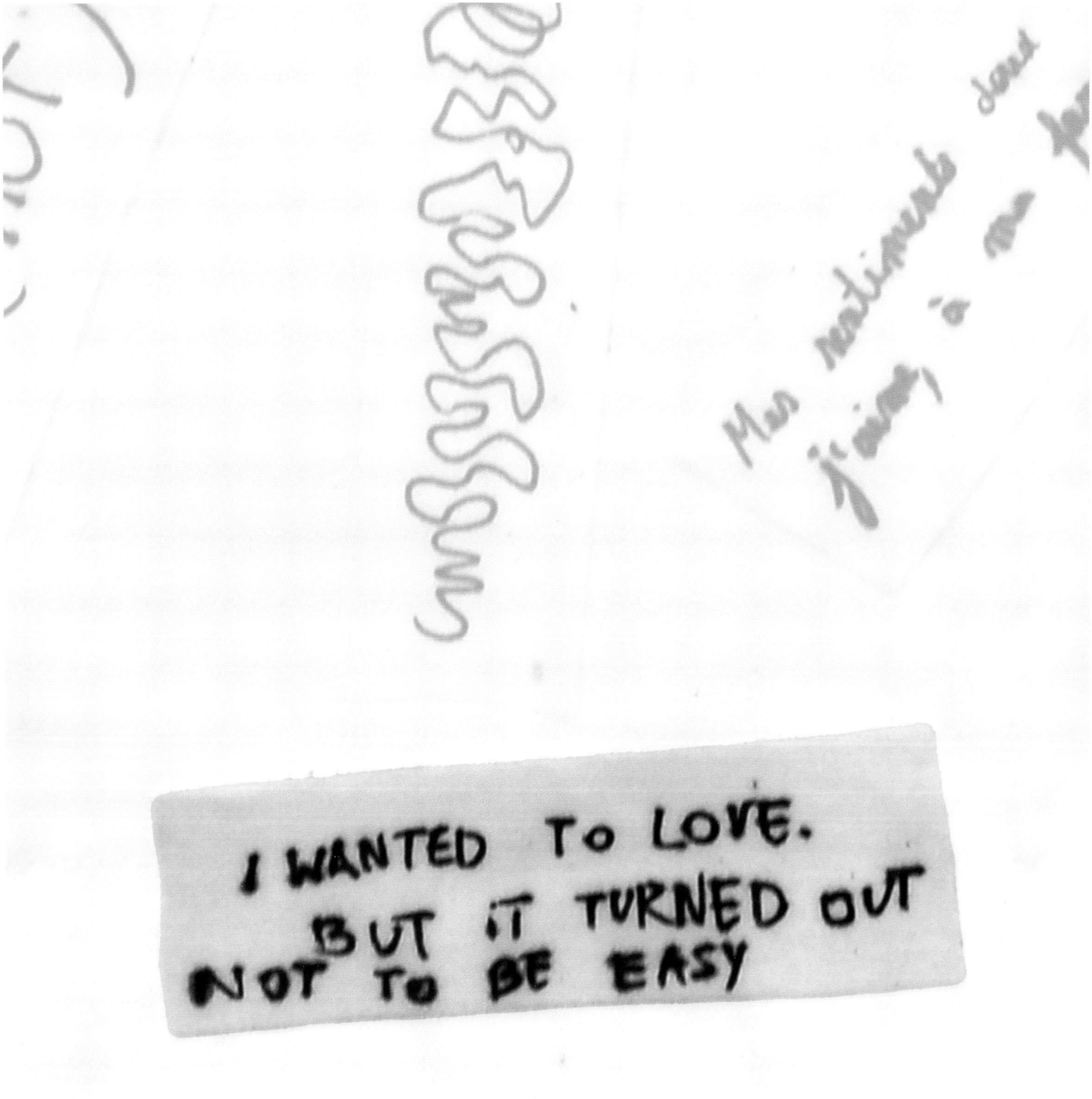
Mes sentiments dans
j'aime, à ma
I WANTED TO LOVE.
BUT IT TURNED OUT
NOT TO BE EASY

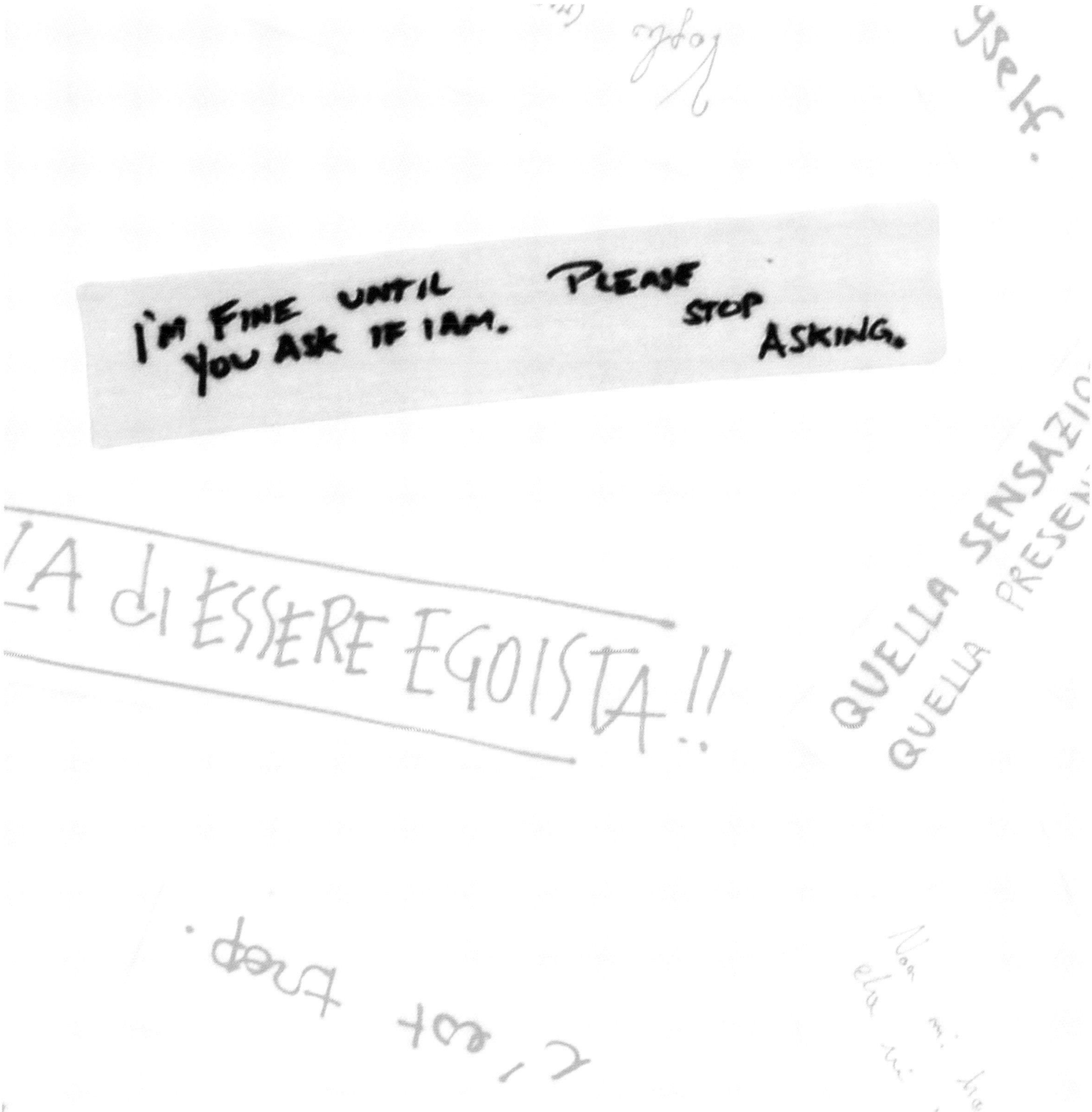
I'M FINE UNTIL YOU ASK IF I AM. PLEASE STOP ASKING.
di ESSERE EGOISTA!!
QUELLA
QUELLA

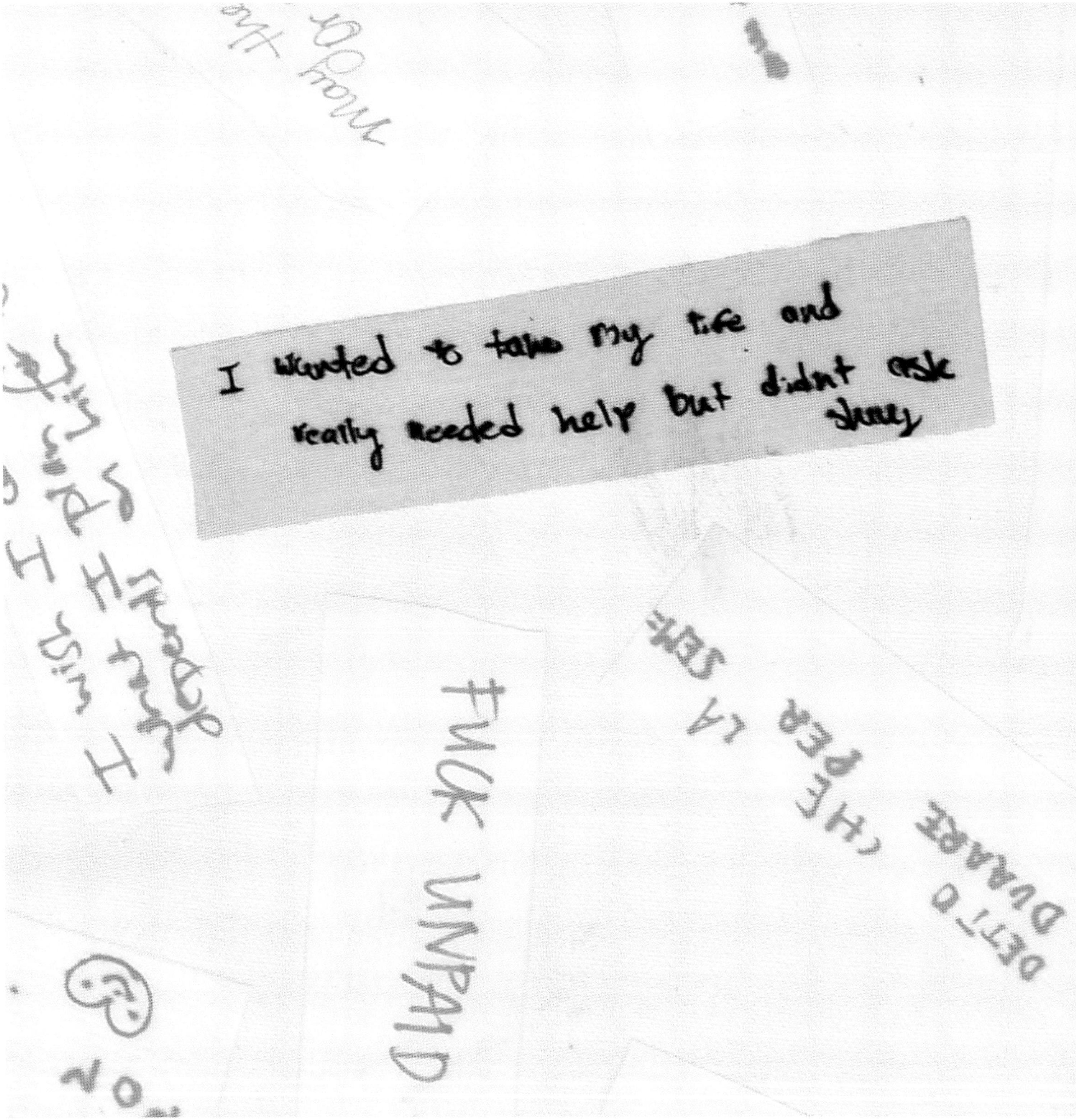
I wanted to take my life and
really needed help but didnt ask
FUCK UNPAID

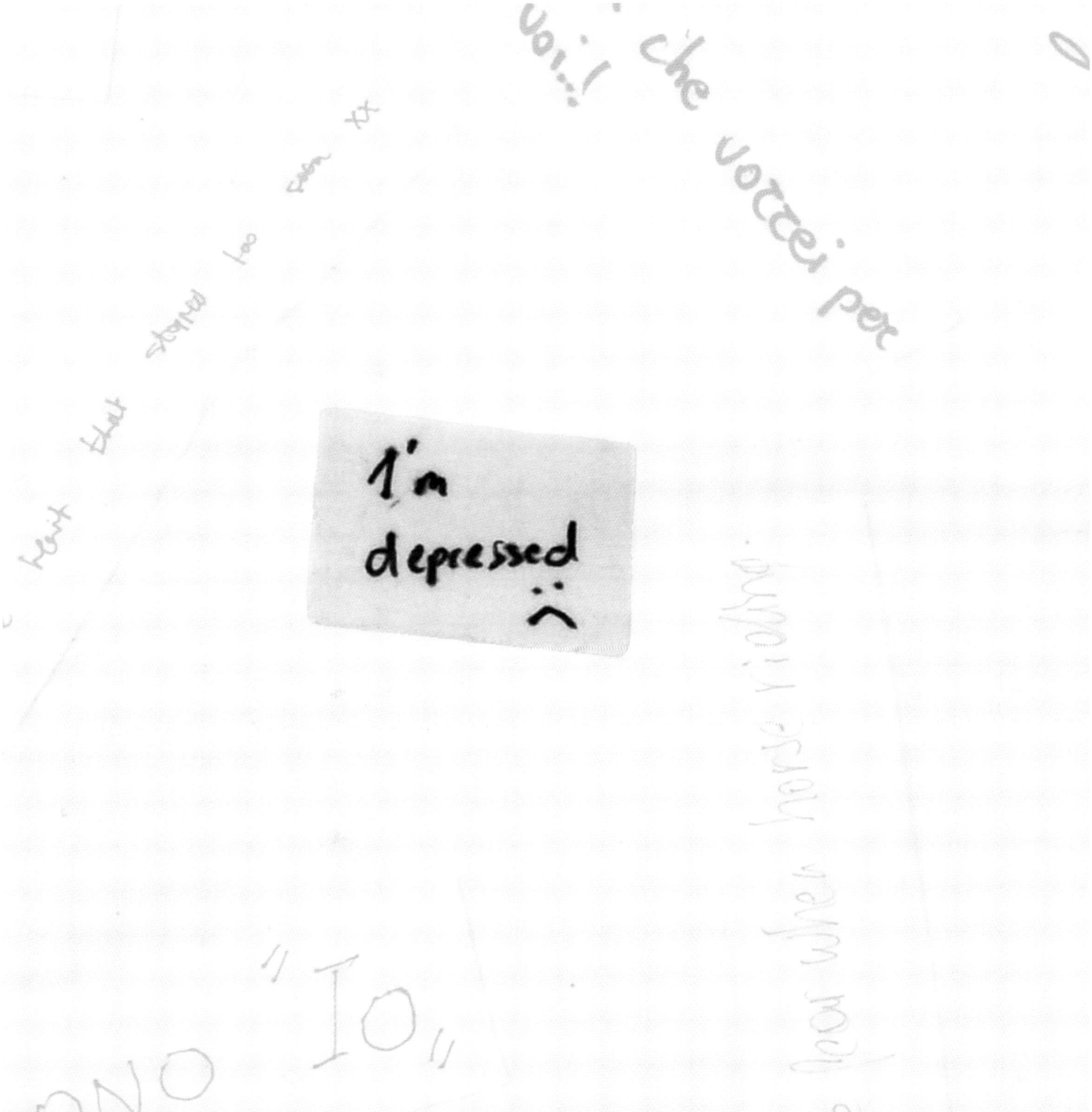
I'm
depressed

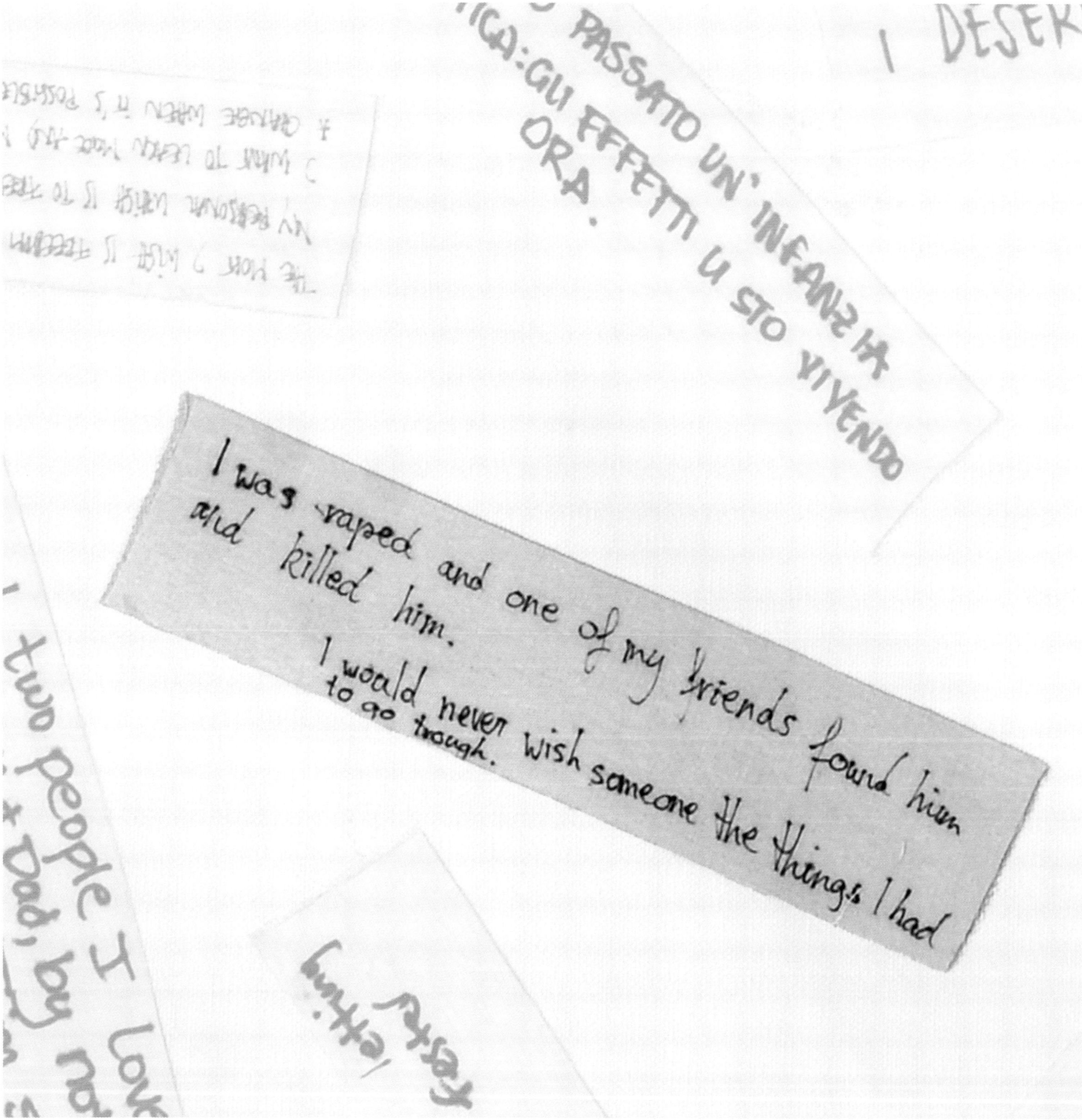
I was raped and one of my friends found him
and killed him.
I would never wish someone the things I had
to go trough.
PASSATO UN' INFANZIA
GLI EFFETTI LI STO VIVENDO
ORA.
I DESER
two people I Lov

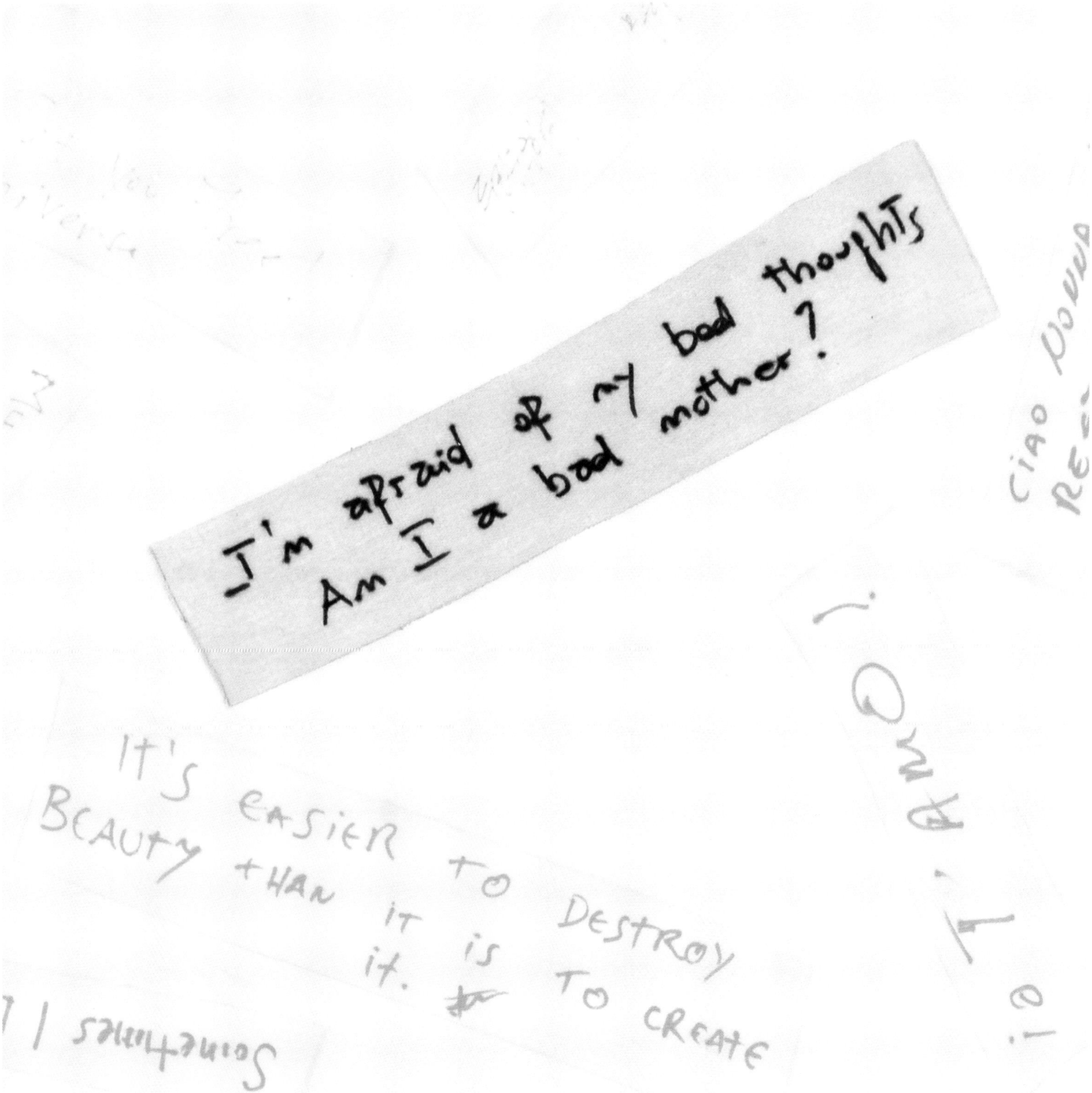
I'm afraid of my bad thoughts
Am I a bad mother?
IT'S EASIER TO DESTROY
BEAUTY THAN IT IS TO CREATE
it.

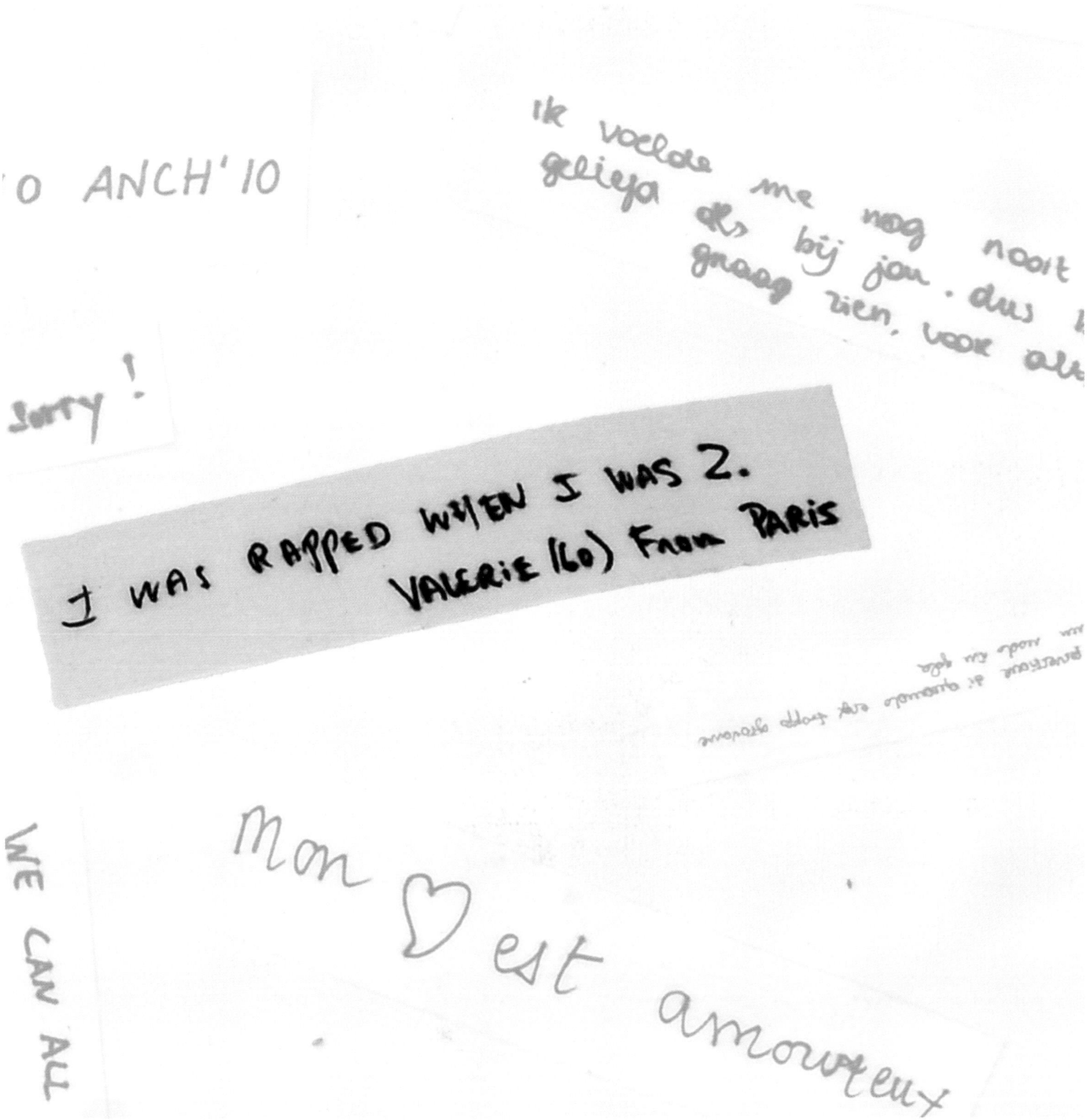
O ANCH'10
ik voelde me nog nooit
geliefd als bij jou. dus
graag zien. voor
sorry!
I WAS RAPPED WHEN I WAS 2.
VALERIE (60) FROM PARIS
Mon ♡ est amoureux
WE CAN ALL

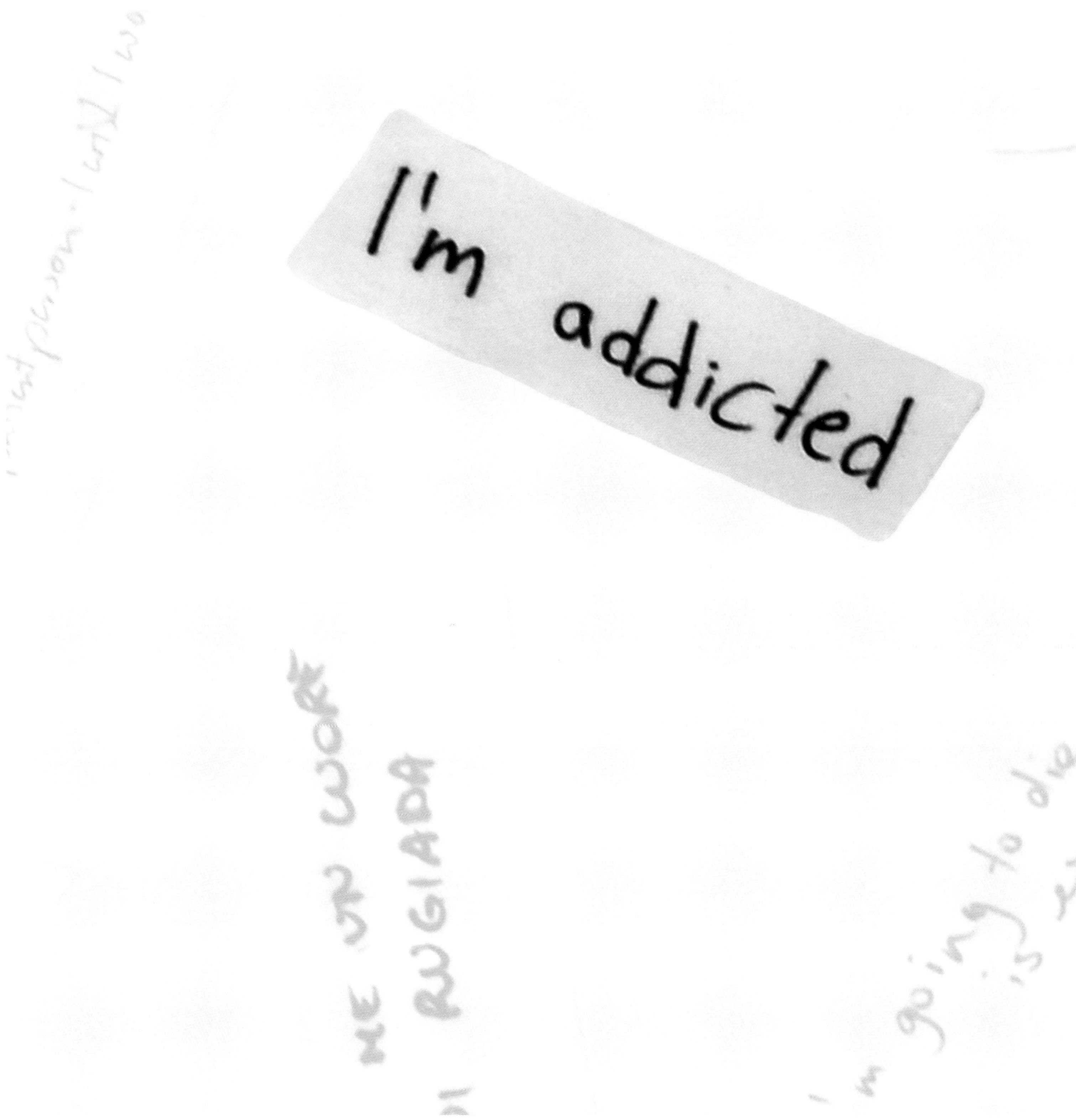
I'm addicted

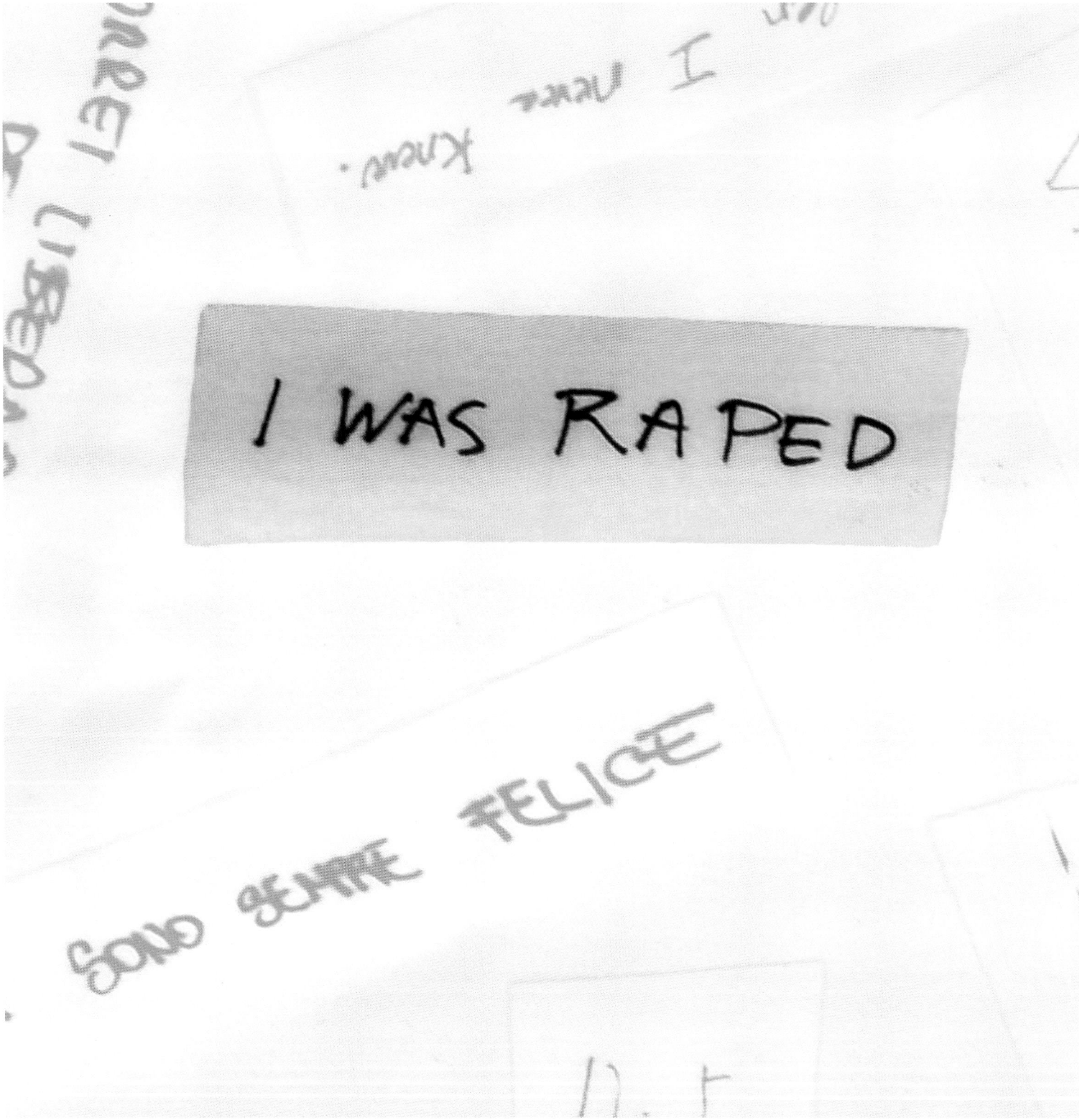
I WAS RAPED
SONO SEMPRE FELICE

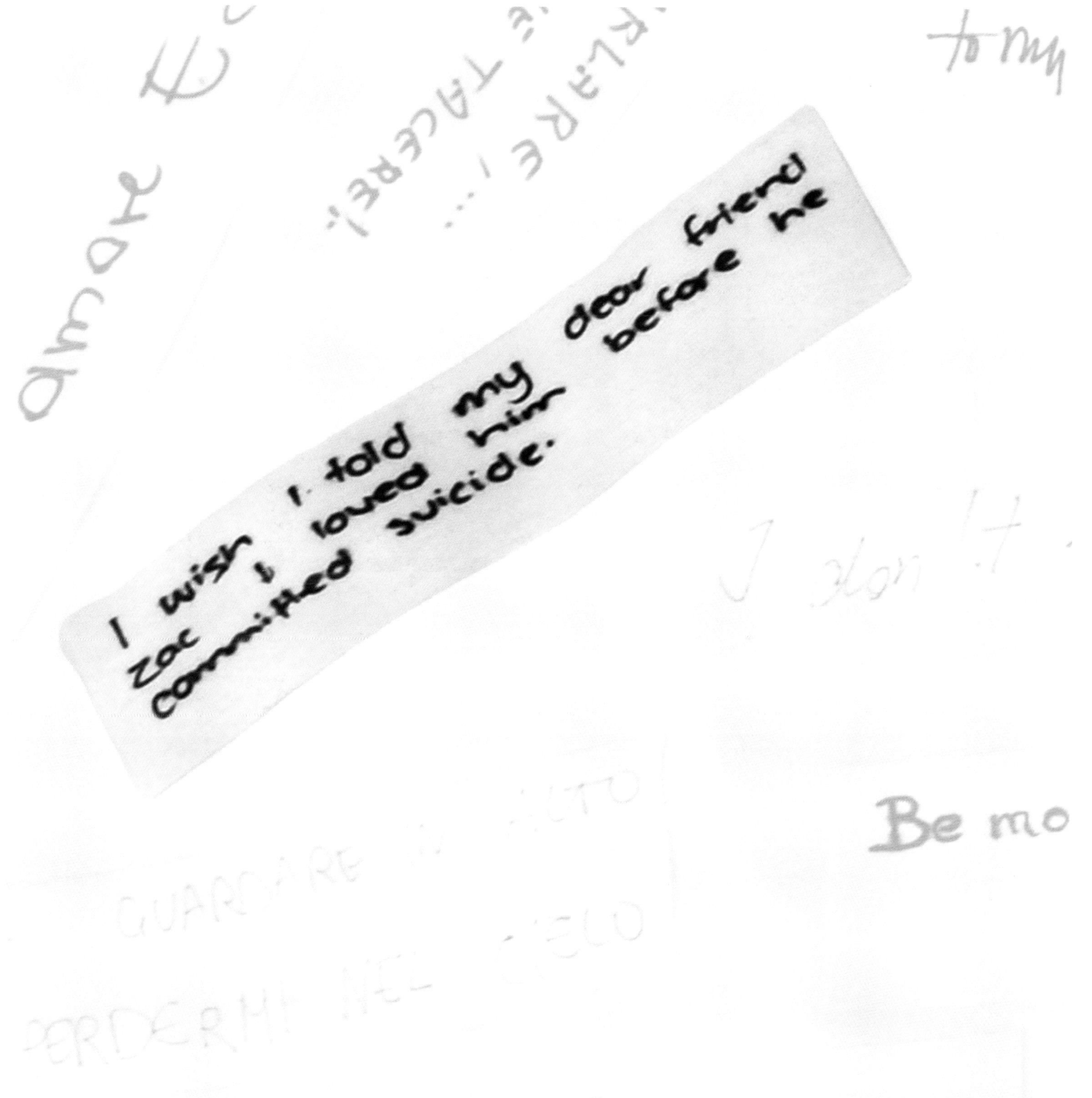
I wish I told my dear friend
Zoe I loved him before he
committed suicide.
amore
Be mo

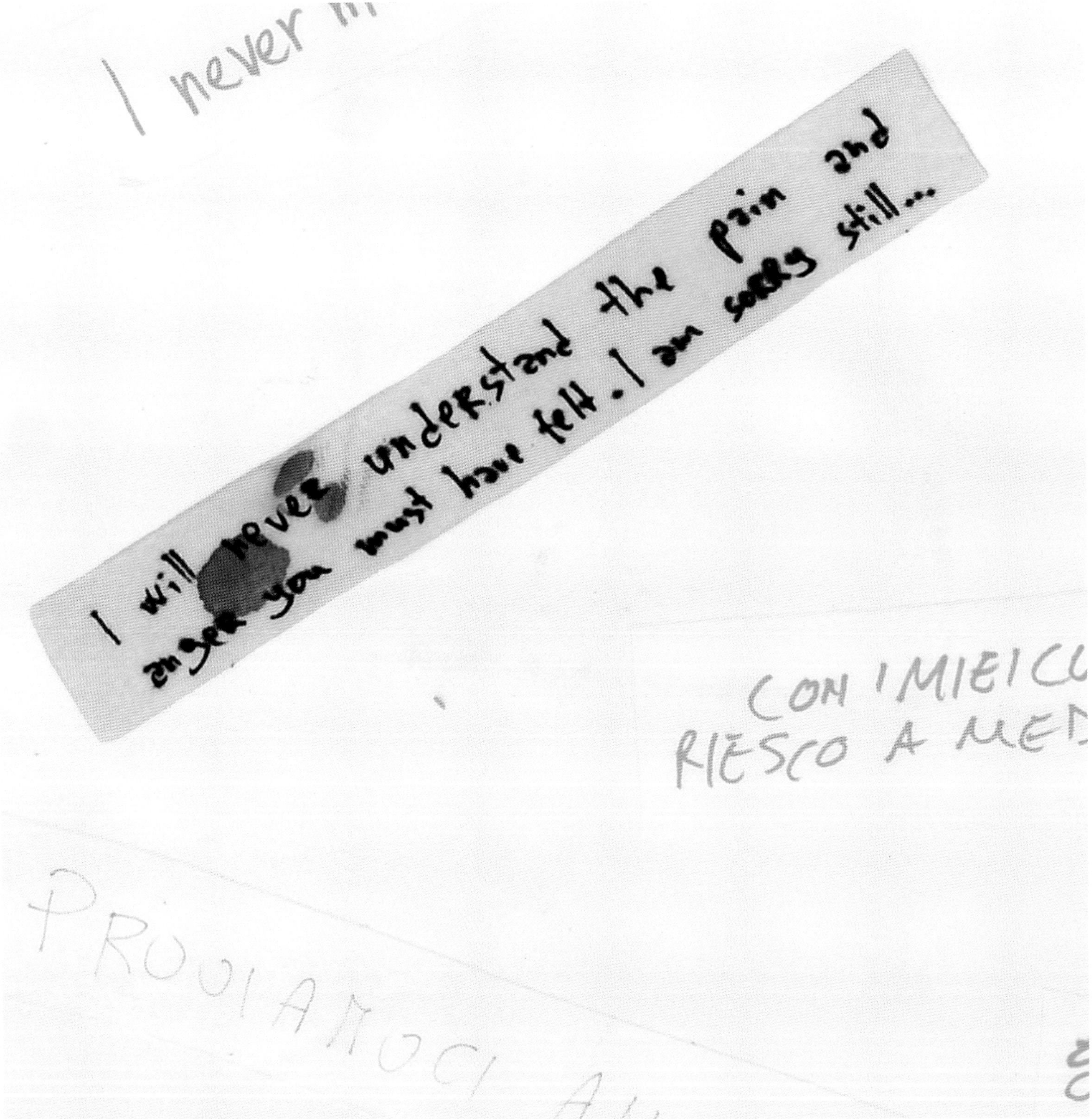
I never
I will never understand the pain and
anger you must have felt. I am sorry still...
CON I MIEI C
RIESCO A MED
PROVIAMOCI A

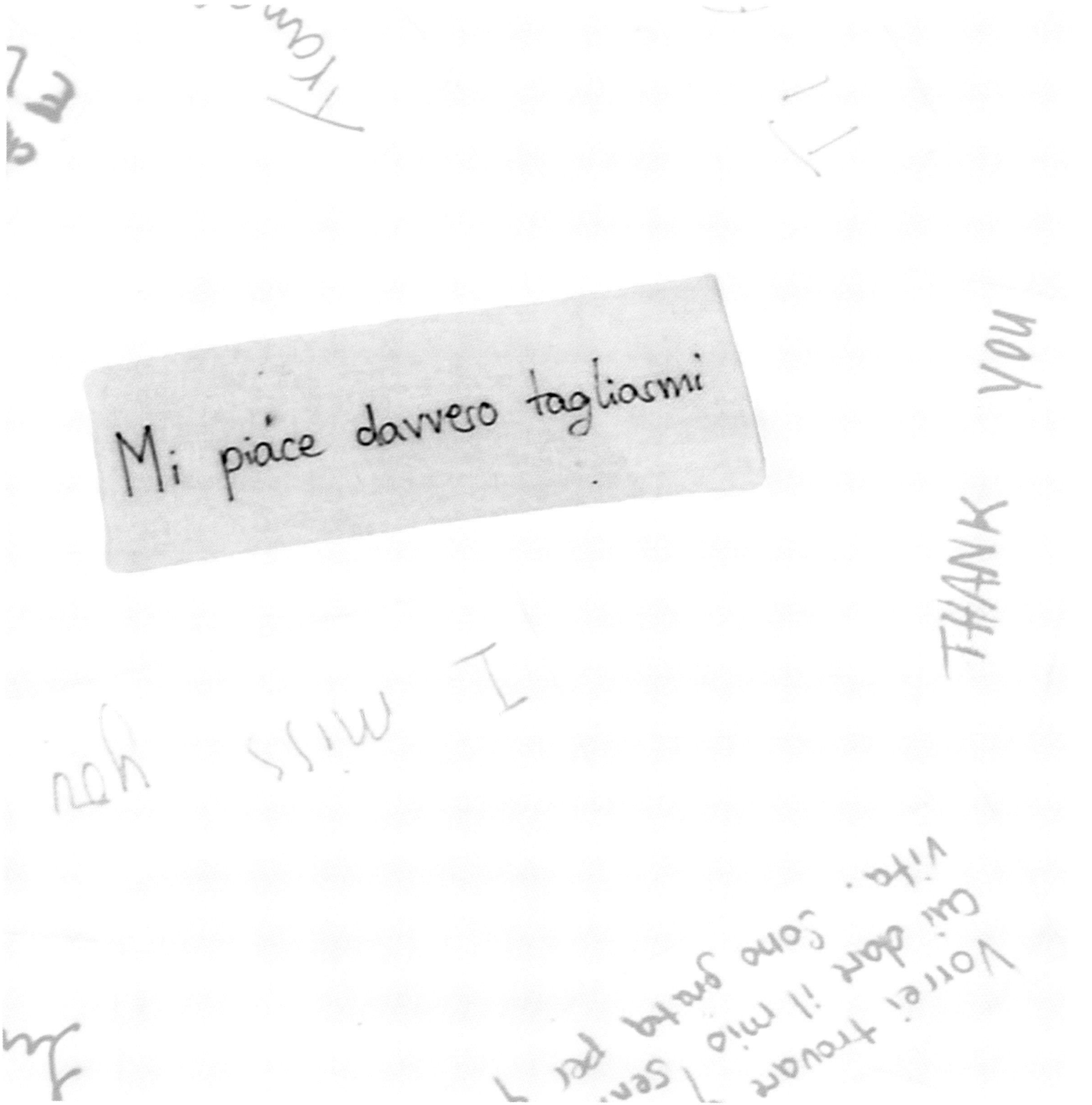
Mi piace davvero tagliarmi
THANK YOU
I miss you

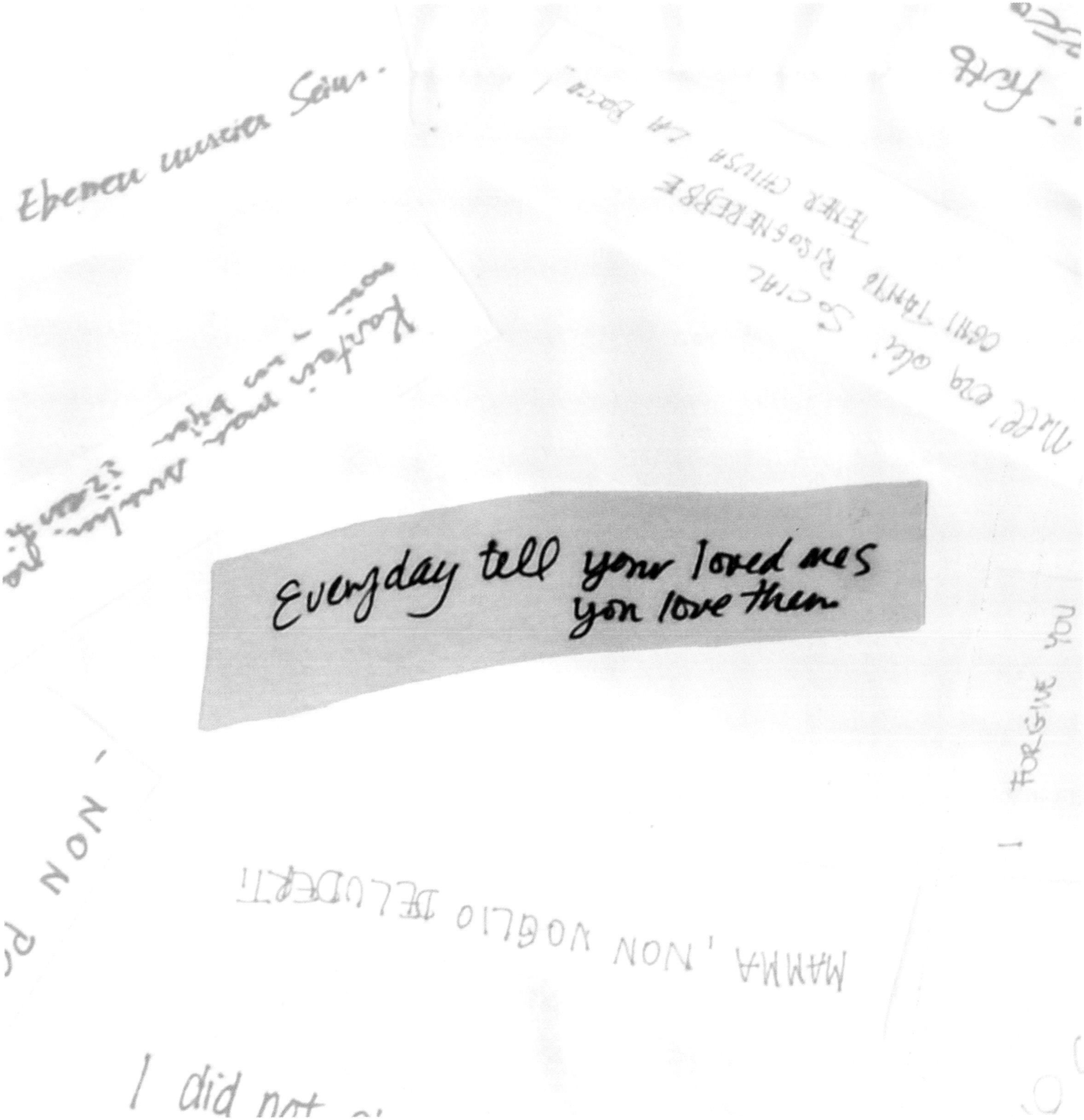
Everyday tell your loved ones
you love them
MAMMA, NON VOGLIO DELUDERTI
I FORGIVE YOU

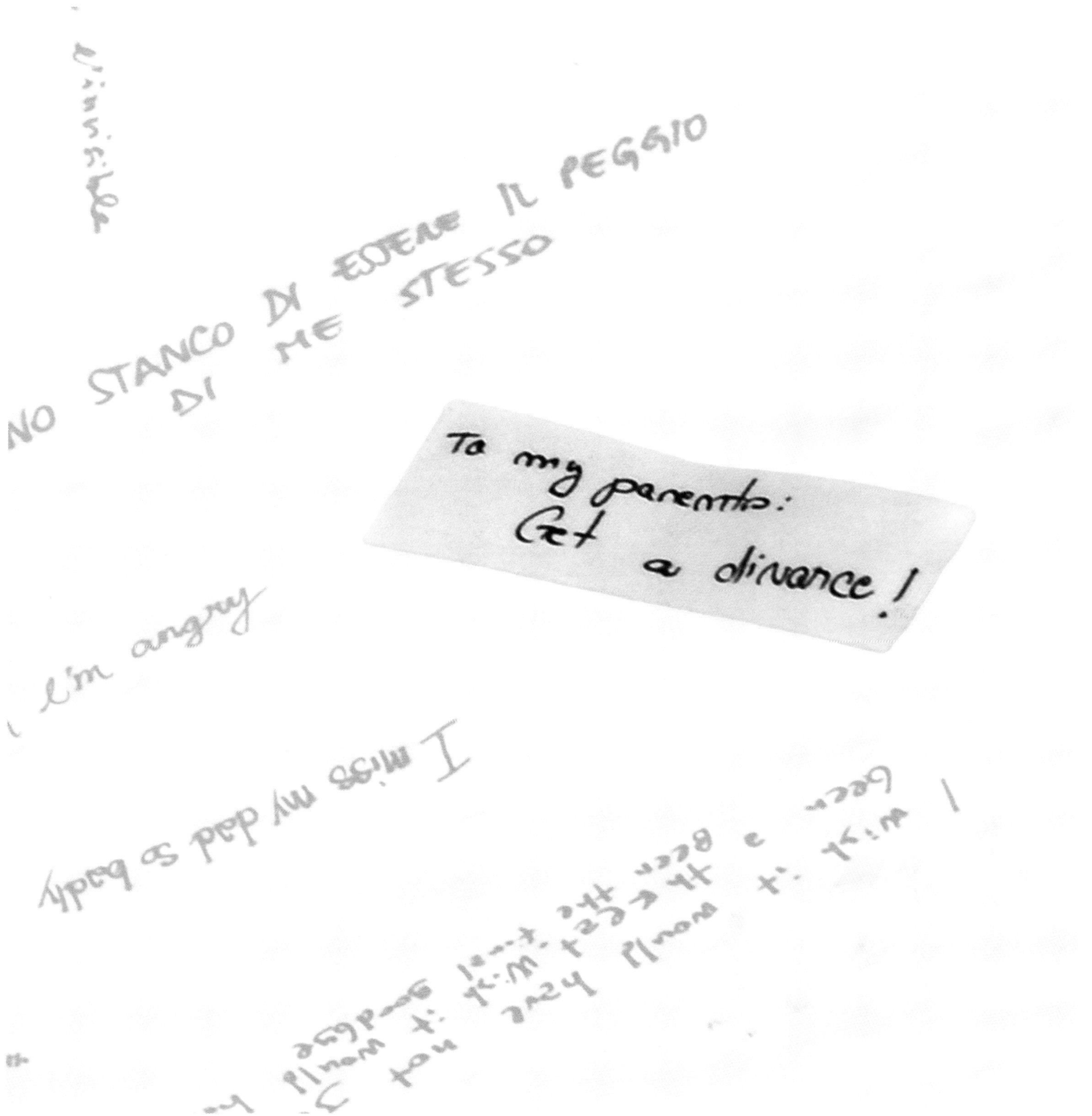
NO STANCO DI ESSERE IL PEGGIO
DI ME STESSO
To my parents:
Get a divorce!
I'm angry
I miss my dad so badly

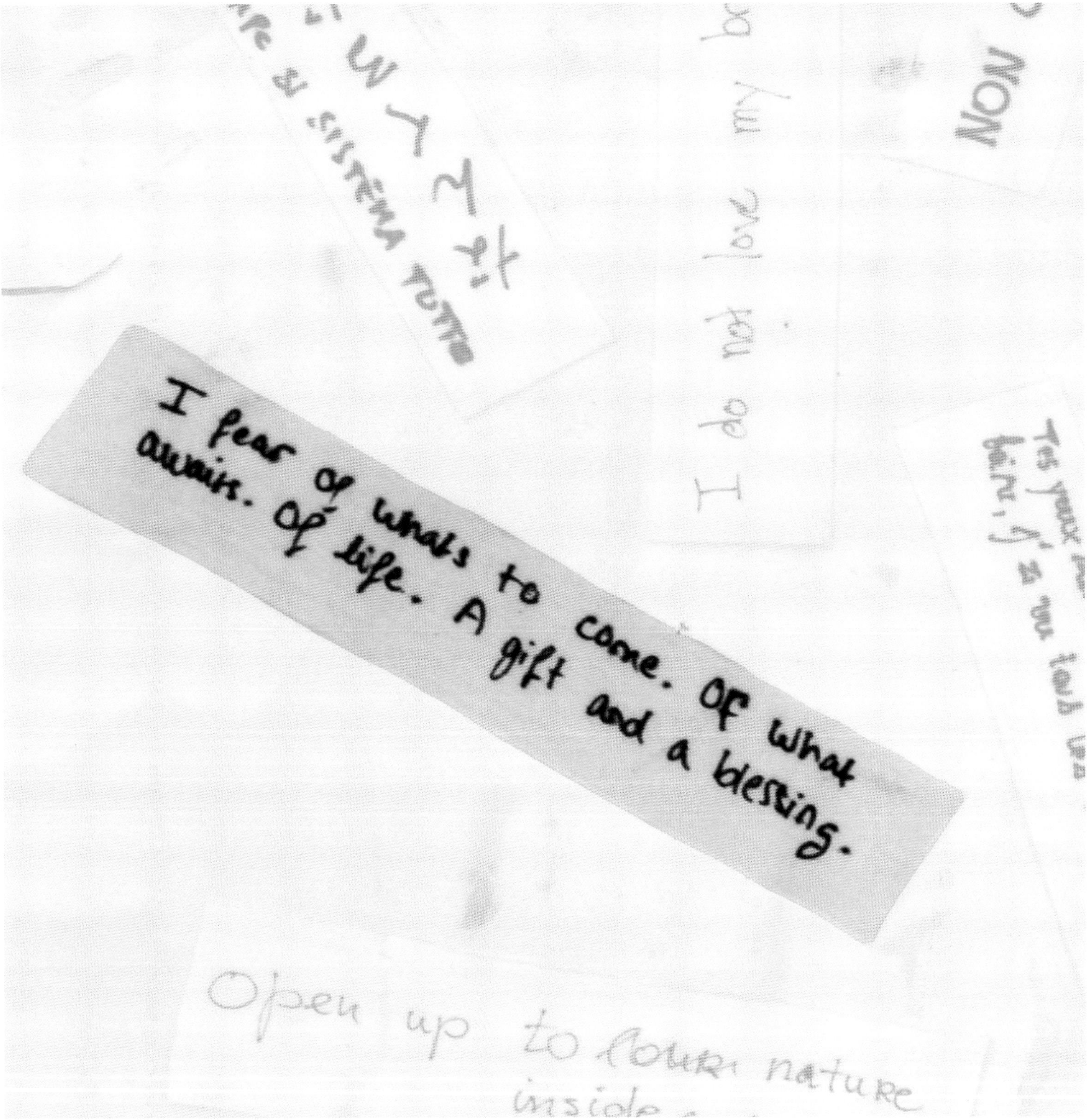
I fear of whats to come. Of what awaits. Of life. A gift and a blessing.
I do not love my
NON
Open up to
nature

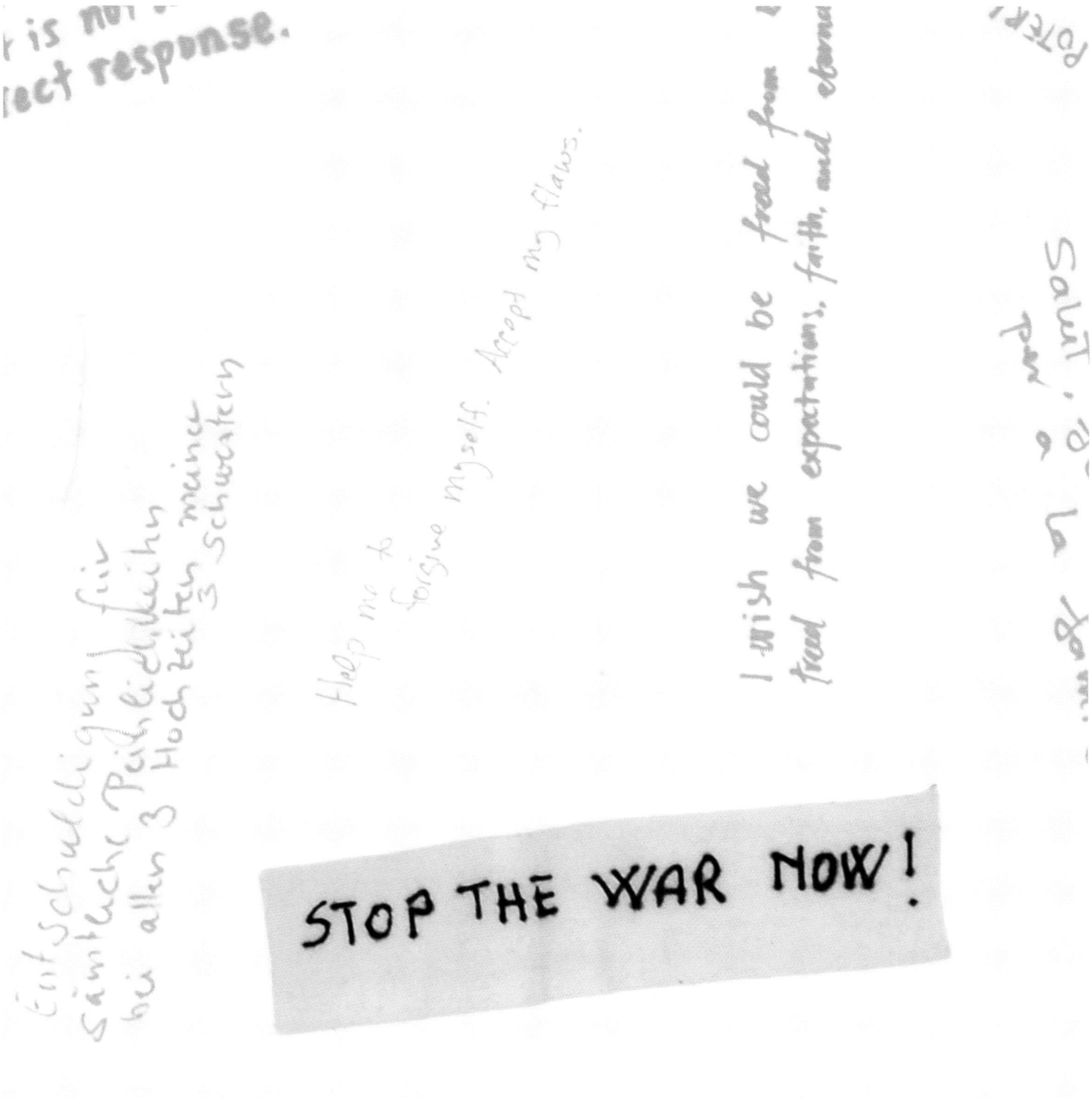
STOP THE WAR NOW!
Help me to forgive myself. Accept my flaws.
I wish we could be
Entschuldigung für sämtliche Peinlichkeiten bei allen 3 Hochzeiten meiner 3 Schwestern

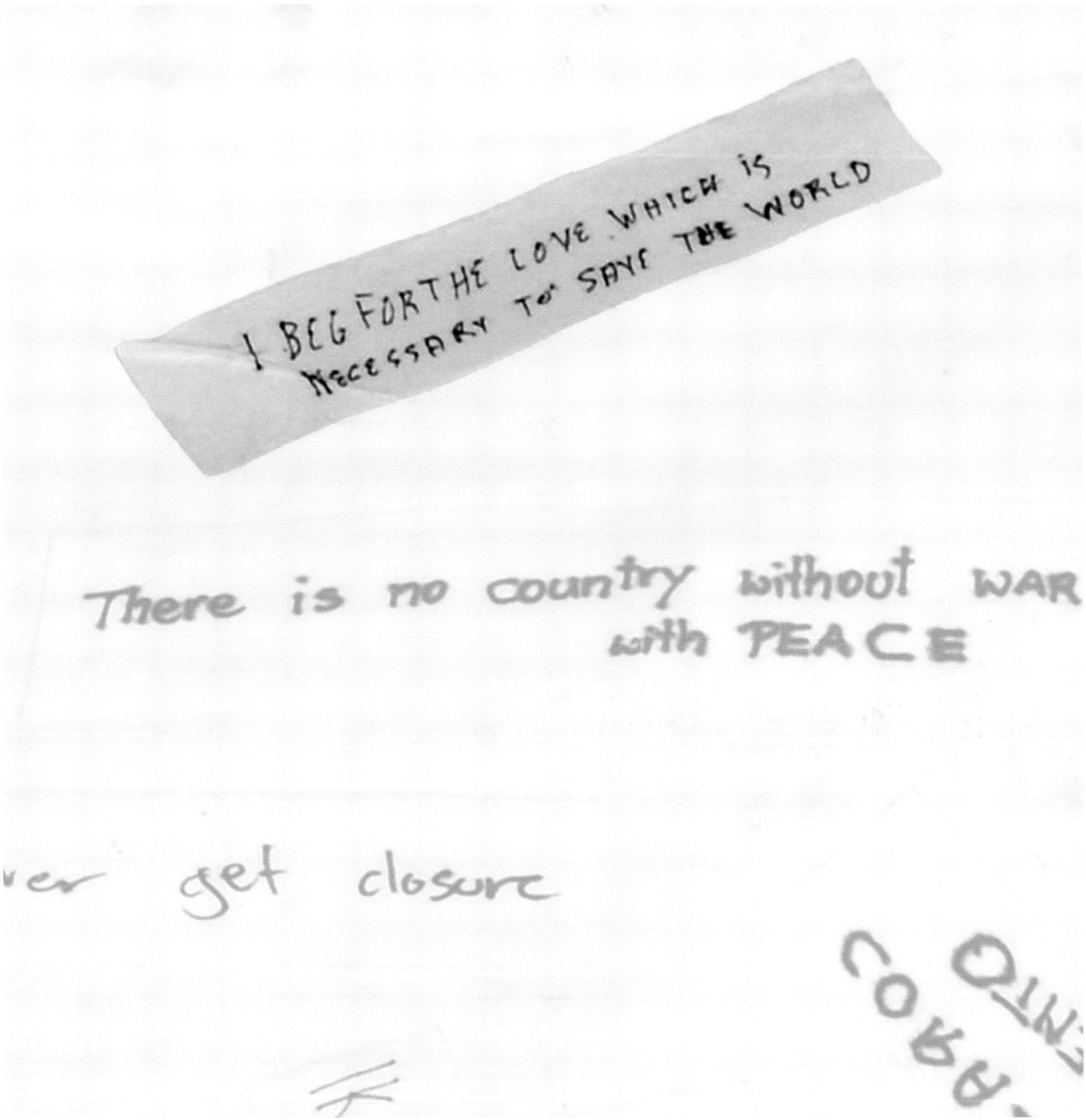
I BEG FOR THE LOVE WHICH IS
NECESSARY TO SAVE THE WORLD
There is no country without WAR
with PEACE
get closure

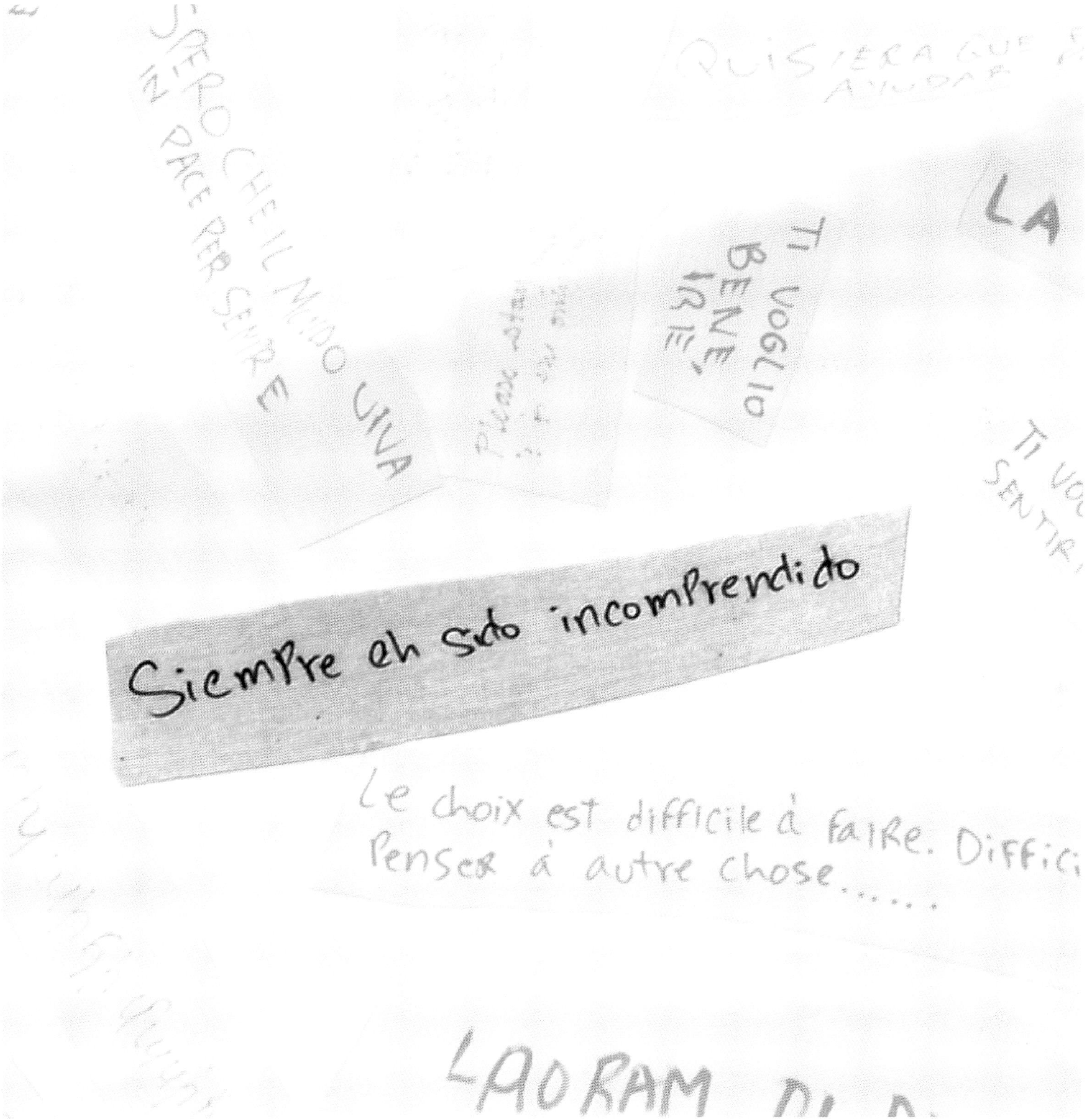

SPERO CHE IL MONDO VIVA
IN PACE PER SEMPRE
TI VOGLIO
BENE
Siempre eh sido incomprendido
Le choix est difficile à faire. Diffic
Penser à autre chose......

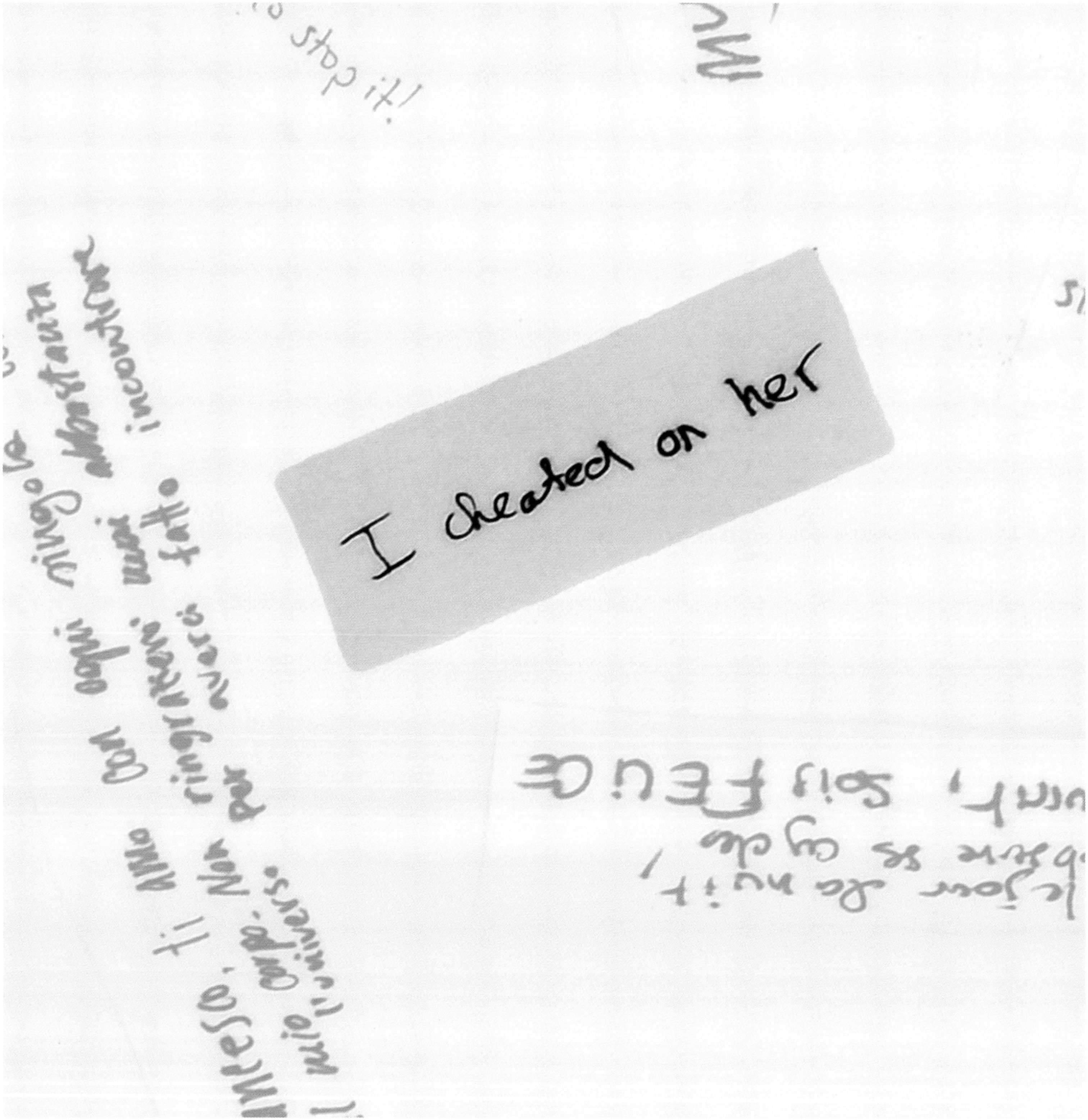
I cheated on her
stop it!

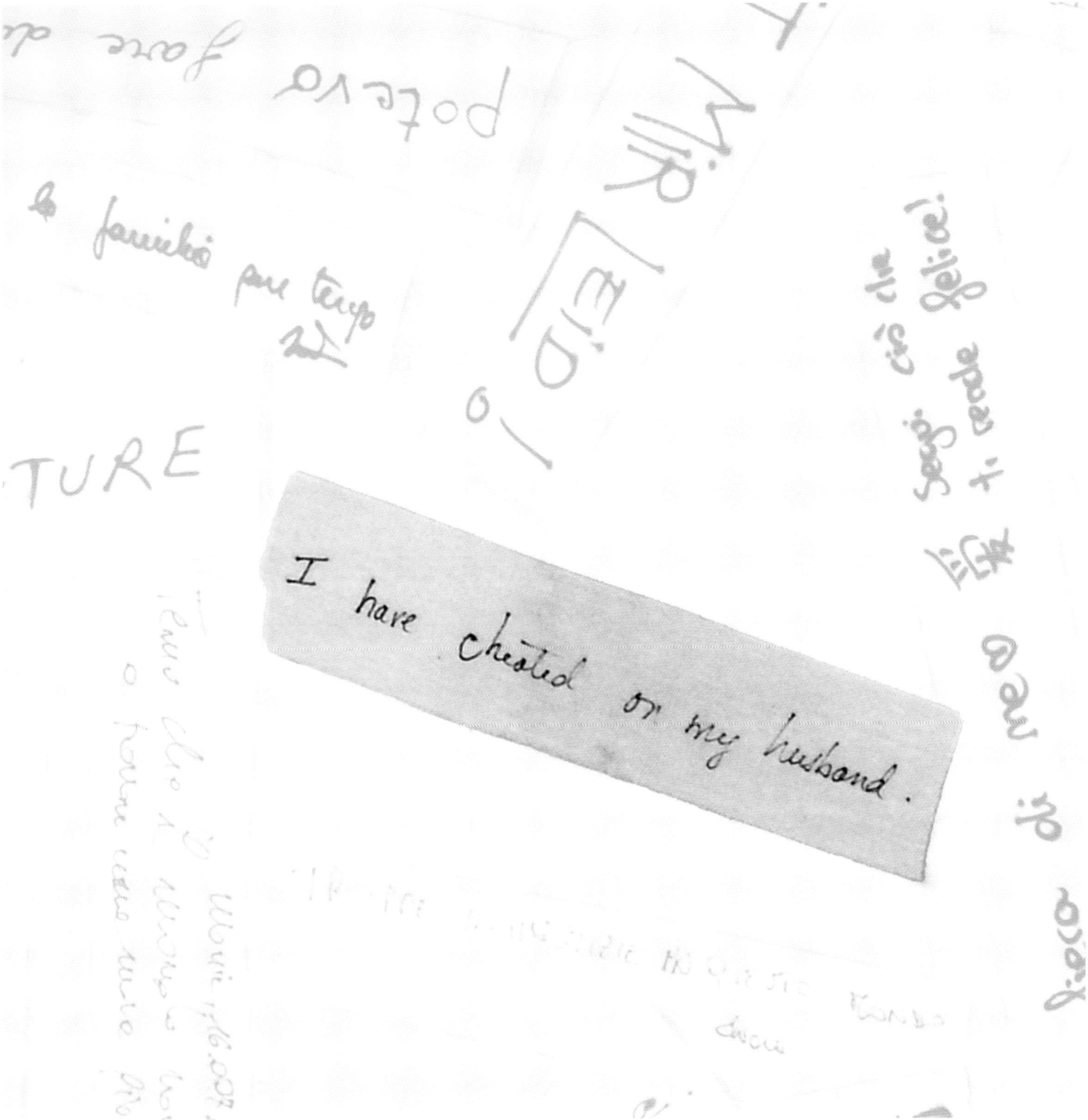
TURE
I have cheated on my husband.

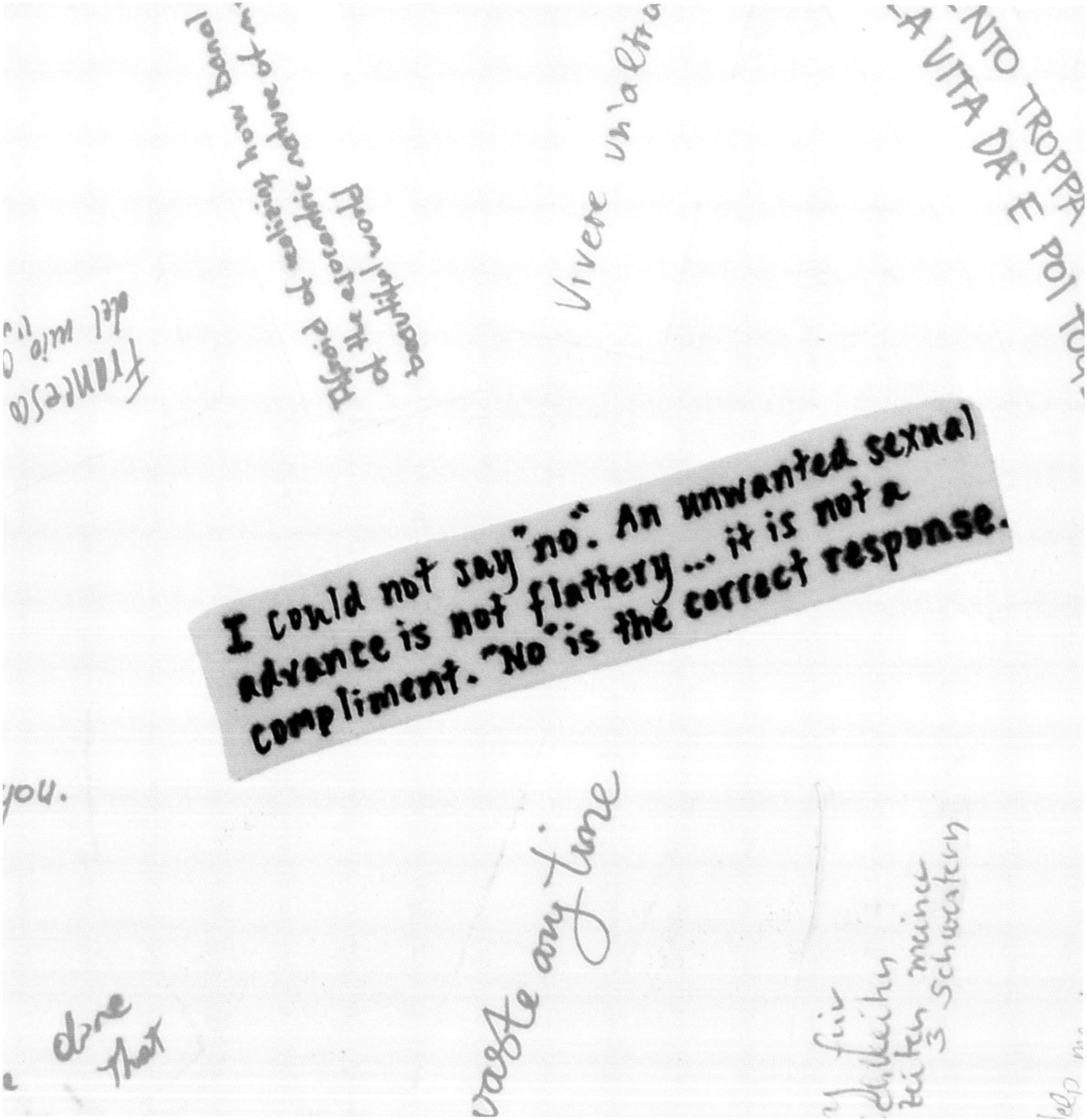
I could not say "no". An unwanted sexual advance is not flattery... it is not a compliment. "No" is the correct response.
you.
waste any time
done that
meiner 3 Schwestern

My mother is old & in pain.
I wish she would die ♡

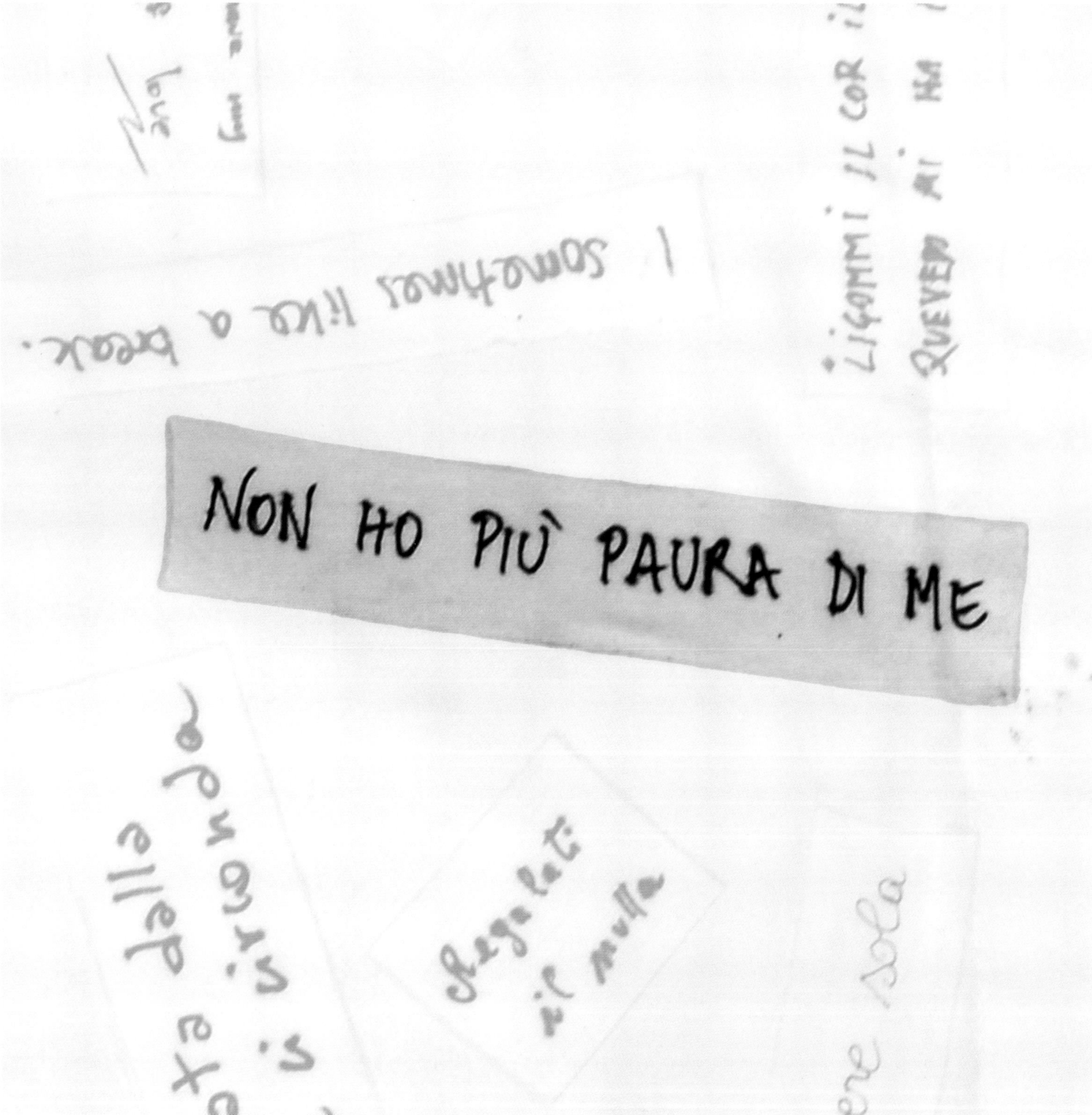
NON HO PIÙ PAURA DI ME

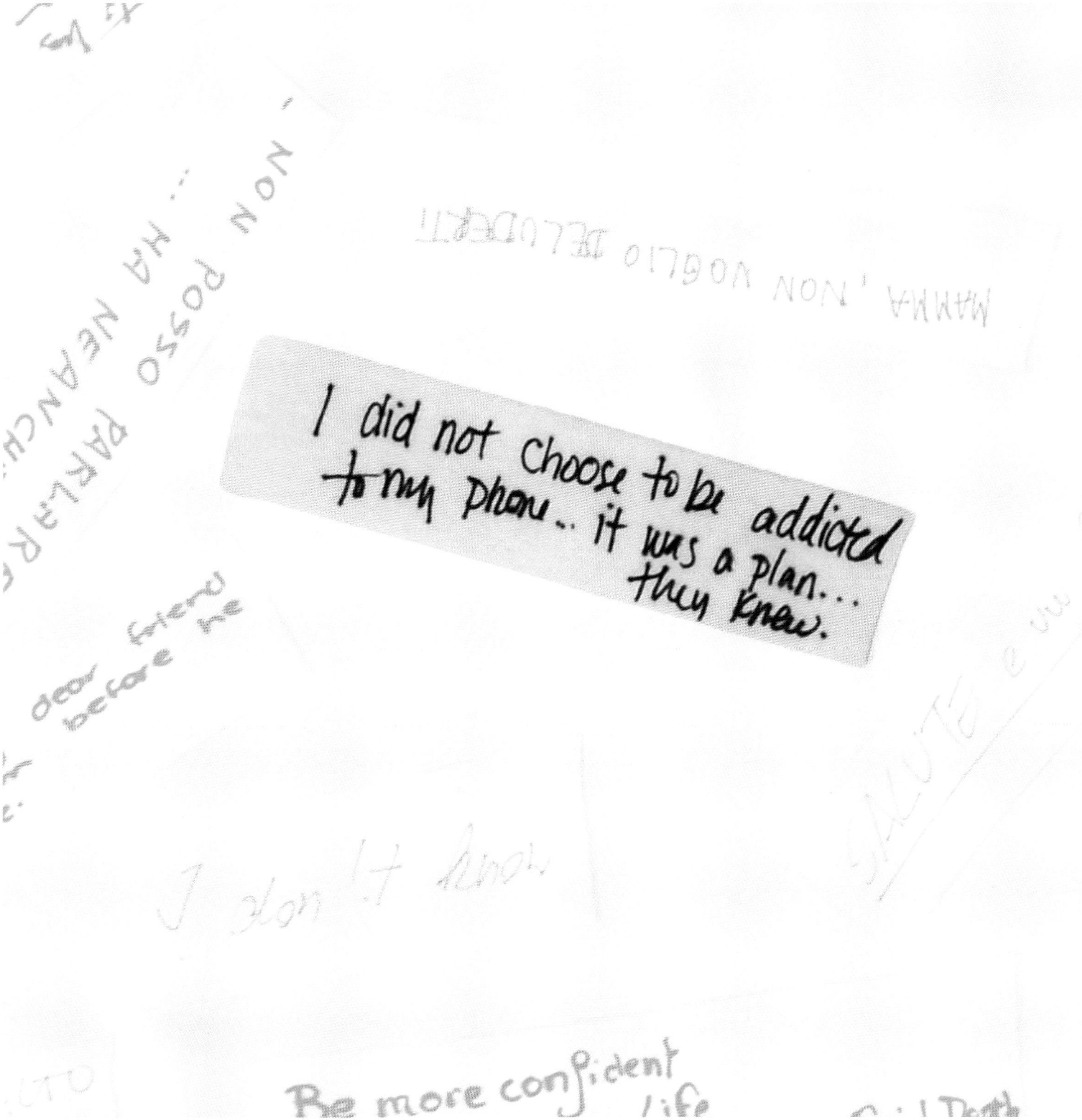
I did not choose to be addicted to my phone.. it was a plan... they knew.
I don't know
Be more confident

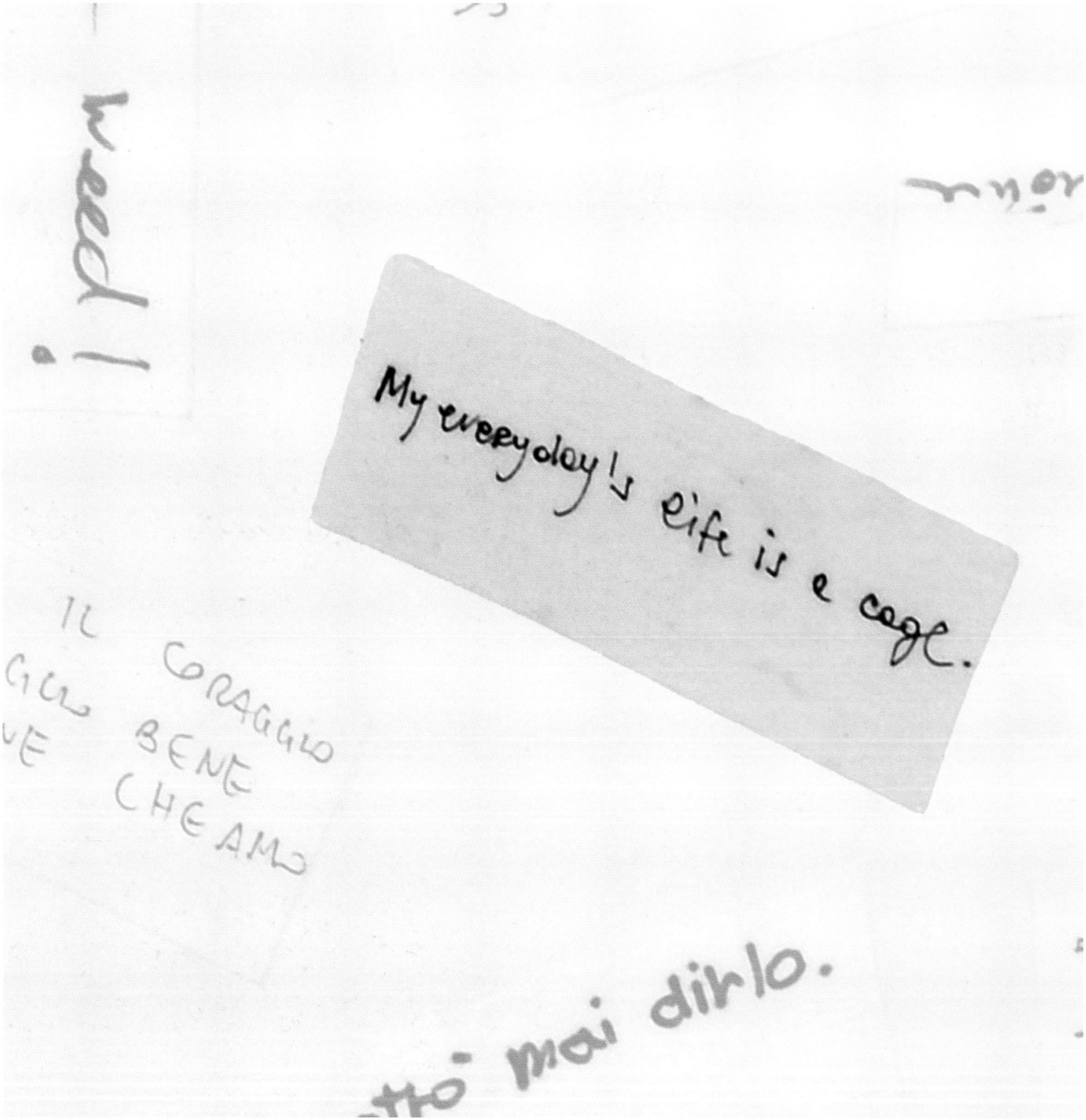
My everyday's life is a cage.
IL CORAGGIO
BENE
CHE AMO
mai dirlo.

Lebe jetzt,
Vive adesso!
I DO NOT KNOW HOW TO STOP FEELING
INADEQUATE. AND IF I KNEW HOW, WOULD I?
Chiara
VIVA LA VITA
E TANTA SALUTE

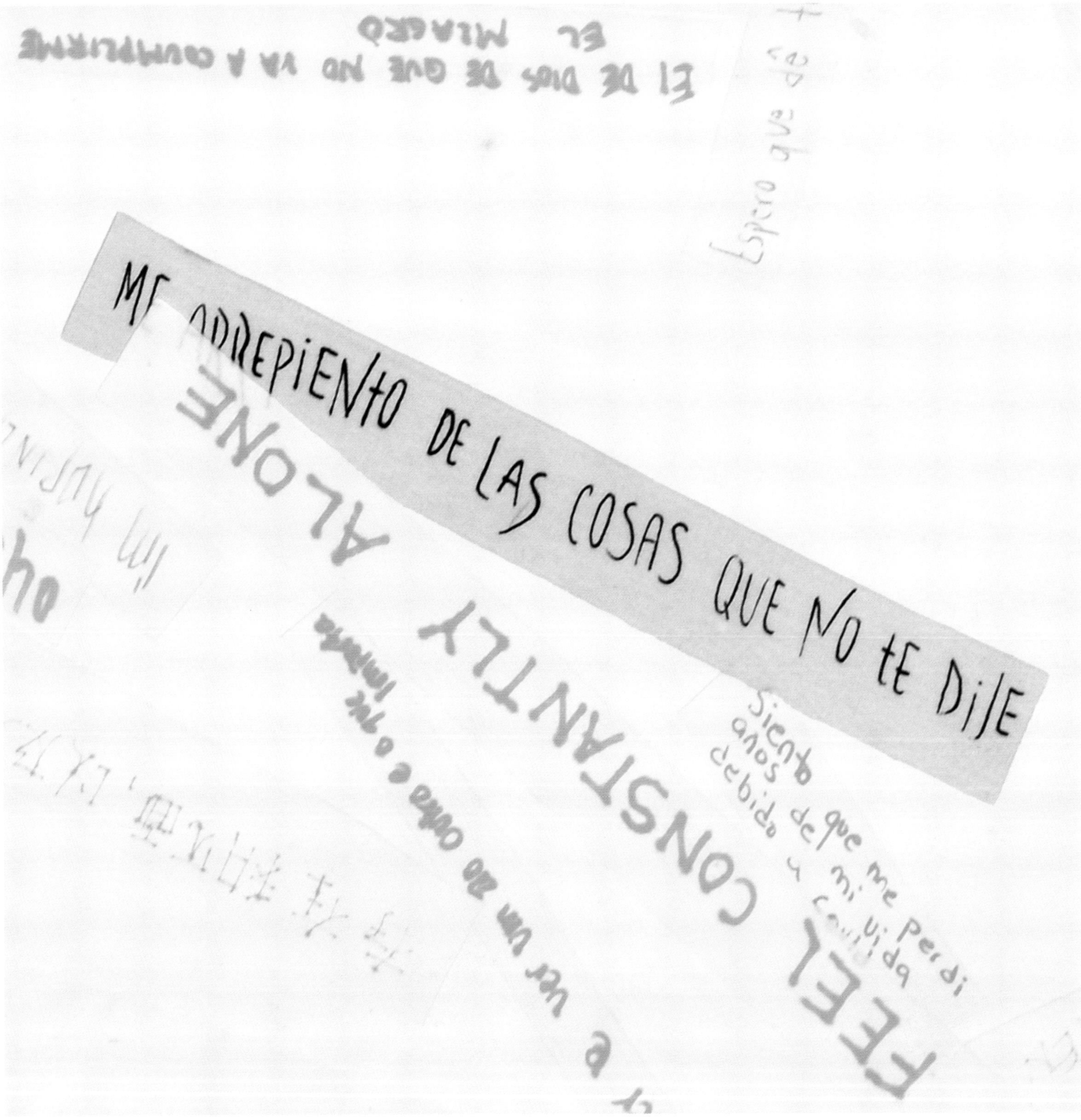
ME ARREPIENTO DE LAS COSAS QUE NO TE DIJE
FEEL CONSTANTLY ALONE

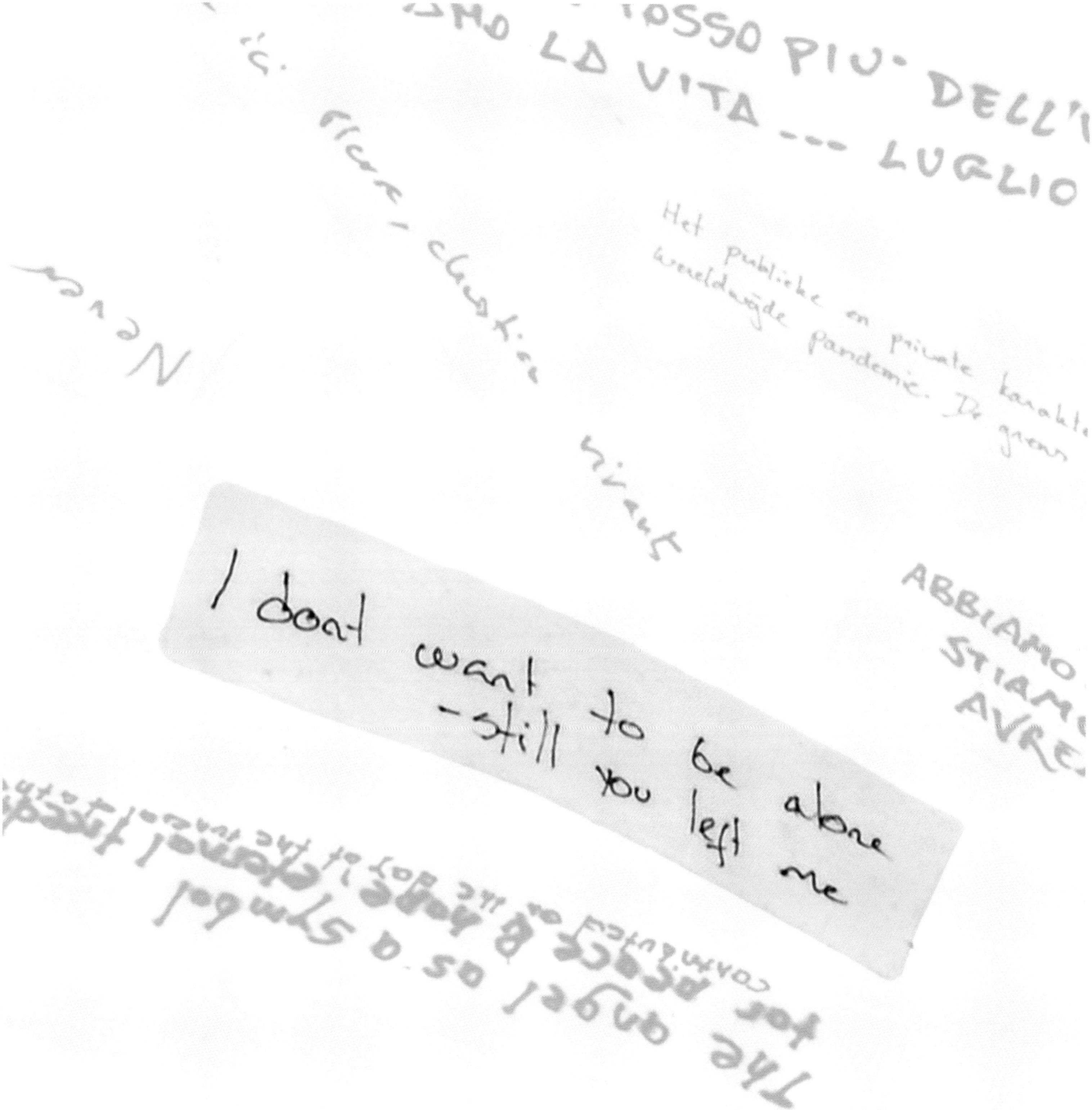
LA VITA ... LUGLIO
ABBIAMO
STIAMO
I dont want to be alone
- still you left me

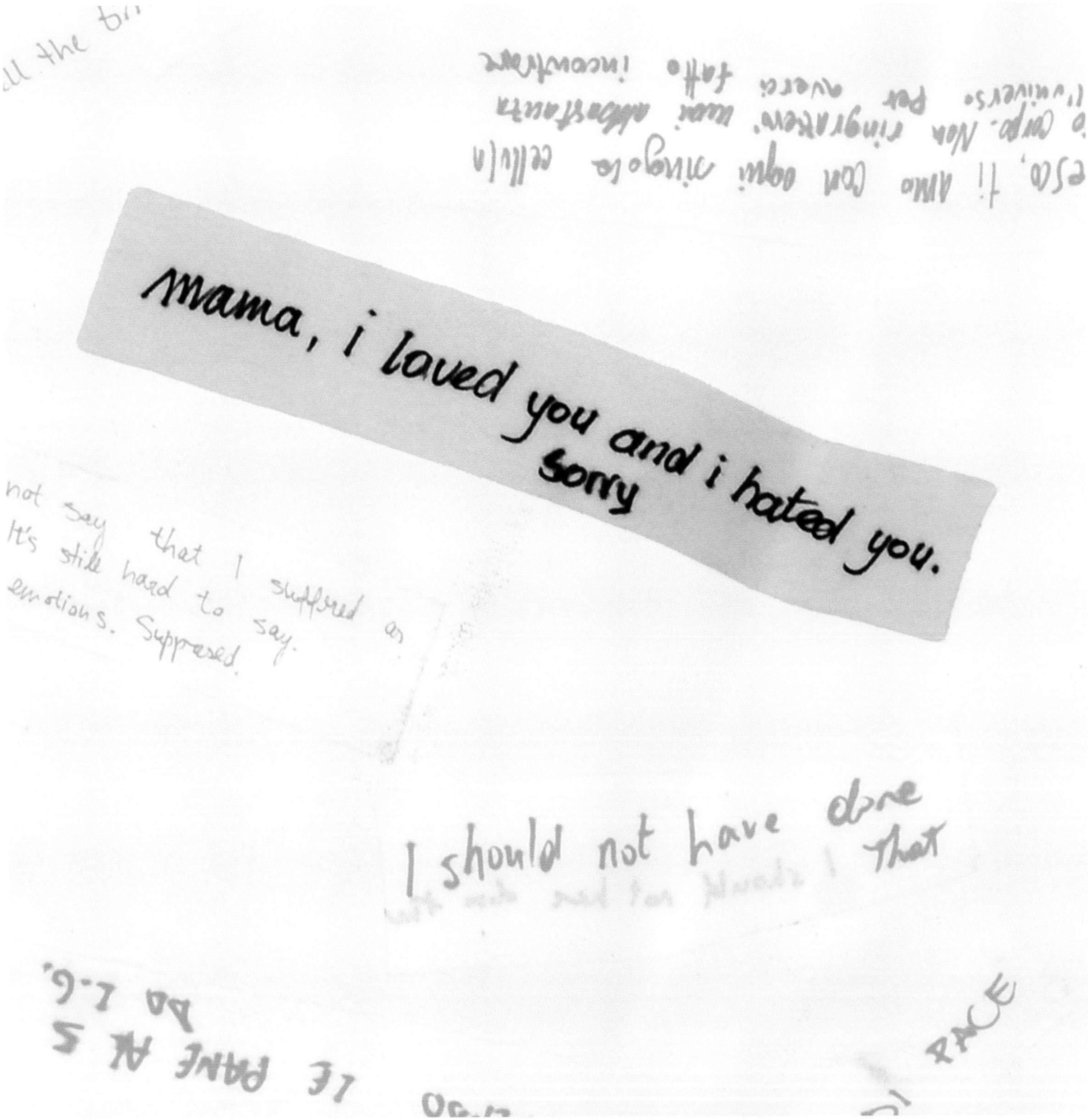
mama, i loved you and i hated you.
sorry
not say that I suffered as
It's still hard to say.
emotions. Suppresed.
I should not have done That

I don't want to be used anymore
without my consentment.
I own my power now

NON RIESCO A SUPERARE LA
PAURA DELLA MORTE, FIN
DA PICCOLA MI TERRORIZZA I
PENSIERO DI SCOMPARIRE

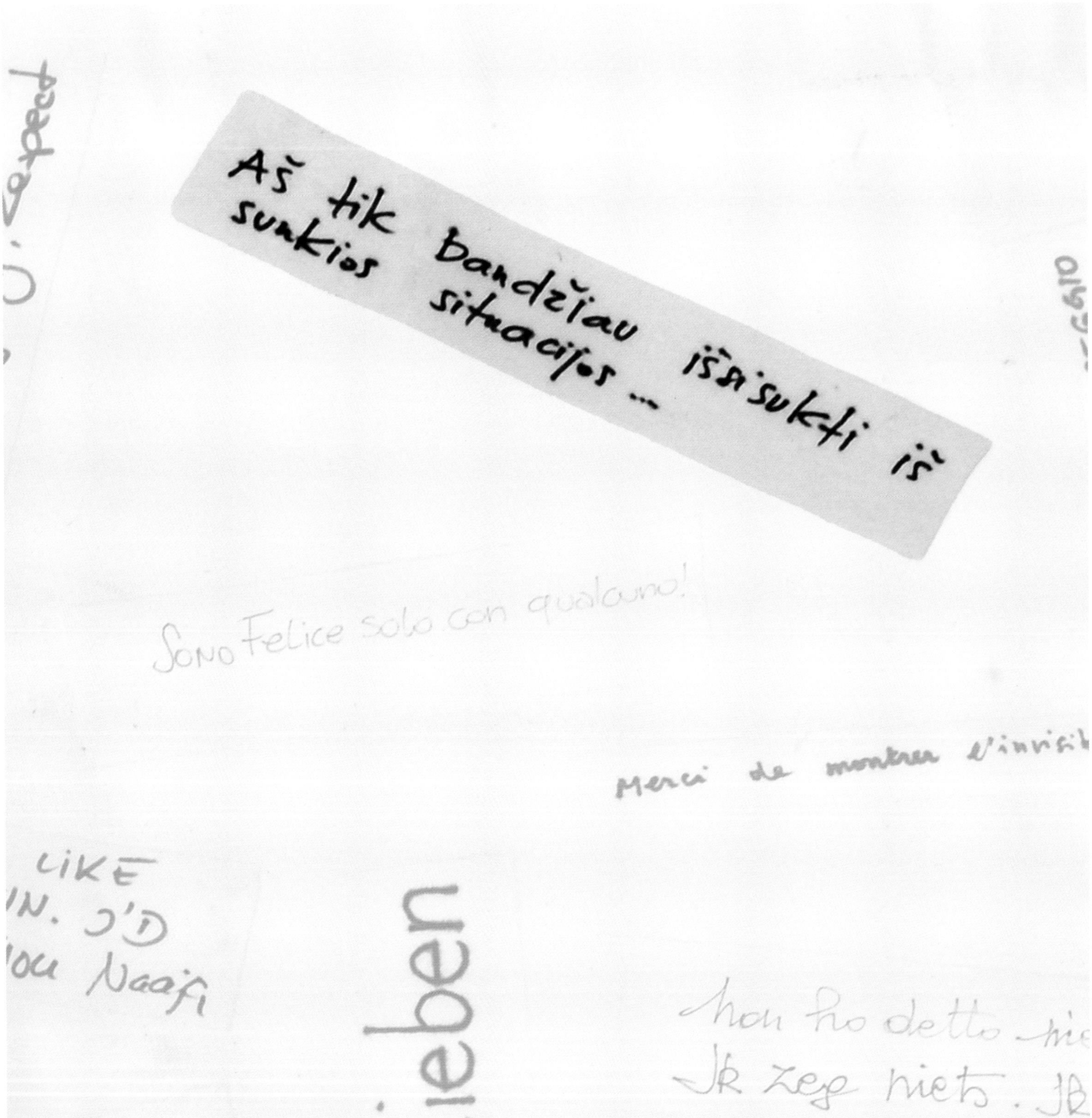
Aš tik bandžiau išsisukti iš
sunkios situacijos ...
Sono Felice solo con qualcuno!
Merci de montrer

SONO STANCO
DI
TO UN PASSATO
ENDO UN PRESENTE
UN FUTURO?
I hate who I am when I'm angry

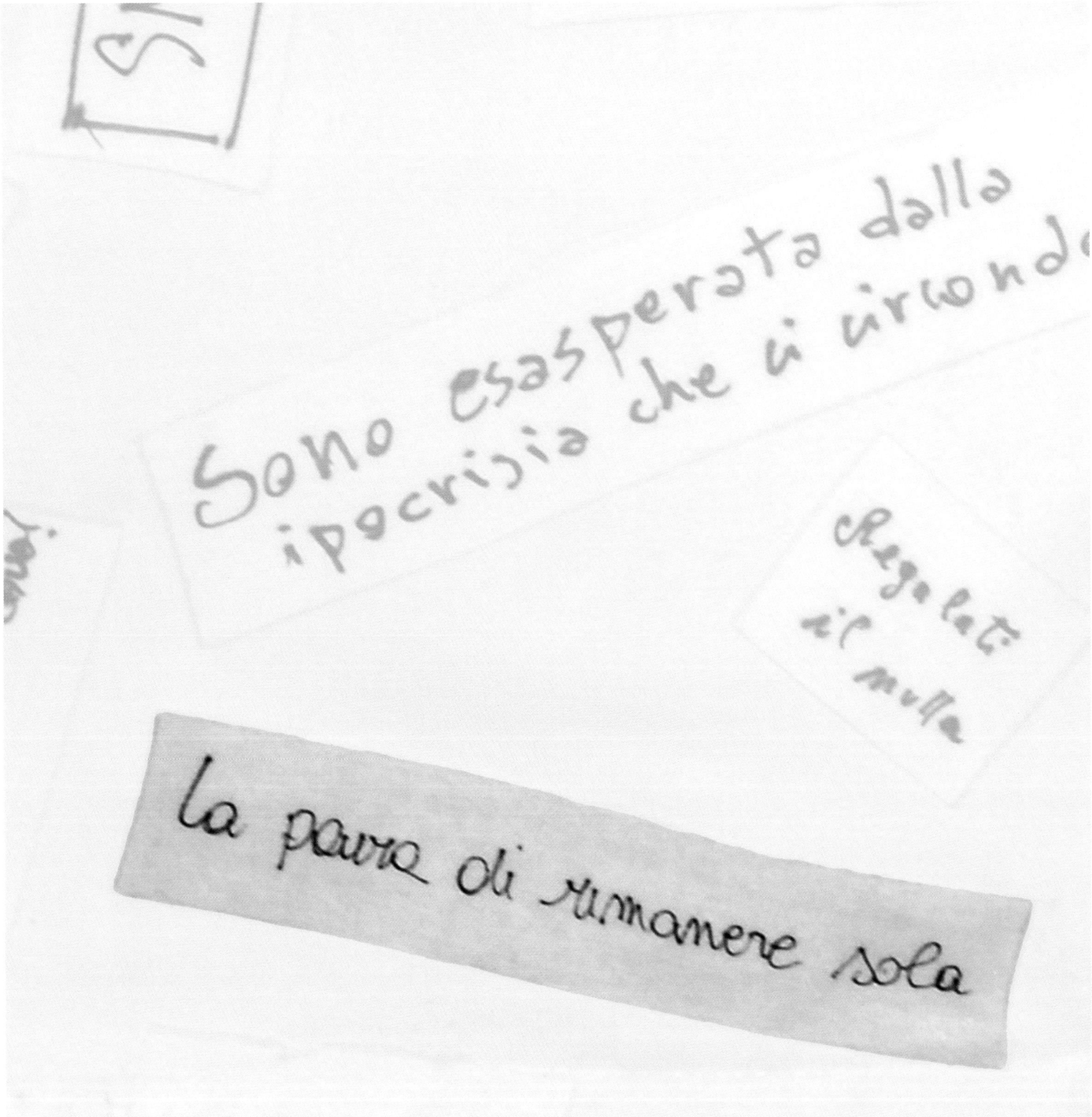
Sono esasperata dalla
ipocrisia che ci circond
la paura di rimanere sola

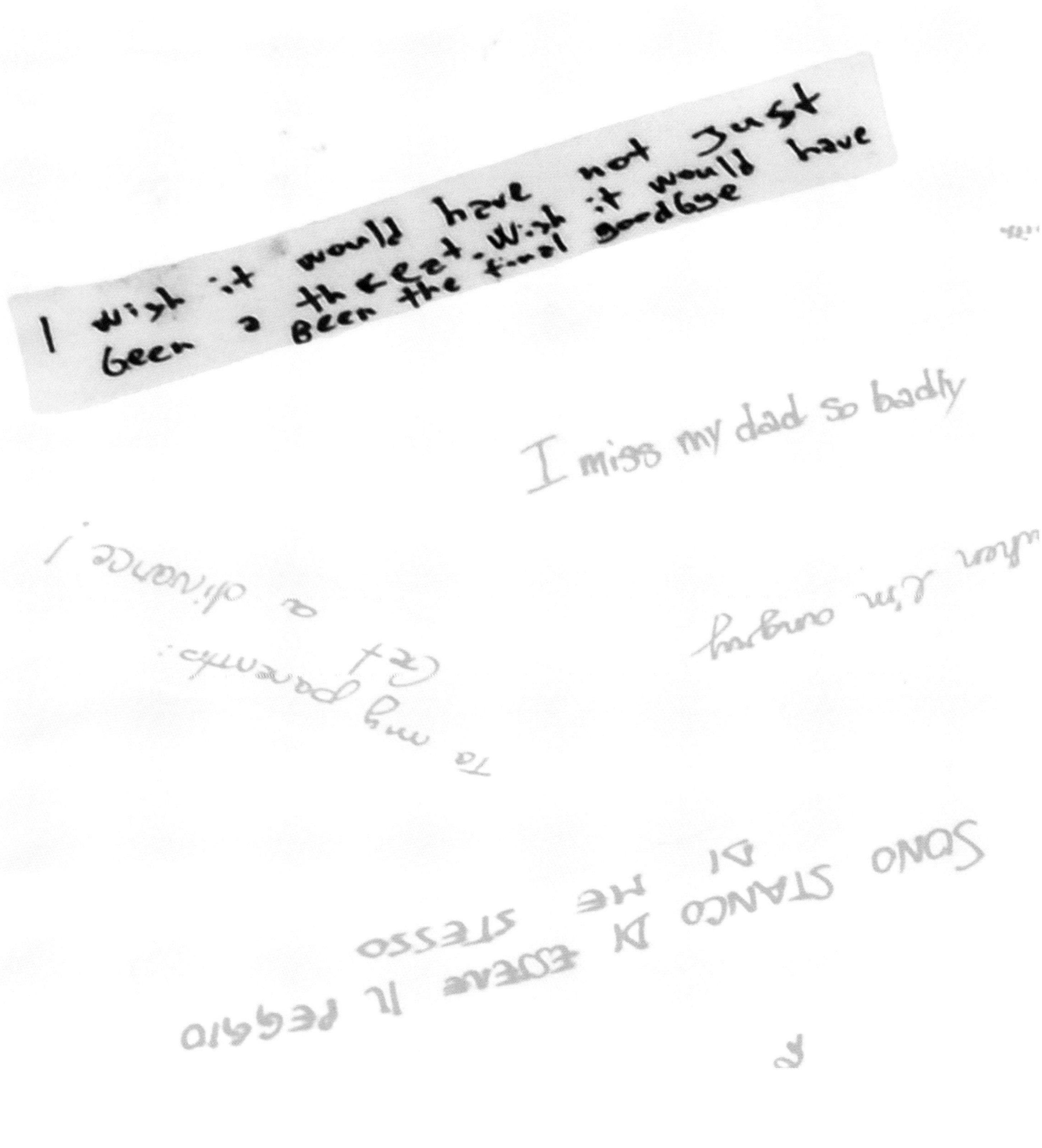
I wish it would have not just
been a threat. Wish it would have
Been the final goodbye
I miss my dad so badly
To my parents: (Ex)
a divorce!
when I'm angry
SONO STANCO DI VEDERE IL PEGGIO
DI ME STESSO

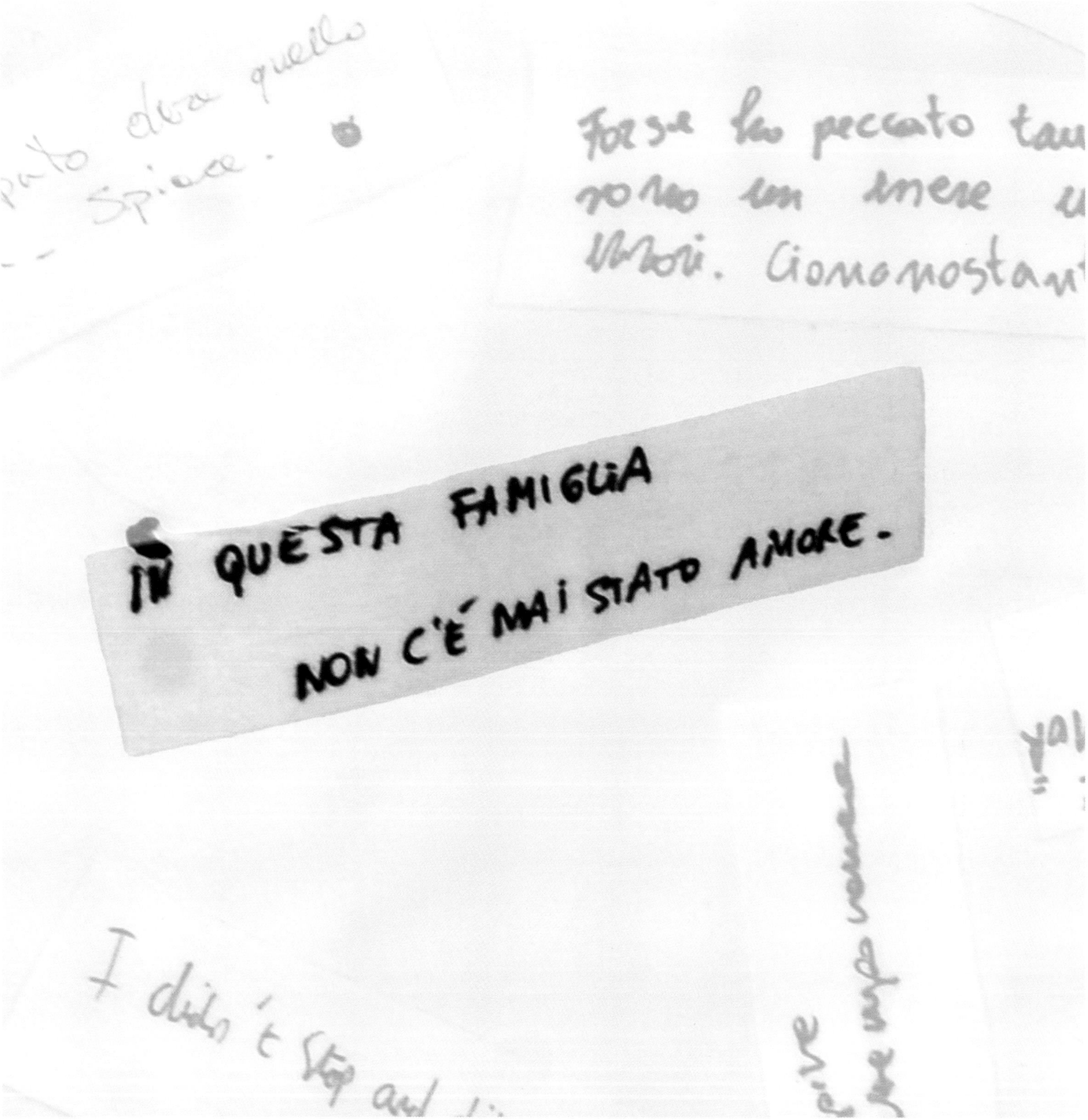
IN QUESTA FAMIGLIA
NON C'É MAI STATO AMORE.

ICH FUNKTIONIERE BESTENS,
DAS IST DAS PROBLEM!

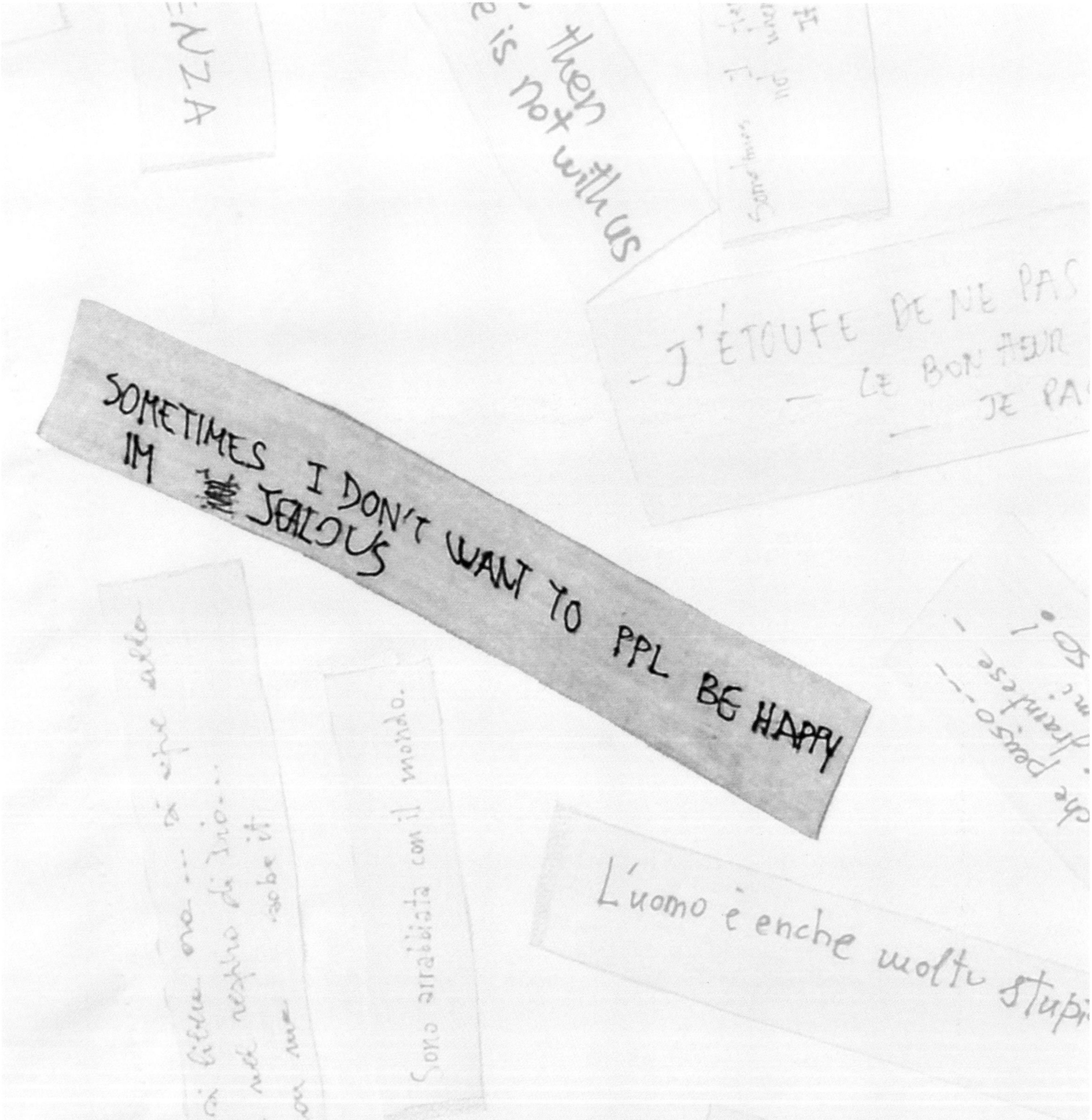
SOMETIMES I DON'T WANT TO PPL BE HAPPY
IM JEALOUS
then
is not with us
J'ETOUFE DE NE PAS
LE BON HEUR
Sono arrabbiata con il mondo.

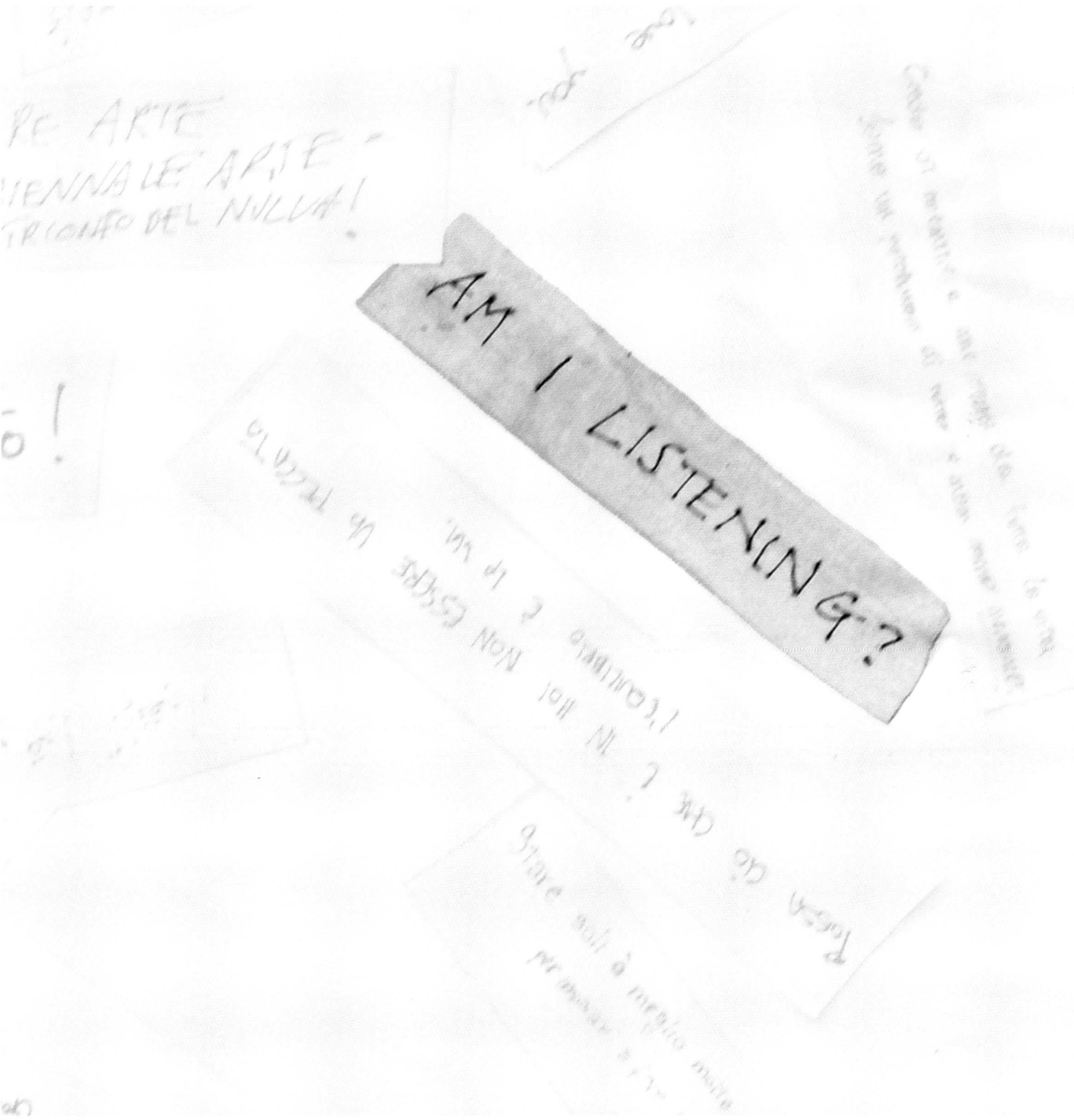
AM I LISTENING?

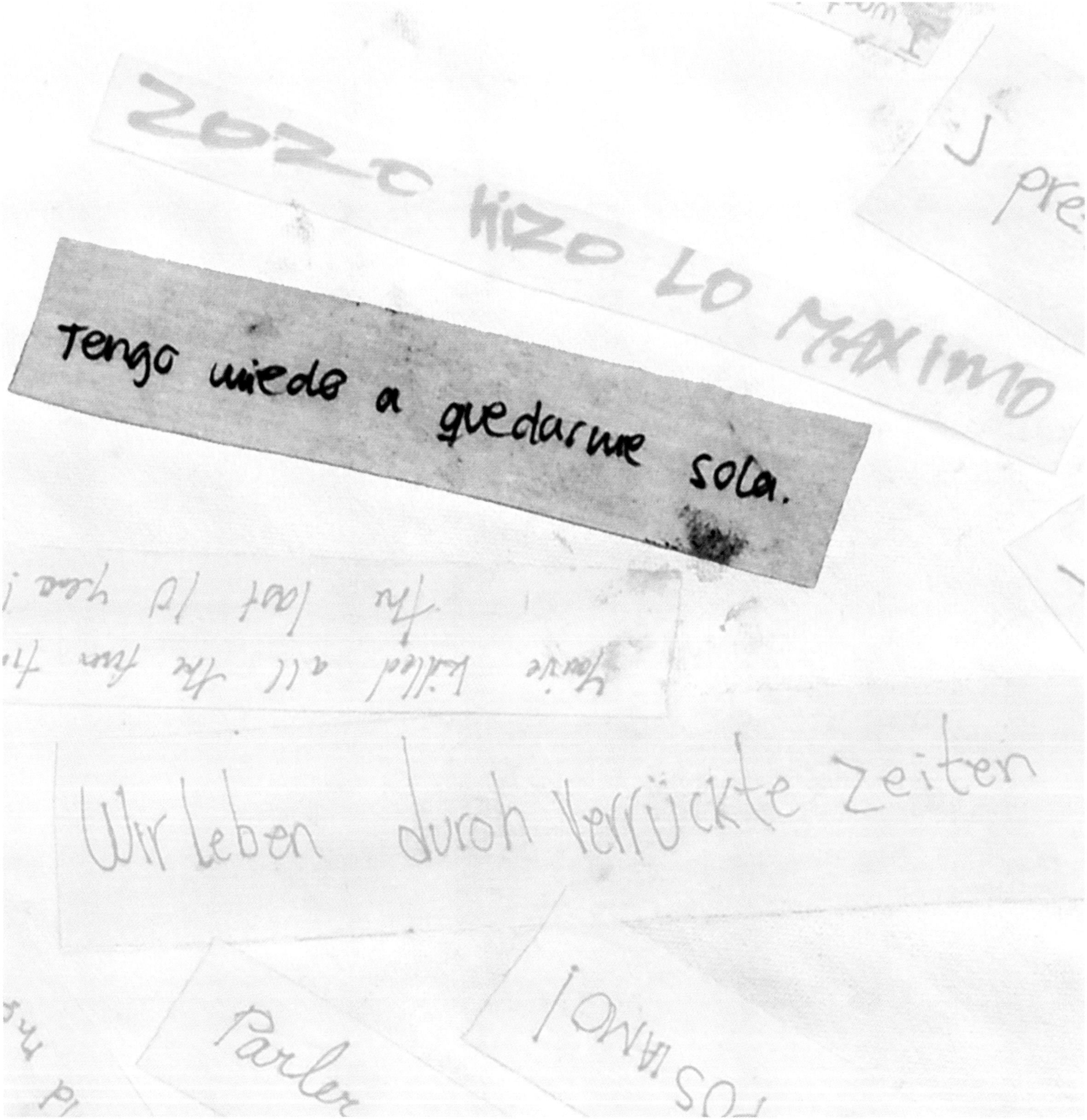
2020 hizo lo máximo
Tengo miedo a quedarme sola.
Wir leben durch verrückte Zeiten
Parler

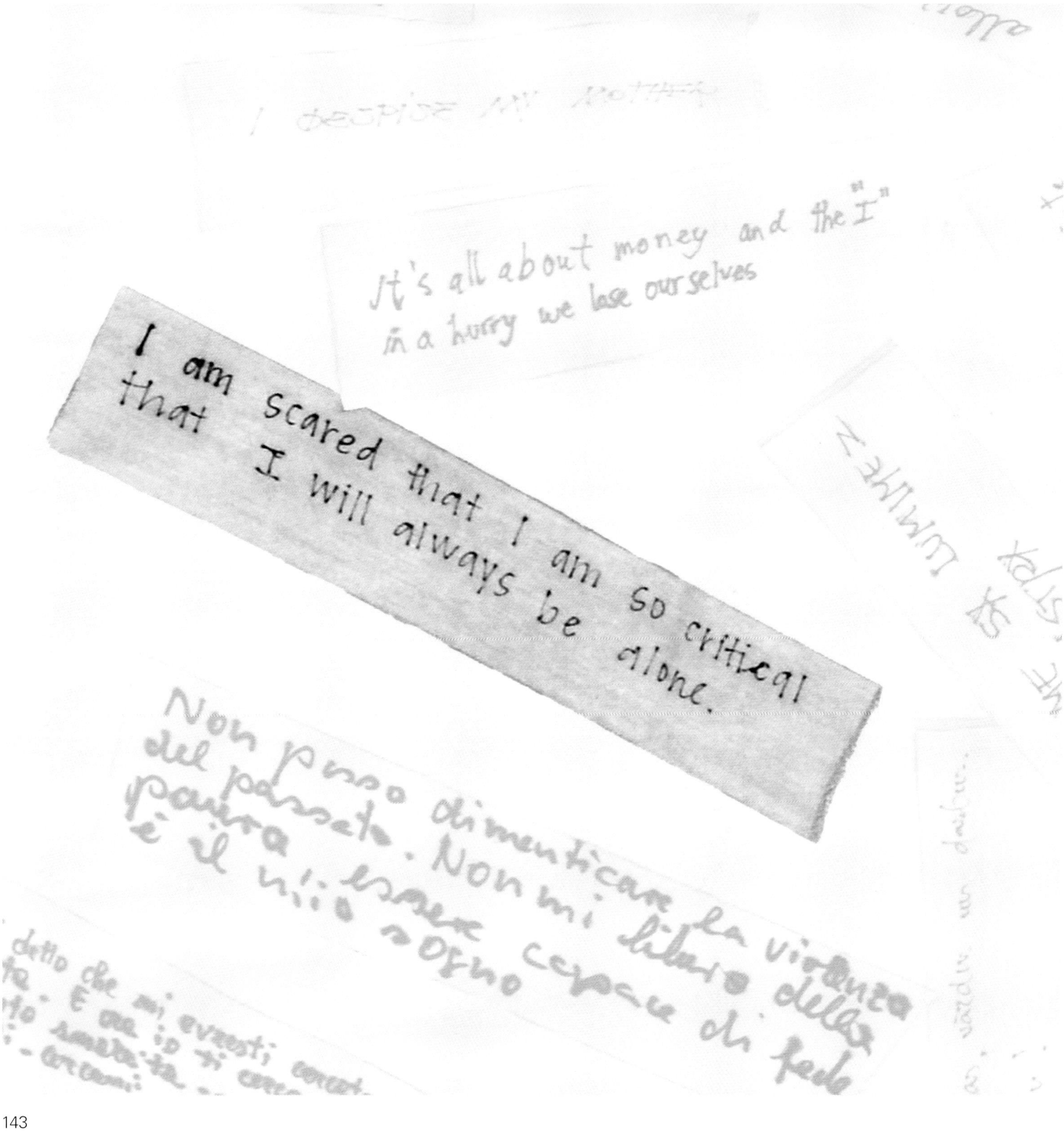
I DESPISE MY MOTHER
It's all about money and the "I"
in a hurry we lose ourselves
I am scared that I am so critical
that I will always be alone.
Non posso dimenticare la violenza
del passato. Non mi libero della
paura

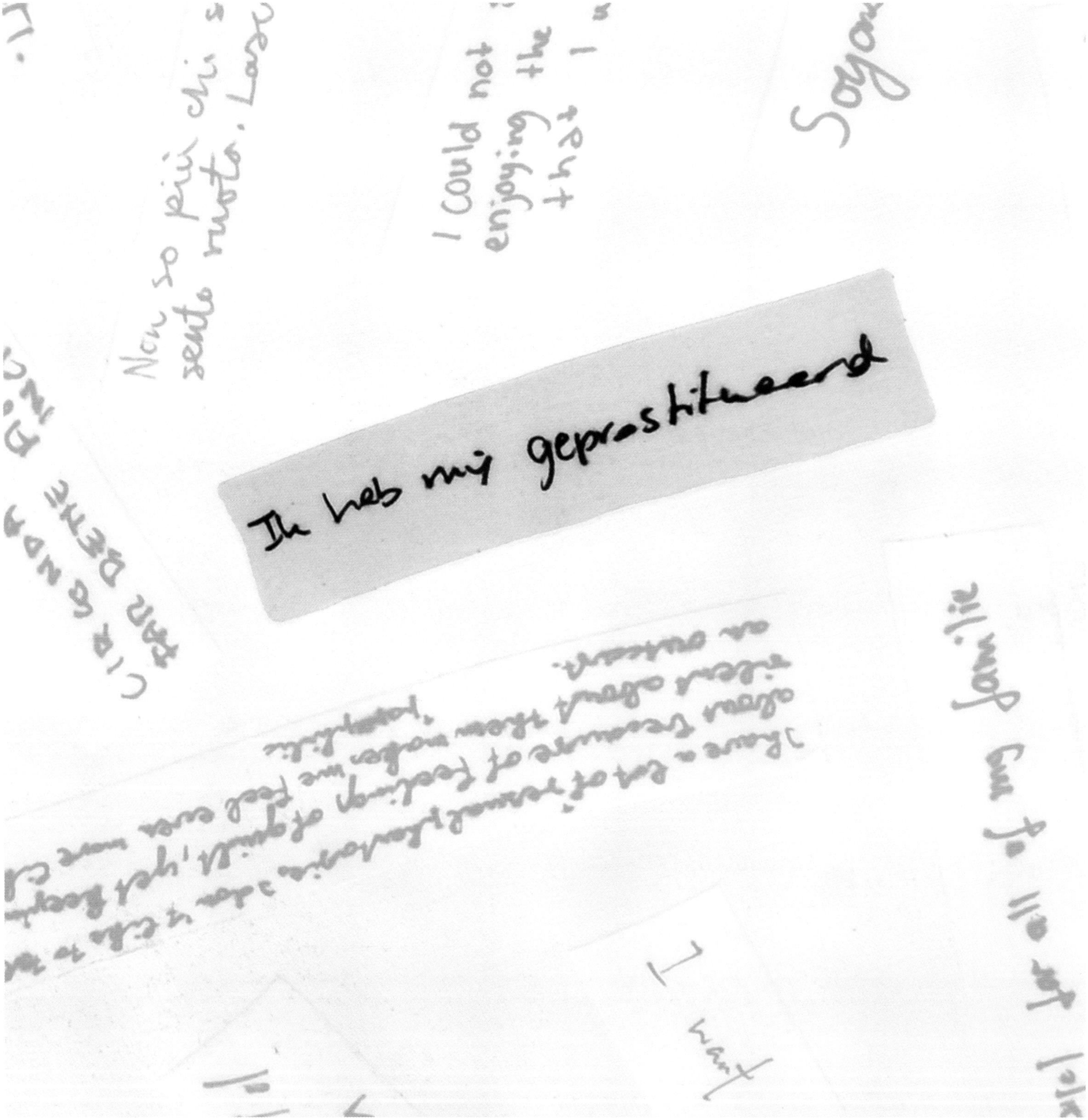
Ik heb mij geprostitueerd

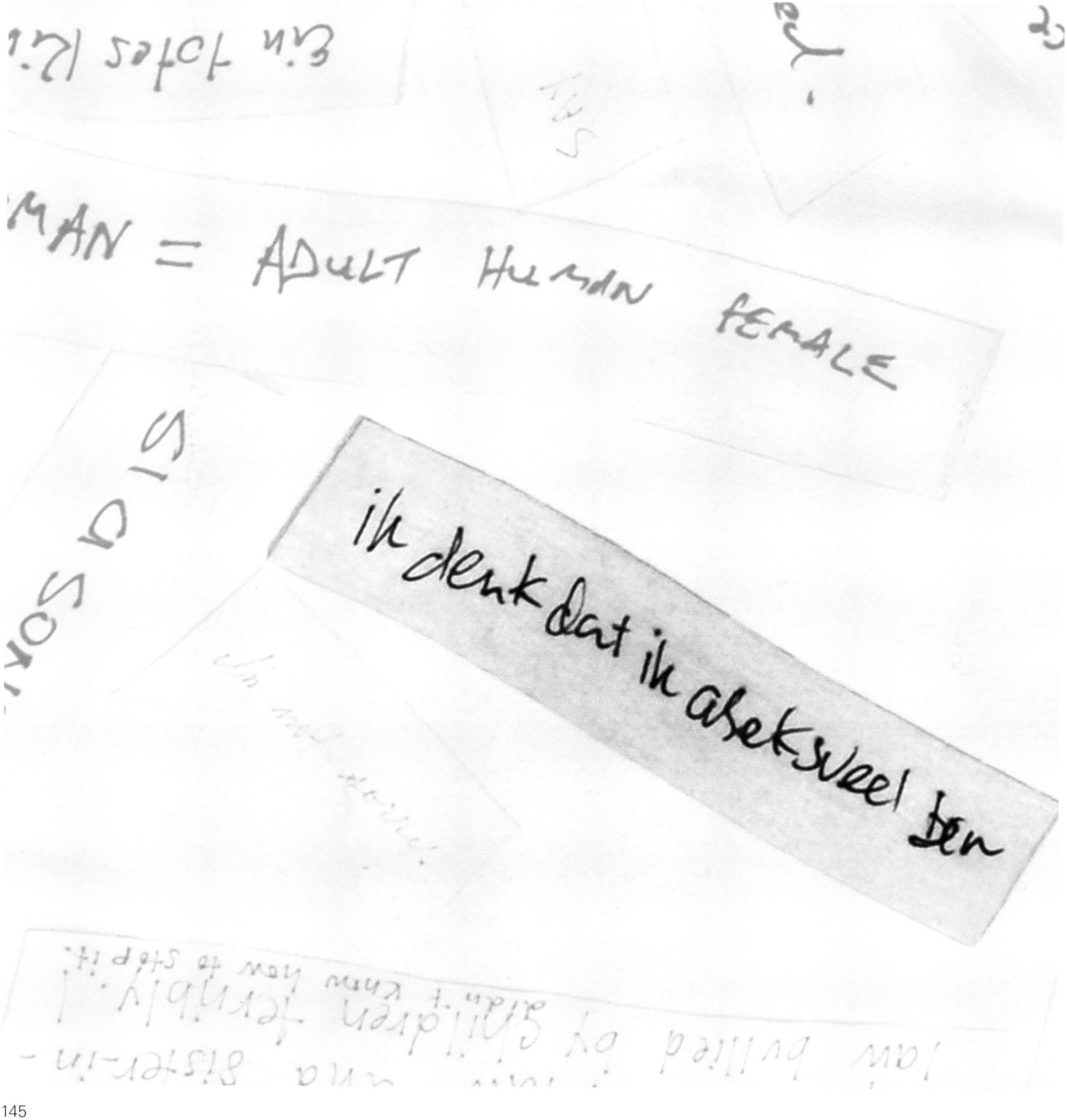
MAN = ADULT HUMAN FEMALE

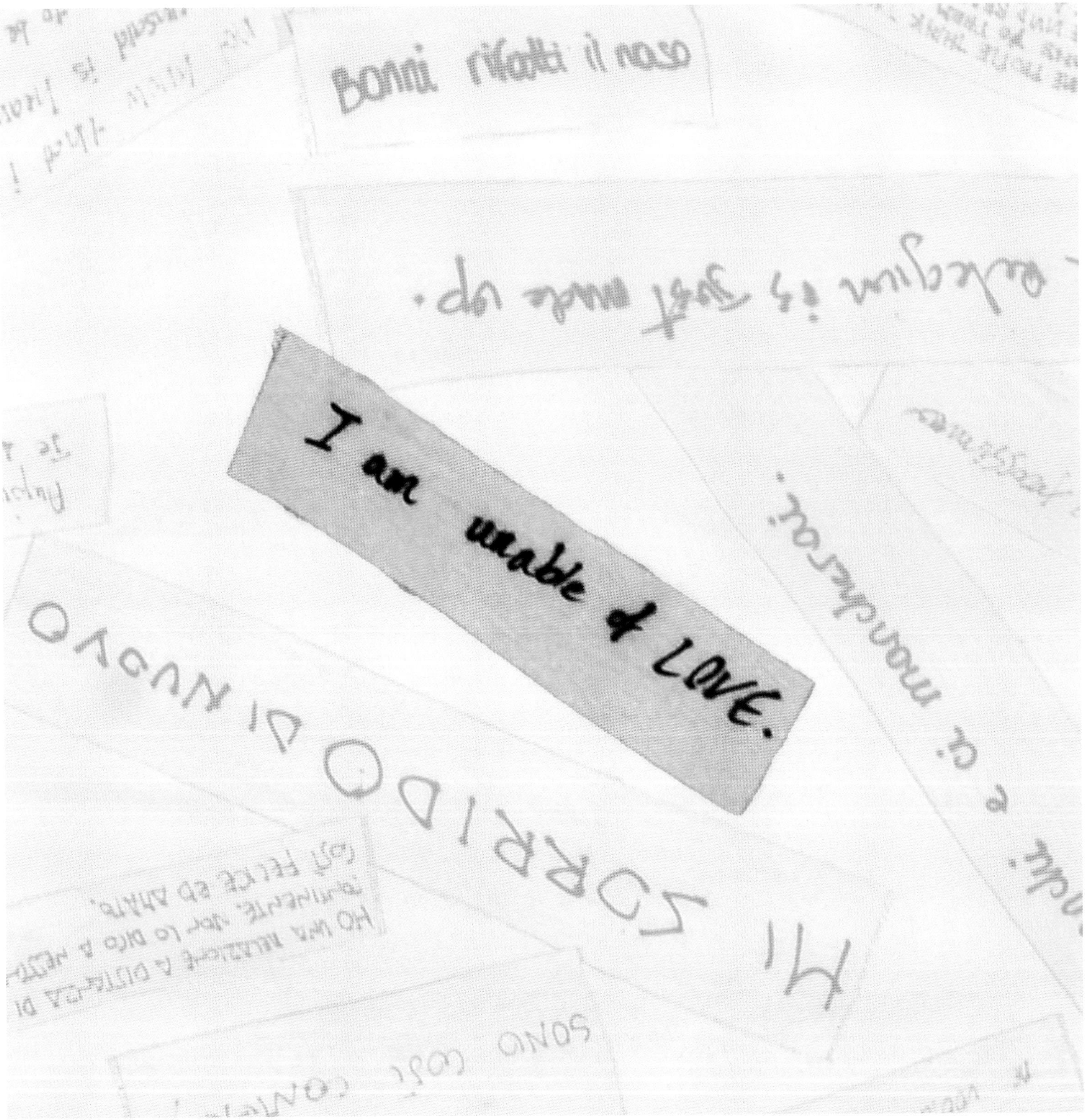
Bonni rifatti il naso
I am unable of LOVE.

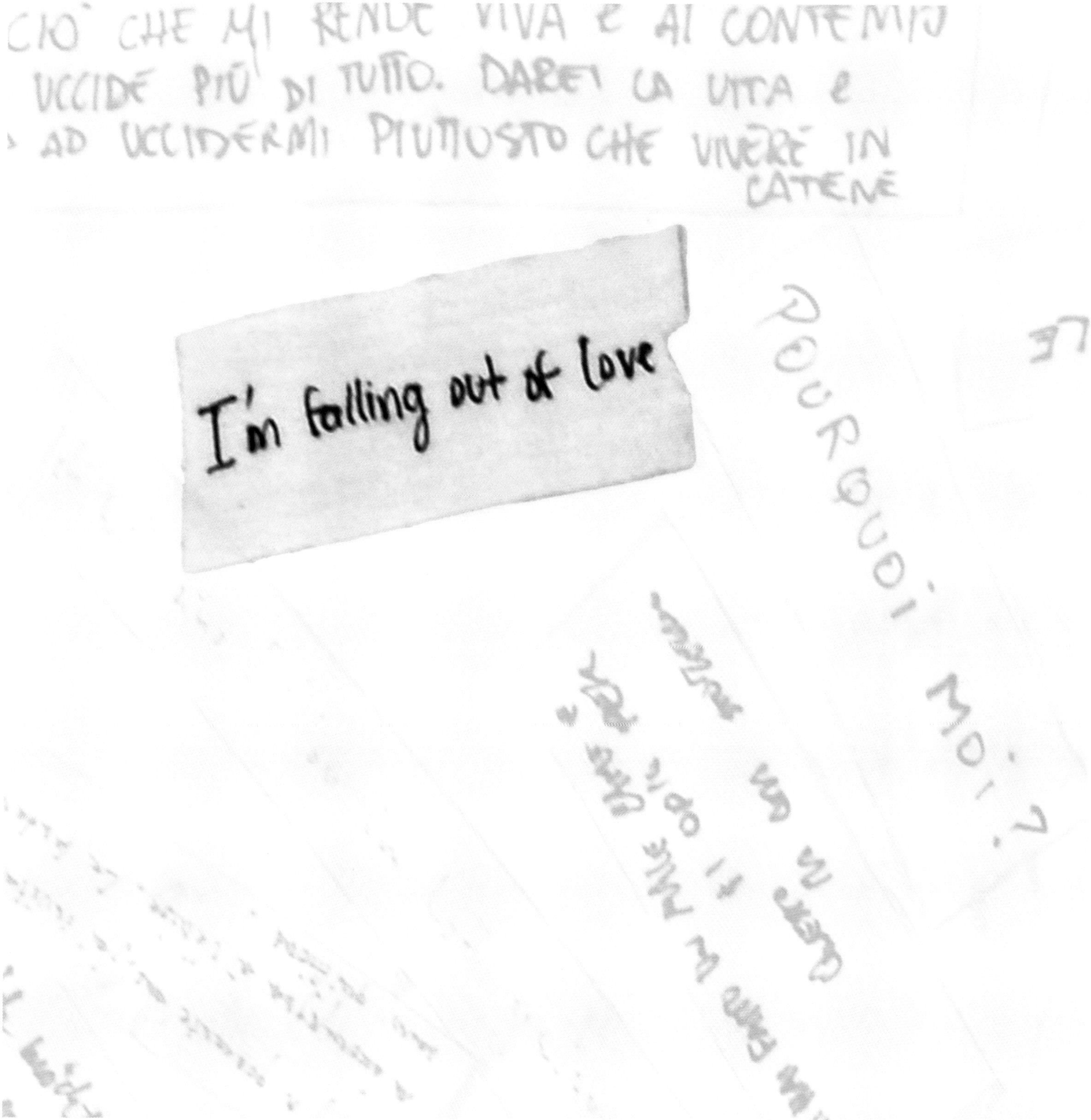
CIÒ CHE MI RENDE VIVA E AL CONTEMPO
UCCIDE PIÙ DI TUTTO. DAREI LA VITA E
AD UCCIDERMI PIUTTOSTO CHE VIVERE IN
CATENE
I'm falling out of love
POURQUOI MOI?

I Don't Feel Like I'm alive.
Molto
è PROPRIO QUESTO SILENZIO CHE
ZIONE E' GRAVE MA NON E' SERIA
SPERIAMO BENE

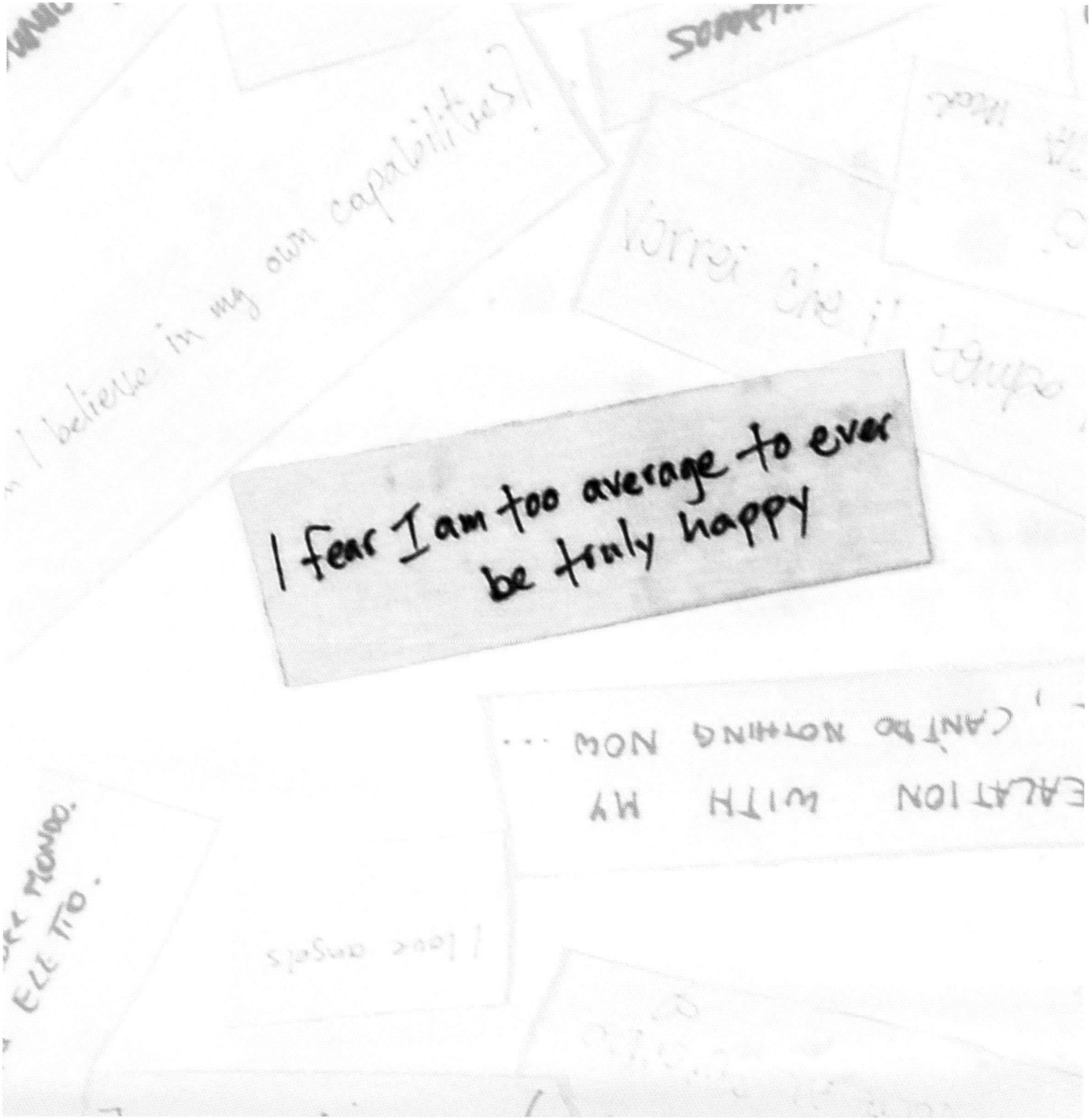
I believe in my own capabilities
I fear I am too average to ever be truly happy
CAN'T DO NOTHING NOW...
WITH MY

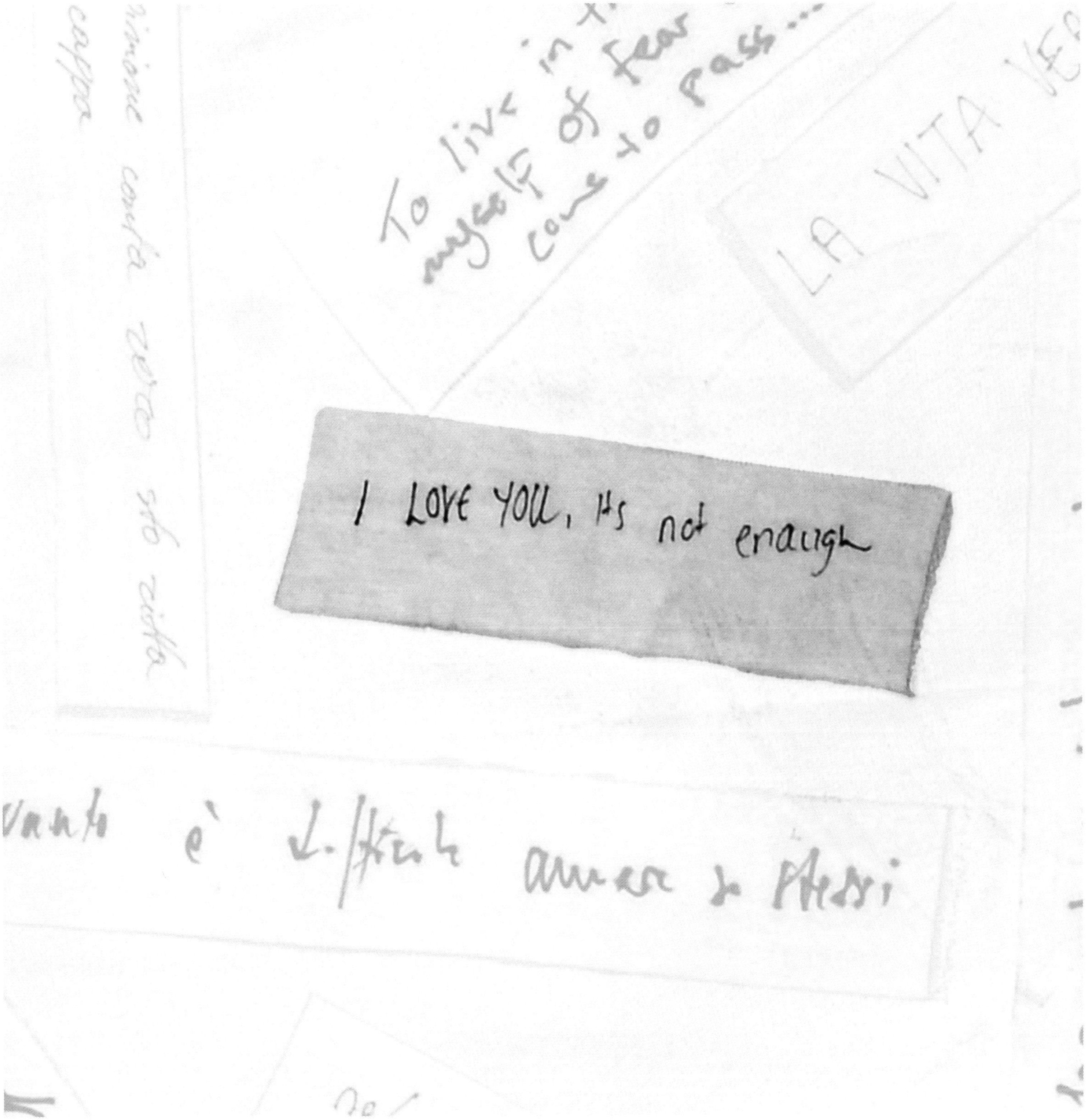
I LOVE YOU, It's not enough
myself of fear
come to pass...

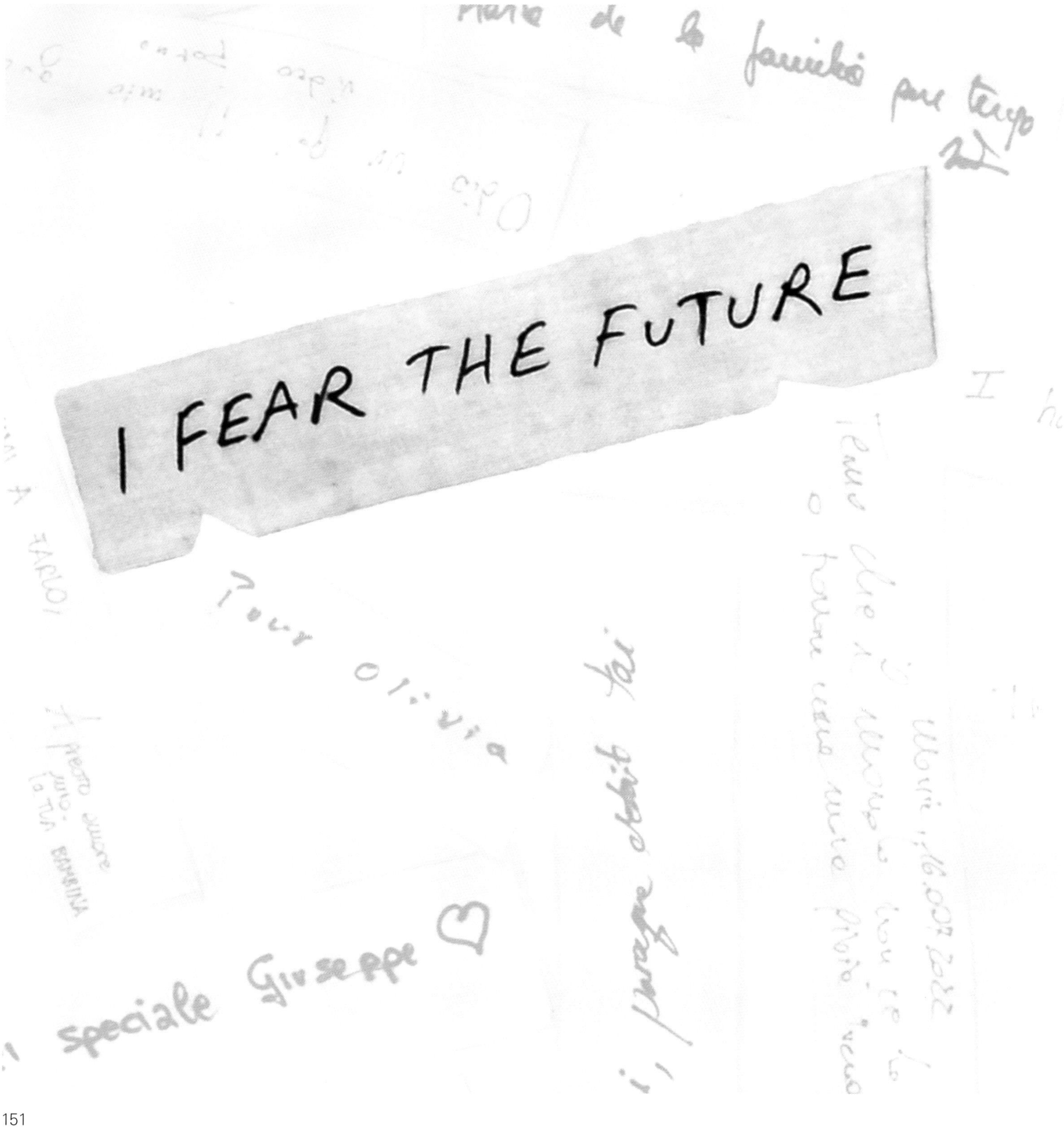
I FEAR THE FUTURE
Pour Olivia
speciale Giuseppe

MESSAGE TRANSLATIONS

Page 26
Italian: *Vorrei stare con un'altra...*
I would like to be with another (girl/woman)

Page 34
Italian: *Ho bisogno di amore*
I need love

Page 36
Italian: *Ho molta paura*
I'm very afraid

Page 38
Italian: *Ho paura di essere bipolare*
I'm afraid I'm bipolar

Page 39
Italian: *Sono soffocato dal peso della vita*
I'm smothered by the weight of life

Page 41
Italian: *Sono pazza*
I'm mental

Page 44
German: *Warum ist mir Sex nicht versonnt?*
Why don't I like sex?

Page 47
Spanish: *Solo pienso en mi mismo y me voy a quedar solo por culpa de mi egoismo*
I only think about myself and I will end up alone because of my selfishness

Page 49
Italian: *Sento il pianto del mondo tutto*
I hear the cry of the whole world

Page 51
Spanish: *Siempre estoy imitando, no soy nadie*
I am always imitating, I am nobody

Page 55
Italian: *Sei un pessimo padre*
You are a bad father

Page 57
Italian: *Prima che te ne andassi avrei voluto dirti: "ti voglio e ti vorrò sempre bene papà"*
Before you left I wanted to say, "I love you and I will always love you dad"

Page 59
Italian: *Pensando di non riuscire ad amare nessuno mi consumo d'amore. Sarà sempre così?*
Thinking I can't love anyone, I'm consumed with love. Will it always be like this?

Page 61
Italian: *Ogni volta che amo davvero finisco per scappare*
Whenever I really love I end up running away

Page 63
Italian: *Non sono felice della mia vita*
I am not happy with my life

Page 65
Italian: *Non mi interessa se stai male*
I don't care if you feel bad

Page 67
Italian: *Non mi fate bene*
You do me no good

Page 69
Italian: *Non faccio attenzione agli altri*
I pay no attention to others

Page 71
Italian: *Non avevo il coraggio di dire che ho paura*
I didn't have the courage to say that I was afraid

Page 73
Italian: *Non so cosa sto facendo perché non so chi voglio essere*
I don't know what I'm doing because I don't know who I want to be

Page 75
Spanish: *No puedo olvidarme de ti, no es justo que tu si de me*
I can not forget you, it's not fair that you can forget about me

Page 81
Italian: *Mi sento estremamente sola e insignificante*
I feel extremely lonely and dull

Page 83
German: *Manchmal bin ich nicht die Person, die ich gerne sein würde. Das macht mir Angst*
Sometimes I'm not the person I'd like to be. That scares me

Page 87
French: *Je n'ai pas assez dit à mon papa que je t'aimais… Il est dans le ciel maintenant*
I didn't tell my dad enough that I love you... He's in heaven now

Page 89
German: *Ich bin so leer im Kopf und kann mich oft nicht erinnern*
My head is so empty and often I can't remember

Page 115
Italian: *Mi piace davvero tagliarmi*
I really like to cut myself

Page 121
Spanish: *Siempre eh sido incomprendido*
I have always been misunderstood

Page 126
Italian: *Non ho più paura di me*
I am no longer afraid of myself

Page 130
Spanish: *Me arrepiento de las cosas que no te dije*
I regret the things I did not tell you

Page 134
Lithuanian: *Aš tik bandžiau issisukti is sunkios situacijos*
I was just trying to get out of a difficult situation

Page 136
Italian: *La paura di rimanere sola*
The fear of being left alone Page 138
Italian: *In questa famiglia non c'è mai stato amore*
In this family there has never been love

Page 139
German: *Ich funktioniere bestens, das ist das Problem!*
I'm functioning perfectly, that's the problem!

Page 142
Spanish: *Tengo miedo a quedarme sola*
I am afraid to end up alone

Page 144
Dutch: *Ik heb mi geprostitueerd*
I have prostituted myself

Page 145
Dutch: *Ik denk dat ik aseksueel*
I think I am asexual

Annalisa Bugliani

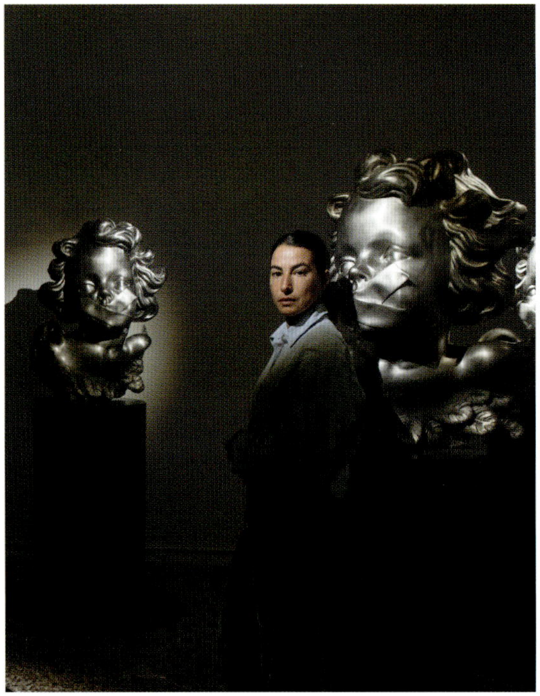

Annalisa Bugliani (1973), studied Literature and Philosophy at the University of Pisa with a focus on art history and specialization in Film History and Criticism.

She worked for many years as a presenter and correspondent for Canal+ (Tele+ Cinema) and later for Sky Cinema. Correspondent and writer for various newspapers including Rolling Stone Italia.

She currently runs her own contemporary art gallery and is dedicated to curating cultural events and art exhibitions. She holds the position of president of the Tg Residency Foundation in Pietrasanta.

Rachel Lee Hovnanian

My job is to elicit conversations. We watch and we participate as technology offers mirrored worlds that resemble reality but remain hollow. What is our culture's obsession with beauty and narcissism doing to our individuality and to our relationships with one another? What impact is technology having on our understanding of time and space?

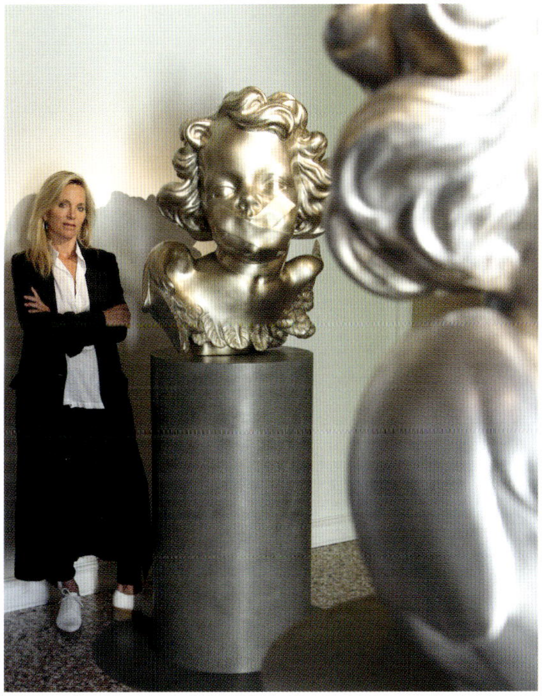

Rachel Lee Hovnanian's multidisciplinary practice explores the complexities of modern feminism through the lens of our cultural obsession with beauty and narcissism, eliciting conversations around contemporary ideals regarding physical perfection and the compounding psychological effects of new media and technology.

In 2022, Hovnanian was selected to participate in the 59th Biennale di Venezia: The Milk of Dreams, where she presented "Angels Listening" (2022). Recently, Hovnanian's "Mind the Bod"y (2023) was selected for the 44th La Versiliana Festival: Of the Multiple Identities of the Body in Pietrasanta, Italy, and again for presentation within "The Divine Feminine" (2023–4) at the Ann Norton Museum and Sculpture Gardens in Palm Beach, Florida.

Over the last decade Hovnanian's work has been exhibited at public and private institutions across the globe, including numerous solo presentations in the United States, Asia, Europe, and the Middle East. She received her BFA from the University of Texas, Austin, and completed postgraduate studies at the Parsons School of Design in New York. Born in Parkersburg, West Virginia, and raised in Houston, Texas, Hovnanian currently lives between Miami, New York, and Tuscany.

Samantha Boardman

Dr. Samantha Boardman is a New York City-based psychiatrist, Assistant Professor of Psychiatry at Weill Cornell Medical College, author of Everyday Vitality, and founder of PositivePrescription.com.

She received a B.A. from Harvard University (1994), an M.D. from Cornell University Medical College (2000), completed a 4-year residency program in Psychiatry at Weill Cornell Medical College (2004) where she was awarded the Oskar Diethelm Prize for Excellence in Psychiatry, and also earned a Master's degree in Applied Positive Psychology from the University of Pennsylvania (2013). Dr. Boardman is also a Distinguished Fellow of the American Psychiatric Association and currently serves as Co-Chair of The Positive Psychiatry Section for the World Psychiatric Association.

Her work has been published in The American Journal of Psychiatry, The Journal of Clinical Psychiatry, Translational Neuroscience, and Nature Reviews Neuroscience. She is a frequent contributor to Psychology Today, The Wall Street Journal, and Thrive Global, and a guest on the Today Show and Good Day New York.

She is a board member at the Metropolitan Museum of Art, Citymeals-on-Wheels, Let Grow, and Millbrook School.

Alessandro Romanini

Alessandro Romanini was born in Lucca on July 15,1967 and graduated in 1992 from the University of Pisa with a focus in Modern Literature and History of Art. He is a tenured professor of Theory of Perception and Psychology of Form, Theory and Analysis of Cinema, and Audiovisual and Psychology of Arts, at the Academy of Fine Arts in Carrara.

From 2017–22, Romanini was the Chairman of the Scientific Committee of the Ragghianti Foundation in Lucca, following his position directing the Fondazione Centro Arti Visive di Pietrasanta, from 2009 to 2016. He has been the Director of the Cinema and Visual Arts section of the Lucca Film Festival - Europa Cinema since 2011 and a member of the scientific committee of the National Park of the Peace of Sant'Anna di Stazzema since 2020.

He has curated numerous exhibitions in Italy and abroad, working across multiple disciplines including art, cinema, video-art, and photography. He is well-known for his work organizing exhibitions with a focus on contemporary African art and for his involvement with film, audiovisual, and video art festivals, specifically surrounding the relationships between art and technology and between visual and musical arts. His curatorial credits include Pietrasanta's "Carve Time" Festival; three editions of Lucca's Festival "Images that Sound Well;" and the Lucca Film Festival, "Art on the Screen," a review of films and documentaries devoted to art, architecture, music and sculpture which he has curated since 2012.

Romanini is a frequent collaborator with art and culture magazines including *AW ArtMag*, and regularly holds seminars and courses at the Athens Academy of Fine Arts; Mimar Sinan University Contemporary Arts Department, Istanbul; and UBV Facultat de Belas Arts, Valencia.

INDEX

Note on p. 13: Alessandro Romanini

RACHEL LEE HOVNANIAN : YOU ARE NOT ALONE, OR THE CATHARTIC POWER OF ART AND HOW TO RECREATE CONTEMPORARY RITES

1. David Riesmann, *The Lonely Crowd: A Study of the Changing American Character*, New York, 1950.

Notes on p. 17: Samantha Boardman

RACHEL LEE HOVNANIAN: ANGELS LISTENING

1. Ellyn Maese, 'Almost a Quarter of the World Feels Lonely', *Gallup Blog*, October 24, 2023.

2. Rachel Lee Hovnanian, *Angels Listening*, at rachelleehovnanian.com.

3. Carla Ross, Tom Postmes, Namkje Koudenburg, 'Feeling heard: Operationalizing a key concept for social relations'.

I dedicate this book to my mother
Peg Lee

Special thanks to
Amy Elias, Fabiola Salazar and Mandragora
for helping produce this book
Minas Lourian
Centro Studi e Documentazione della Cultura Armena

Mandragora s.r.l.
via Capo di Mondo 61
50136 Firenze
www.mandragora.it

isbn 978-88-7461-686-2

Printed in Italy
March 2024

Editor
Marco Salucci

English translation (pp. 13-15)
NTL, Florence

Design
Paola Vannucchi

Pre-print
Puntoeacapo, Florence

Printed by
Grafiche Martinelli, Bagno a Ripoli
(Florence)

Bound by
Legatoria Firenze